DEDICATION

This book is dedicated to my mother, Angeline Langas, who inspired me to write this story. I am constantly moved by her strength, patience, humor, resilience, and positive attitude.

She is pictured on the cover with her mother, Olga, in the late 1940's. Almost seven decades later, Mom still has the same joie de vivre and beauty that is evident in the photo.

Contents

Part I

ZOITSA

    Beginning 1

OLGA

    Arrival 11

ANGIE

    Childhood 14
    Coming of Age 20
    Greek Lessons 25
    Chicken Every Sunday 34
    War Years 40
    Secrets and Gossip 54
    George 59
    Boulevard 71
    Separation 77

RITA

    Kids 81
    Suburban Life 85
    Adventure 88
    The Greek Picnics 94
    Return to Greece 100
    College 103
    Newlyweds 111
    Teacher 117
    Sunsets and Sea Urchins 124

Greek Lessons

Rita Langas Wilson

Copyright © 2016 Rita Langas Wilson
All rights reserved.

ISBN-13:978-1534900950
ISBN-10:1534900950

Part II

ALEXANDRA

    Beach Scene 138
    Young Love 158
    Daddy 164
    Learning 167
    Greek Night 175
    The Village 179
    Connections 192
    Roots 202
    Athens 212
    Santorini 225
    Reunited 229
    Discovery 236

Epilog 241

Acknowledgements 242

Gaia's Gift

> *And Gaia, Earth, presented to Hera*
> *branches of the golden apple*
> *to celebrate her marriage to Zeus...*

In Xirokambi oranges grow
round and large and sweet
golden spheres of fragrant fruit
suspended from the trees

I dig my thumbnail deep
into the thin and dimpled skin
sticky pulp under my nail
I peel away the rind

Naked slices cradled by
a thin web of white lace
I plunge my thumbs into the core
to break apart a slice

The sticky juice explodes,
a fragrant, sweet aroma
I taste the liquid gold
Hesperides' ambrosia

The Prison of Palamidi in Nafplion, Greece stood sentinel over the Venetian trade route to the Middle and Far East. Elias Savellos, from Xirokambi, spent several years in a cell in this former Venetian fortress for allegedly killing a man. I don't know whom, I don't know why, and I don't know if he was guilty. During this time, he was married to Zoitsa Laskaris, a young woman from the village, 26 years his junior. These were my great-grandparents. What I am able to put together of my family's story begins here.

PART I

Meros I: ΜΕΡΟΣ I

ZOITSA
(Zo-eetsa)

Zoitsa with sons Vagglis (l) and Mike (r)

BEGINNING - *Arhi*: APXH

The prison of Palamidi looked out over the Argolic Gulf on the east coast of the Peloponnese, which opened into the Aegean Sea, but the prisoners saw nothing of this. Elias Savellos, who had been prosecuted for murder, dwelled in an underground cell in the Militiadis bastion, which had been converted into a prison for serious criminals. He was supervised by guards who could observe him through the iron bars on top of the cell. In the 1800's there were no rights for prisoners and no parole; as criminals, society had discarded them. The availability of water depended on how much rainwater was collected in the tanks. Water was scarce, especially in the summer, and food was always meager. Visitors were infrequent, due to the arduous climb to get to the prison - the only way to approach Palamidi was by climbing nine hundred and ninety nine steps from the bottom to the top of the mountain. But Elias's wife, Zoitsa, was a determined woman.

Once a month Zoitsa left her daughter Chrysoula in the care of Kuria Laskaris, her mother. She would have wrapped freshly baked bread in a woven cotton towel, and loaded the donkey's worn brown leather saddlebag with late summer legumes, hard cheese, oranges, and smoked pork covered in *siglino*, the pork fat, to preserve it. I imagine her peering through the early morning mist surrounding Mount Tayetos, hoping for clear, dry weather for the journey. Because it was dangerous for a woman to travel the 140 kilometers from Xirokambi to Nafplion by herself, Zoitsa met with other travelers in Sparta to form a caravan of those traveling east on horseback, donkey, or mule. They rode for several days, stopping at night at a *chani*, or inn, before they arrived at Palamidi. Perhaps Zoitsa tied the donkey to a post at the bottom of the mountain, or perhaps she rode him slowly up the worn stone steps. If the guard was in good humor, he might let Elias out to see her. If not, she would be lucky to have him take the food and pass it down to Elias through the iron bars.

Legend has it that upon his deathbed, the man who actually committed the murder said, "It was not Savelakos, it was me." In any event, Elias, now in his fifties, was set free. For years, month after month, Zoitsa gave Elias food and hope. After he was released from prison, Elias gave Zoitsa five more children: Loukia, Vaggelis, Odysseas, Mihali (Mike), and my grandmother, Olga.

The Savellos family lived in Xirokambi, a village in the southern Peloponnese region of Greece, at the foot of Mount Taygetos. Like most people in the Greek countryside, they were farmers. In the front of the house they tended fragrant orange groves. In the back, they planted a garden with tomatoes, beans, onions, garlic, lettuce, and root vegetables to last through the winter. They probably raised some small livestock – chicken, ducks, or rabbits. They would have had a goat or two for milk, and a pig when they could afford one. Years of Turkish occupation had wreaked havoc on the economy, and families tried to increase their income any way that they could. Elias's family did this by cultivating silkworms on the ground floor of their home. Zoitsa fed the silkworms with mulberry leaves. When they had satisfied their need for the nutrients in the leaves, the caterpillars spun silk cocoons with the tiny spinnerets in their lips. They rested on the dry brush that was spread over the floor until they were ready to emerge as creamy white moths, leaving the precious silk threads to be harvested. The rest of the ground floor was used for storing grain, flour, olive oil, and the fruits of the garden. The upstairs living area consisted of the kitchen and three bedrooms, which the children shared.

    While Zoitsa tended the silkworms, Chrysoula, as the oldest daughter, often had the chore of taking care of the younger children. This included putting the children to bed at night while Elias went on his nightly ritual to the *kafeneio* – by day a coffee shop, at night a place to relax and drink an *ouzo*. (The clear liqueur with its strong taste of anise brought him home inebriated many nights.) Elias was known to call over his shoulder, "Chrysoula, don't forget to put the children to piss before they go to bed." She eventually married a man named Rotzikos, had five children, and in time owned a *kafeneio* of her own with her husband. Once Chrysoula moved out, it was difficult for Zoitsa to manage the home, the silkworm production, and the children. Year after year of drought conditions made food scarce and life difficult. One by one, the children left home.

    Loukia became romantically involved with a young man named Panos, and found herself the target of mean-spirited gossip. A decent young lady was not supposed to fall in love; marriages were arranged by the parents and often by a *proxenitis* - a matchmaker. But Loukia was intelligent and independent, and cared little for tradition. The ladies of the village began to question Zoitsa, and the whispers of *morosa*, or mistress, grew louder and more frequent. One night, Loukia left her home, family, and the only place she had ever lived, and headed for Athens. She found work as an apprentice to a seamstress. She learned quickly, and soon started her own business. She traveled to Paris to attend fashion exhibits by well-known designers like Paul Poiret and Jacques Doucet. As she watched the models glide down the catwalk, she appeared to be making notes in a small notebook. She was actually sketching the basic features of the dresses, with their fluid silhouettes and loose waistlines, so different from the stiff, form-fitting dresses of her village. Upon her return to the hotel, the designs still fresh in her mind, she perfected the sketches with greater details, adding her own ideas. Once she returned to Athens, she sewed these dresses herself, and held her own exhibition of haute couture. She eventually founded a fashion house and served clients of high society. After a brief, unsuccessful marriage to a man named Chadzaras, she married a retired army General named George Platos, with whom she lived until his death.

After Platos died, Loukia was reunited with Panos, her first love. The feelings that they had for each other so many years ago still lingered. Panos asked Loukia to marry him. Loukia had a large pension from the Greek army as the widow of a general, which she stood to lose if she remarried. Many years had passed since she has been called *morosa*; times had changed. People, she hoped, were less judgmental. And if they weren't...the hell with them. Panos and Loukia moved together to the island of Kos. They were no longer young, and both now had health concerns. Panos doted on Loukia with her back problems, and she kept a merciless watch on his diet because of his heart condition. She had a knack for sitting in the living room and hearing the slight creak of the refrigerator door as Panos quietly tried to steal a morsel of food. "PANOOOOOOOO...." she would yell, as he would try to answer with a full mouth without being caught eating. They lived together happily until well into their eighties.

Odysseas also moved to Athens, but did not fare as well. An unbelievably strong young man, he was also temperamental, and found himself losing his composure with little provocation. He had been known to lift up and throw a donkey in anger when the burro refused to move. One day he became angry at his younger brother Mike, and threw him into a nest of *fragosykies*, a type of thorny cactus. Mike suffered from the thorns of the cacti for days, laying on his stomach while Zoitsa anointed his sore back with olive oil. Oddyseas' strength and temperament led him not to a career in boxing or wrestling, but to a relationship with hashish, and involvement with the underworld in Athens. During the German occupation of Greece, he was arrested by the Germans. One story goes that he was executed by the Germans, not as a resistance fighter, but as a criminal. Another version is that he was imprisoned for drug addiction and was knifed by another inmate. In any event, Odysseas met a sudden end in prison.

Vaggelis, the oldest son, was thought to be his mother's favorite. His sister, Loukia used money that she had earned as a dressmaker to help him move to Athens, where he met his future wife, Matina. After several years of trying to conceive, Matina became pregnant. Her pregnancy was difficult, and most of it was spent in bed for fear of a miscarriage. Their only son, Elias, was born in 1949. It was a difficult birth, and Matina feared losing her son. She christened him Panagiotis, promising him to the *Panagia*, the Virgin Mary. Her husband took Spartan pride in the birth of a son, and their clever child was doted on by both parents. Vaggelis was active in politics and forged a career with the National Post Office, where he retired as Director General. He had been a chain smoker who, it has been said, would use only one match a day, lighting his first cigarette in the morning, and using the butts of cigarettes to light others for the rest of the day. Vaggelis finally stopped smoking in his sixties, but continued to spend every evening in the kafeneio, earning himself a reputation as a *kafenovos*. In the winter, when the doors were closed to the chill outside, the captive smoke lay in a stagnant cloud inside the building as the men played *tavli* – backgammon - and drank their whiskey. Vaggelis succumbed to lung cancer within ten years.

Mike was the youngest son of Zoitsa and Elias. Like his nephew, Vaggeli's son Elias, he was somewhat spoiled and quite clever. He was also adventurous, strong-willed, and resourceful. By the time Mike went to school, his family had sunk into poverty. School was a luxury, and he did not have the money to buy pencils or notebooks, or any of the supplies needed for school. He approached his father.

"Can I have some money to buy pencils?" he asked Elias.
"Pencils? For what you need pencils?"
"I need them for school," Mike explained.
"School? For what you need school? You don't need school to work on a farm."

Mike would scavenge where he could, writing with the pencil stubs his classmates had discarded, so tiny he could barely hold them in his fingers, and reading from his friends' books. As he got older, he began selling oranges in the market, and did any odd jobs that were available.

When Mike was a teenager, the family home burnt to the ground. A burning coal from the kitchen on the upper floor fell between the slats in the wooden floor, and landed on the brush on the ground floor. The combustion was instant. As Mike fled the house, he remembered money that his parents kept in an earthenware pot. He ran back into the burning house, grabbed the money, and ran through the black smoke out into the yard. Elias, knowing that nothing could save the house, sat in a chair several yards away, calmly smoking a cigarette and watching the flames destroy his home. Mike rushed over to his father and opened his hand, producing the money for which he had risked his life. Expecting thanks and praise, he was shocked to receive a powerful backhand to the head. "You didn't wake me up!" Elias yelled. "I could have died!"

When Mike was in his late teens, he met a man he knew from the village who had left Sparta some time before, and had come home to visit his family. Mike was impressed with his handsome uniform and asked about it. "I am an aviator," the man replied. Mike did not understand. "I fly airplanes," he explained.

A few days later Mike hiked with a friend to the top of Mount Taygetos. As they sat to rest, Mike looked down at the town of Sparta, tiny in the distance, and wondered what it would be like to fly from that altitude down into the valley.

He approached Elias, who was sitting in the kitchen. "Baba´," he said, "I want to become an aviator." Elias listened closely as he told him about meeting the man and finding out about the military school for aviators in Thessaloniki. Mike would need money for the train ticket to Thessaloniki. At this part, Elias laughed, and spoke, "The priest who has the beard has the combs, too." In other words, the rich keep getting richer, and Elias was not rich. Zoitsa had also been listening closely, and quietly left the room. When she returned to find Mike sitting alone, she took his hand in hers.

"*Pare afto*, take this," she said, and pressed into Mike's palm the small sum of money she had tucked away in case of emergency. It was enough for his train ticket to Thessaloniki and some food.

Mike arrived in Thessaloniki and went straight to the military unit to submit his application. He was accepted into the military aviation school, but faced a problem: school was not beginning for a month. In the meantime, he had no money and needed food and a place sleep. He went to a small tavern near the airfield and spoke to the owner about his plight. Convinced of his honesty and impressed with his ardor, the man gave him food on credit until the school opened, trusting Mike to pay him back with the first salary he would receive.

Flight school nurtured Mike's spirit of adventure and his desire for speed. Upon finishing school near the top of his class, Mike was transferred to Tatoi, an airfield outside of Athens near Parnitha Mountain. To keep him challenged when he wasn't flying, he bought a motorcycle which he stripped of all unnecessary parts, including the muffler, to make it lighter and faster. He and his friends loved to show off, and revved up the noise level as they raced on the streets of Athens. One can only imagine the dust that would be stirred up and the decibel level of a bike without a muffler as he kicked it up into fourth gear, and the surprise of the widow who found him at the threshold of her first floor apartment after he hit the wall of the building during one of these displays of recklessness. Although he was injured and told that he would be unable to have children as a result of this accident, it didn't keep him from continuing with his brash behavior. While stationed at Tatoi, the troops regularly participated in flying maneuvers. Because of a prior accident, the commander had prohibited flying upside-down at a low altitude. This did not sit well with Mike Savellos, and he proceeded to turn his plane upside-down, passing close to the control tower. Upon landing, he was arrested and placed in jail for a few days, which also did not sit well with him. When he came out he suited up, climbed aboard his aircraft, took off, and buzzed the control tower – upside-down. Upon landing, once again, he went to the brig. When he came out, he repeated his arrogant show of disdain for rules. But this time, after buzzing the control tower, he didn't land at the airfield. He grounded the plane at a strip of land close to the railway station where he boarded a train to Athens. There he contacted a friend at the Parliament, a renowned doctor, who somehow got him off the hook.

The fact that Mike was such a skilled aviator most likely worked in his favor. Until the outbreak of World War II, with the exception of minor scrapes with authority, life in the army suited Mike. He filled his days with flying, riding, wine, and women. When the Germans invaded Greece, Mike was transferred to

Egypt, where the wine and women were replaced by whiskey, and more whiskey. Whiskey was the only thing to help him sleep at night because of the mosquitoes, and Mike wanted to make sure that he didn't feel any bites. On one particularly sleepless night, Mike had more than his share of whiskey and stumbled to the officer's mess to eat. It was closed.

"Why is it closed?" he demanded.

"There is an official dinner tonight," the mess sergeant replied. "Prince Peter of Greece is the honorary guest. All of the food has been transferred to the dinner." Prince Peter was serving as Representative of the King of the Hellenes in the Middle East. His father and brother had been evacuated to Alexandria with the help of the British army after Germany invaded Greece in 1941, but Prince Peter was already an officer in the Greek army.

"*Vlakies*, fools," Mike spat out, and turned around, angry that royalty should receive special privileges. He swayed his way to the room where the official dinner was taking place. He turned his hat sideways on his head, barged through the door, and shouted, "You take this food from us, who give our blood every day to defend our country, to feed this mutt? Shame on you!"

The guards closed in on him, and dragged him to the brig. He was condemned to prison for his insubordination towards Prince Peter, but the camp in Egypt had no prison, so Mike was sent to a Greek warship in the harbor of Alexandria, which had a jail in the hold for insubordinate sailors. The ship captain asked Mike what he had done and why he was sent there, and Mike answered him honestly. As luck and fortune would have it, the captain was a socialist and an anti-royalist. He gave Mike a crate of whiskey and sent him back to the base, reporting that his jail was full.

Mike reported back to the base carrying the crate of whiskey, and delivered it to his superiors, along with the news that there was no room for him in the jail. He had gotten away with something...again. He was becoming a headache for his superiors, and the popular opinion was that they had to get rid of him. Taking into account that he had been drunk during the incident, and that he was an excellent pilot, they decided that the best course of action for all concerned was to send Mike to Rhodesia as a flight instructor.

If they thought this was a punishment, they were wrong. Mike took to the terrain of jungle and grasslands like a hawk takes to flight. He charmed the natives, who called him Chee-ou-esee after an ancient chief, because he could shoot with his double barreled rifle using only one hand. The exotic locale lent itself to his thirst for adventure, and he learned to ride a horse and hunt wild game. He did not neglect his duties. He not only taught his pupils to fly, but how to land a plane in the jungle and survive without a compass or supplies. Life in Rhodesia clearly suited Mike, but as the war ended, Mike was called back to Egypt, where he found that being a Greek in uniform was quite a draw to the women of Alexandria. The Greek communities in Alexandria and Cairo were generally wealthy, educated, and cosmopolitan, and they welcomed their heroes back from the war. Once again, alcohol played a part in directing Mike's life when, one evening at a friend's engagement party, under the influence of good company and whiskey, he proposed to Popi, a young Greek woman from Alexandria. He awoke the next morning in a whiskey-induced haze to his friend knocking at the door to take him to Popi's home to ask her parents formally for her hand. The marriage lasted only a few years.

After the war ended, and the Greek armed forces returned to their homeland, Mike met a man named Stefanos Zotos who would become the founder of the first Greek postwar airline, Technical and Aeronautical Holdings - TAE National Greek Airlines. Mike, along with several other pilots, went back to the Middle East, where they recovered DC3 Dakotas which had been abandoned in the Allied camps. They purchased the planes, along with whatever spare parts and tires they could gather, for next to nothing, and painted them with the new logo and stripes of TAE. In 1950 Mike purchased shares of stock in the company, becoming a partial owner and chief pilot.

Comfort was not an option in these early planes, which had long benches across the fuselage, not unlike those used by the paratroopers in the war. As the company profited, newer, more modern airplanes were acquired, and hostesses were hired. The requirements for these stewardesses were that they were to be beautiful, but not provocative, multilingual, mannerly, and sophisticated. One of these new hostesses was a Yugoslavian woman from Smyrna named Zorka. In the midst of a divorce and living in Athens, she needed to work to support herself and her young son. She met Mike; they fell in love, and they married.

Michael, Chrysoula, and Vaggelis were married, Odysseas had met his tragic end in prison, and Loukia had a thriving career as a seamstress and designer. This left Olga, my grandmother. One April evening in the spring of 1922, Elias met Achilles Nefopulas at the kafeneio. Achilles had emigrated from Xirokambi to the states, and was now experiencing some success as a painting contractor in Pittsburgh. He had come back to the village to find a wife. He and Elias made arrangements for Olga to sail to America, where Achilles would meet her in New York at Ellis Island. Achilles was fifty. Olga was twenty seven. She was leaving the only place she had lived and the only people she had ever known. Going from a small village in Sparta on a ship to New York would have been terrifying – but it was also necessary. The Savellos family had fallen on hard times. She would be provided for in America where she would have a husband and a home.

Olga (right) and friends in Xirokambi.

OLGA

Achilles and Olga circa 1924

ARRIVAL - *Afiksi*: ΆΦΙΞΗ

The air was crisp as the *Byron* approached New York Harbor on November 1, 1923. Olga waited in line to climb the stairs to the ferry boat that would take her to a new life. Although she had not known any of her fellow travelers when she boarded the steamship, she soon realized that she was not the only woman leaving her homeland to become a bride in America. Dozens of women from villages and islands all over Greece traveled to Ellis Island to be met by fiancées who would take them to strange sounding places like Chicago, Newport News, and even as far as Los Angeles. As Olga carried her suitcase up the steps to the deck, she heard a commotion. Cheers and shouting erupted in several languages, as passengers spotted "the lady," the impressive copper statue which stood high on her pedestal, her hand raised in the air holding the torch that welcomed them to their new lives. The passengers who had boarded the steamship two weeks before in Patras, Greece anxiously pushed each other aside. Olga was jostled with the crowd as it funneled into the exit and onto the double-decker ferry to *Ellie-Silie*, as she called Ellis Island. The sun's reflection on the water cast an orange glow on the windows of the large building, and its turrets gave the impression of a castle. Once on the ferryboat, Olga searched the crowd on shore for Achilles, the butterflies in her stomach coupled with the fatigue of sailing across the Atlantic in her lower class berth. Although she was 27 years old, she probably had not been told much about what to expect on her wedding night. They would soon be consummating their marriage, and I wonder what she must have been thinking about this man she did not know. Her relief at being off the ship was short lived, as the passengers were made to wait in front of the building until being ushered into Ellis Island for the three-hour inspection and processing. Recorded by the officials as healthy at five feet five inches, with brown hair and brown eyes, and no money to her name, Olga was finally released into the custody of Achilles Nefopoulas. He waited outside of the Great Hall at the "Kissing Post," as the tall pillar was called by the employees of Ellis Island who had seen so many families unite and reunite at this plain wood column. Olga spotted Achilles in the crowd who waited for their loved ones, so handsome in his black derby hat and thick dark mustache. Achilles approached Olga and kissed her gently on each cheek. They wed two days later, on November third, in the Manhattan County Courthouse.

      The newlyweds arrived in Pittsburgh where Achilles, or Archie as he was called, had a flat on Fourth Avenue which he shared with his widowed sister, Marigo, who was accustomed to being the lady of the house. Marigo cooked and cleaned for Archie, and served coffee to his fellow painters when they visited. As Olga and Archie grew into their marriage, Marigo's attitude soured. Marigo resented the gentle, pretty bride whom Archie had brought into their home. Olga was shy and spoke no English, and Marigo attempted to maintain control of the household. When Olga gave birth to her first son, Marigo insisted that he be named Nicholas after her deceased husband, rather than following the Greek tradition of naming him after Archie's father, Efstratios.

Archie was not a fighter, and gave into Marigo's demands. With the household no longer her official domain, Marigo took over care of the baby. Olga would warm a bottle in a pot on the stove; Marigo would take it out of the pan and feed the baby. Olga would wash her son's clothes; Marigo would rewash them. Although Archie realized that Marigo was out of control, he was not one to put his foot down.

When Nicholas was two years old, Olga became pregnant again. Marigo continued to cause the couple unnecessary stress. Many evenings were spent in hushed conversation as Archie and Olga tried to figure out what to do with Marigo. They could not just throw her out - Marigo had been an attentive sister, and had kept house for Archie ever since her husband had passed away. The couple offered to send Marigo to Greece for a visit with her sister Stavroula. This would give Olga and Archie a few months of peace, and they hoped that upon Marigo's return they would be able to establish a new order. But Marigo refused to go unless she could take Nicholas with her. Olga and Archie decided that as much as they would miss their son, the trip would only be for a few months; this would allow Olga to run her household, care for the new baby, and prepare to deal with Marigo upon her return.

    With Marigo away, Olga took over as woman of the house. She and Archie were happy, and while they missed Nick terribly, they had a new baby to take care of. They honored Archie's father by naming this son Efstratios, or Stanley. The household was running smoothly and they hoped that things would continue to do so upon Marigo's return. But Marigo did not return. At first she extended her stay, ignoring Archie and Olga's pleas for her return. And then she died. Achilles could not afford another round trip ticket to Greece. His painting contracts had slowed, and his financial situation worsened.

    Olga and Achilles continued to plead with Marigo's sister to return their son, but by now Stavroula had fallen in love with her nephew, and made no attempt to return him to the states. While Nick was in Greece, he did not know about his growing family in Pittsburgh. The year after Stanley was born, Olga gave birth to a daughter, Angie. Two years later Angelo was born, along with a twin Louis, who was stillborn. The following year, Peter was born. Angie, my mother, would be their only daughter.

ANGIE

CHILDHOOD - *Paidiki Ilikia*: ΠΑΙΔΙΚΉ ΗΛΙΚΊΑ

By the time Angelo and Angie were five and six years old, they would walk up McKinley Street to greet the 7754 streetcar which brought Archie home from work. The orange car squealed to a halt on the metal tracks, the clang of the trolley signaling its arrival at the Carrick station. Archie got off the streetcar, and upon seeing his children, a big smile grew under his formidable mustache. He took Angie's hand, and with Angelo in the lead, they walked to their yellow brick house on the corner. Large round flowers with small white petals bloomed on the trees in the front yard. A sturdy rope line stretched between two large oak trees in the backyard where Olga had hung the heavy Oriental rugs to clean them, dust flying off the rugs as she beat them with a large wooden paddle. Archie had a playful side to him; sometimes he would pull himself up on the line and hang upside down, letting coins fall out of his pockets as Angie and her brothers scrambled to pick them up.

    Archie often traveled because of his painting business, leaving Olga to be the disciplinarian for the family. With three boys under the age of 10, Olga knew that speaking softly and carrying a big stick was not enough. "*Ela tho!*" Olga would demand, "Come here!" as she waved a large wooden spoon menacingly. Although the wooden spoon was feared, the accompanying threats were often more effective. "*Tha se skotoso!*" she would threaten young Pete, "I'm going to kill you!" as he would back away, whining, "Maaaaaaaaa."

    One day Mrs. Kairys, a tall, slim woman who had befriended Olga soon after she arrived in the United States, came to call on the family. "Hello, Koula," Mrs. Kairys greeted Angie by her nickname, as she placed her large black handbag on the hall table and went into the living room. Olga had laid out a plate of *koulorakia*, sweet butter cookies twisted like braids, and cups of black coffee to dip them into. Angie went upstairs to play in her room while the ladies chatted, and the house was peaceful with the boys outside in the yard. Mrs. Kairys finished her coffee and sweets and left, and Angie came downstairs to help Olga get ready for dinner.

The front door opened, and Angelo walked in grinning, wearing a brown felt cowboy hat and a black plastic gun belt, with two toy guns in the holster.

"Where did you get that?" Olga asked.

Angelo's smile faded.

"*Apo pou epires afto*? Where did you get that?" Olga demanded.

As Olga questioned Angelo, the telephone rang. "Olga," Mrs. Kairys said. "I'm missing a dollar from my handbag. Could you check to see if it fell out on the floor?"

Olga glared at her son as she hung up the telephone. "*Ela tho* - Come here!" she yelled at Angelo, her anger intensifying as she realized that not only had her young son walked up the street and crossed a busy intersection to buy the outfit, but he had taken the money from her friend's purse to do so.

"*Tha se kapse*, I am going to burn you!" she threatened, as Angelo cringed and Angie looked on, horrified that her little brother was going to be lit on fire. Of course, Angelo was not burned, but this may have been the moment that made him an honest man.

The borough of Carrick experienced an extensive program of beautification in the early 1900's: workers paved streets, planted trees, and expanded the borough park. After being annexed to the city of Pittsburgh in 1927, property values continued to rise, and the house in Carrick symbolized prosperous times for the Nefopoulas family. There was room not only for all of the children, but for guests from Greece. Three Karambelas cousins from Xirokambi, hoping to make a living in America, came to stay with the Nefopoulas family. Within a short time, Gus, the oldest, found a job delivering bread, and Taki found a job working for Frank and Seders department store downtown. But the person who most impressed Angie was their sister, Kiki. She had long, dark hair and clear, white skin, and spoke softly in Greek. Not only was Angie stricken by her beauty, but she loved having another girl in the house. Living with three brothers provided much in the way of entertainment - as the only girl, she was used to being treated as one of the boys. Birthdays brought the requisite number of punches, and playing a card game of war left her open for sharp smacks on the hand with a deck of cards. Kiki's brief stay brought a feminine serenity into an otherwise boisterous male-dominated household.

When Angie was nine years old, Archie moved his family to an orange brick row house on Melba Place in Oakland, a 10-minute streetcar ride from Pittsburgh. All of the families on the block, except for one Jewish family, were Greek. On warm summer evenings the kids gathered their bats and a soft leather ball to play mushball in the empty lot across the street, setting up large rocks for bases. Their parents kept vigil on their front porches, while they visited with one another, and Greek conversations echoed up and down the street. It was the 1930's, and only the well-to-do families had cars. Oakland was a sidewalk community with schools, churches, banks, and stores within walking distance. The walk to St. Nicholas Greek Orthodox Church from Melba Place took about a half hour, and even though Archie and Olga did not often attend church, the children walked to Sunday school every week. Angie awoke one Sunday morning to a cold, driving rain. The walk to Sunday school would be wet and miserable, but she was not about to give up the perfect attendance pin that she would soon be receiving.

"Where do you think you're going?" Olga asked, as Angie came into the kitchen where Archie and Olga were having their toast and coffee.

"I'm going to Sunday school," Angie said, perplexed that her Sunday dress hadn't made that obvious.

"Not with this rain," Olga said.

"But, I want to go," Angie said.

"No. Go change your clothes."

"I have to go," Angie insisted. "I want my pin."

Olga refused to budge, and Angie skulked out of the room. It wasn't fair, she thought. She wanted that pin. She *deserved* that pin. As she turned to go up the stairs to her room, she spotted her mother's umbrella leaning in the corner by the front door, and made a quick decision.

A couple of hours later, Angie quietly walked up the wooden steps to the kitchen door, soaking wet and a little peevish. Olga was at the door to meet her. "Your father wants to see you," she stated. Surprise and relief flooded Angie, as she realized that Olga was not going to yell at her. She knew that Daddy would never be mean to her, but to be on the safe side, she took a deep breath and put a cheerful smile on her face as she entered the living room.

"Yes?" she said to Archie. "You want to see me?"

The look that greeted her was not the kind, affectionate expression that she expected, but a stern, angry one. "Didn't your mother tell you not to go outside because it was raining?"

"Yes," she replied hesitantly.

"But you left anyway?"

"Yes," Angie's voice came out, now an unsure whisper.

"Listen to your mother," Archie said, and patted her lightly on the cheek. Tears smarted in her eyes, and Angie ran from the room, crying uncontrollably. To her, it felt like a slap in the face from this gentle man who had never raised his voice, let alone his hand, to her.

Melba Place represented happy times for the family. Archie took the streetcar to work and Olga took care of the kids and housework. Once in a while, she would go to visit her friends, Fotula and Koubara. The ladies visited in the parlor, where the hostess served coffee and a glycko, a sweet delicacy made with sour cherries and thick syrup, which they bought at the Greek Store (and often served with a shot of whiskey!) The kids played "fox in the morning, geese at night," with their friends on Wellsford Street, trying to run across to the other side without getting caught. Once night fell, it was only a matter of time until they heard Olga calling, "*Vageli, Koula, Strati!*" and Angelo, Angie, and Stanley reluctantly went home.

One morning Angelo woke up lethargic and feverish, and Olga knew that it was time for *ventouzes*. She instructed Angelo to lay on his tummy. She washed his back with a warm cloth, and dried it. Olga went into the kitchen and returned with a tray of six small narrow juice glasses. Angie watched as Olga placed loose cotton in each of the glasses, then sprayed the cotton with alchohol. She lit the first one with a match, igniting a small flame, then quickly turned the glass upside-down and placed it on Angelo's back. The skin swelled into the cup drawing the blood to the surface, and Angie thought, *It looks like a puffy pancake!* Olga repeated the process with the other five glasses, and watched carefully until the skin under the glasses became a light shade of pink. Then she tilted the glasses sideways and popped them off. All of the kids endured these ventouzes, which must have worked, because trips to the doctor were rare. If their throats were sore, Olga treated them with iodine. She would wrap a pencil tightly with cotton, then dip in in iodine and swab their tender throats. Although Olga preferred to apply her home remedy, the common solution for sore throats in the 1930's was to undergo a tonsillectomy. As was customary, all of the children eventually had their tonsils removed, and enjoyed the cold ice-cream that followed the operations.

The Depression brought with it a souring economy. Both Archie's painting business and his health slowly declined, and the family was forced to move to a row house on Forbes Street. Archie and Olga had not given up trying to get their oldest son back from Greece. Hope arrived in the form of Emily Paraskevas, a distant cousin from Chicago who was visiting the Nefopulas family in Pittsburgh the summer of 1937. As she spoke of her planned trip to Greece the following spring, Archie talked to her about the situation with his son. The letters he had sent to Nick had gone unanswered, and he worried that they were never given to him. Emily volunteered to help in any way she could. Over the next few months Archie sent her copies of Nick's birth certificate and baptismal certificate, and letters explaining the situation to be given to the authorities in Greece. When Emily travelled to Greece, she met with authorities in Sparta and provided them with the documentation necessary to prove Nick's American citizenship and his legal guardianship. She then broke the news to the heartbroken Stavroula that arrangements were underway to send her beloved nephew home to his parents.

Archie and Olga were elated; Nick would finally be returning home. But the joy that the family felt in anticipation of Nick's return was marred by continuing concern over Archie's declining health. He now stayed upstairs in his bedroom. Olga did not explain the nature of Archie's illness to their children, perhaps not fully grasping it herself. Angie, now eleven, did not understand why she could not go to the Strand Theater with her friends to see the release of *Snow White and the Seven Dwarfs*. She knew that her father was upstairs in his bedroom, but that was all she knew. Archie died in Mercy Hospital in April of 1938 – one month before Nick was scheduled to return home.

At the funeral home in the Northside of Pittsburgh, eleven year-old Angie slowly approached the casket, where her father appeared to be sleeping. She stood on tiptoes to peer at her father who lay in the pine box in front of her, his trimmed gray mustache covering his lips. She bent down to kiss his forehead, and was shocked at how cold it was. She drew away from the casket and made her way into the parlor where two rows of metal folding chairs faced each other. Angie sat down in one of the chairs across from three women with weathered faces. Their heads were covered with thick black scarves, their bodies clad with long black dresses. "Ahhh," one wailed loudly. The second let out a cry, and soon the third began to wail. Intermittently, they raised their hands and undulated their bodies as they cried out. Angie's mouth opened in awe, as the old ladies continued to mourn, sobbing tearlessly. *Oh my*, Angie thought, *They must have really loved daddy!* Later she would learn that the women were professional mourners who would visit funeral homes to pay their respects to the dead.

Olga told the children that her husband died of a "busted appendix." The death certificate read colon cancer. Archie died at the age of 65, with no life insurance. Widowed at age 42, and with no command of the English language, Olga had no way of working to support her family, which would soon be getting an additional member. With her husband's death came yet another move to a row house on the Boulevard of the Allies. As difficult it must have been to move herself and four children at this time, and as poor as the family was, there were others less fortunate. Olga was still able to bake, and the rich, yeasty smell of the crusty loaves drifted from the open windows. The smell drew hobos to the house, and Angie answered a knock at the front door to find a man asking, "Do you have any food to spare?" Olga gave the man some bread, and even some of the cheese and butter that Angie and Stanley had waited in a long line to receive from the government welfare program.

Soon after the move to the Boulevard, Olga received word from Emily Paraskevas. Nick was finally coming home.

Nick's Passport Photo

COMING OF AGE - Enilikiosi: ΕΝΗΛΙΚΊΩΣΗ

Nick was fifteen when he arrived in Pittsburgh in 1939. He did not speak English. Authorities met him upon his arrival in New York, and boarded him on a train to Pittsburgh for the overnight trip. He watched the landscape change from the bright city lights of New York to an occasional cluster of lights as the train chugged on toward Pennsylvania. Soon the darkness, fatigue, and rhythm of the rails lulled Nick to sleep. He woke as the sky turned a soft, pale blue, to a green landscape quite different from the one he had left in New York. As the ticket taker walked past him, Nick tugged on his jacket. "Yes?" he asked the boy.
"Peetsborg?" Nick asked.
"No, not yet."
He repeated the process, and the ticket taker smiled. "No," he said each time, "Not yet." Heavy smog slowly dulled the landscape, and the stops became more frequent. The squeal of the train on the metal tracks and Nick's *Peetsborg?* were now a familiar refrain. The hazy outline of a grey cityscape took form outside of his window. The ticket taker stopped by and tapped Nick on the shoulder. Nick looked up as the man pointed out the window.
"Pittsburgh!" he said.
Nick arrived at Penn station, and as he got off the train he searched for his mother. He recognized Olga immediately because she looked so much like her sister, Loukia, whom he had met in

Athens at the beginning of his homeward journey. Olga, tearful and smiling, watched as her son walked up the platform towards her.

When Olga brought Nick home, Angie, who had not been feeling well, was resting in bed. Hearing the front door open, she peered through the French doors of the room off the living room, where she had been sleeping. Olga introduced Angie to this quiet, dark-haired young man who was her older brother, and she thought, "My, how handsome he is!"

Nick's new home in Oakland was worlds apart from life in the small village of Xirokambi. Nestled at the foot of Mt. Taygetos, fifteen kilometers south of Sparta, the village was surrounded by ancient olive trees and orange groves. Aunt Stavroula's home sat on top of a small hill above the stream that flowed down from the mountain. In the summer the streambed often ran dry, but in early spring when the snow melted, Nick would have to wade through the stream to get to and from the house. In the small house were a kitchen, two bedrooms, and a cool cement cellar to store cheeses and meats. The kitchen housed a large wood burning *fourno*, or oven. In the summer, the baking was done in the large dome-shaped clay oven in the back yard. Nick awoke each morning to the sound of roosters crowing. He tended to his chores – gathering dried brushwood from the olive grove to build the fire in the fourno, or milking the goats who grazed in the field behind the house. After drinking a glass of the fresh, warm milk for breakfast, he walked to school on worn dirt roads, passing farmers selling their fruits and vegetables out of carts drawn by donkeys. "*Karpouzi, rothakia* - watermelon, peaches!" Wildflowers bloomed in profusion along the side of the road, and the sky was a constant crystal Mediterranean blue.

While the Nefopoulas family on either continent was not well off, this economic status was reflected differently in Pittsburgh. Nick was unprepared for his new neighborhood on a busy Boulevard with concrete sidewalks and constant traffic. Nor did he have much time to get used to the house on the Boulevard. The family's already dire financial situation worsened, and they could no longer afford to stay in their home. Lizzy Pappas, a friend of the family who spoke English and Greek, helped Olga to obtain Mother's Assistance, a government sponsored program which provided her with food for her family. Additional help arrived from the Greek Philoptohos Society, literally translated to mean "friend of the poor." The family was situated in a small house on Utica Way, an alley behind the St. Nicholas Greek Orthodox Church on Forbes Avenue in Oakland. They lived in two bedrooms – the boys in one, and Angie and Olga in the other. There was no bathroom in the house – just a toilet with a door in front of it off of the kitchen. The family washed and shampooed in the kitchen. A black pot-bellied stove provided heat for the kitchen and small living room.

      The kids never thought of themselves as poor. They could walk down the alley to Forbes Street, and cross over to the Carnegie Museum and Free Library, where Angie borrowed books from the library or sat in the reference area to read or do her homework. The high-ceiling rooms of the museum held a glorious display of life-sized dinosaur skeletons and lifelike wild tigers and lions. Angie was amazed by the skeleton of the 78-foot long diplodocus with its long neck and tail, and liked to picture it roaming the earth millions of years ago. The cool marble floor led her down the hall to a room that displayed magnificent Greek statues carved in white marble. Angie's favorite was the statue of Athena, the goddess of wisdom, who stood larger than life in the center of the room, staff in hand, overlooking the smaller marble pedestals. Not far from the museum was the Stephen Foster Memorial, which held rooms of the composer's memorabilia and music, from *Camptown Races* to *Suwanee River*. With the Museum, Schenley Park, the high school, and the church all in walking distance, and a neighborhood full of instant playmates, Angie enjoyed her new home on Utica Place in spite of the cramped quarters.

      Nick had only a few months to acclimate to city life before starting school at Schenley High. To ease the transition to public school, he walked uptown on Forbes Street every day to learn conversational English at the English language school which had been established for the many immigrants who moved to Pittsburgh in the 1930's. Luckily he could communicate with his mother and siblings, who all spoke Greek, and all of the kids in the neighborhood. The entire street was made up of Greek families: Diaconis, Papandreas, Belegris, Condoyiannis, Puntzis, Sarantopoulos, Diacoyiannis, Floratos, and Nefos, to which Nefopoulas had been unofficially shortened.

The five Floratos girls loved to sing. Angie might hear *In the Mood* echoing from the Floratos's living room in five-part harmony, or perhaps a duet of *A Tisket, A Tasket* as the sisters walked down the street. Angie and her friends sang constantly, walking to school, washing the windows, or working in the kitchen. Every family had a radio, and if they weren't listening to music, they were tuning in to a radio show. Listening to *Stella Dallas* or the sound of the creaking door signaling the beginning of *Inner Sanctum* while ironing, or the *Jack Benny Show* while scrubbing the floor made Angie forget she was actually doing chores, and there were plenty of those.

While the boys were outside playing, Angie helped her mother with the laundry. She filled the kitchen sink with water, and scrubbed the clothes on a washboard, adding an extra teaspoon of *Rinso* to her brothers' shirt collars and cuffs, and rubbing the fabric together until the dirt stains were out. After all of the clothes were washed, she emptied the sink, rinsed out the soapsuds, and filled it again with rinse water. She wrung out each piece of clothing, and then carried the laundry outside in a basket to hang on the clothesline to dry. Once dry, she gathered up the clothes, and in a conundrum of the times, sprayed them with water and rolled them in balls to dampen them so that they could be ironed. The lace curtains were too delicate to iron, so Angie stretched them across a wooden frame and pinned them in place to dry.

When chores and homework were finished, Angie went outside to meet her closest friend, Virginia Diacoyiannis. Angie and Virginia walked to school together, went to Greek School together, and played cards and jacks together. Every evening after dinner, they met behind the church and sat on the low cement wall, chatting into nightfall. Often it was just the two of them, sometimes they were joined by others. One evening one of the neighborhood girls approached them. Yvonne lived a few streets over from Utica Place. By virtue of the fact that she was older, blond, and non-Greek, the girls were awed by her. Yvonne hopped onto the wall and swung her legs as she chatted about her boyfriend. "You have a boyfriend!" Virginia said. She and Angie giggled. They listened in wonder to Yvonne who, sensing that she had an eager and naïve audience, decided to teach them about the birds and the bees. The girls leaned in close when Yvonne told them just how the male anatomy fit into the female anatomy. Angie and Virginia were shocked. "Eeeuuwwww," they said. Olga had never talked about anything to do with personal hygiene, let alone sex, and when Angie first got her period at a movie theater, it was only because of girls like Yvonne that she knew what was happening. When she went home and told her mother, Olga showed Angie how to cut flour sacks into layered strips to serve as sanitary napkins, which she would launder and re-use. As a twelve-year old, Angie knew nothing about deodorant, makeup, or styling her hair, but then, neither did her girlfriends.

GREEK LESSONS - *Mathimata Ellinikon*: ΜΑΘΗΜΑΤΑ ΕΛΛΗΝΙΚΩΝ

All of the kids in the neighborhood went to church together, sang in the choir together, and went to Greek School together. Greek lessons were held in a classroom at the back of St. Nicholas Church every day after school. Although all of the kids spoke Greek in their homes, it was at Greek School where they learned grammar and reading. Mr. Rudy Agraphiotis was both their Greek School teacher and the choir director, and the kids affectionately called him "Aggie." Mr. Sidirigo was the handsome, dark-haired cantor of the church and also taught Greek School, and the kids unaffectionately referred to him as "Cedar Chest." When Athena Xides took Aggie's boots and hid them, he feigned anger, but chuckled to himself. He only brought the ruler out when the boys misbehaved. Cedar Chest, however, tolerated no shenanigans, and if the boys got unruly, he would grab their ears and twist them.

    The church was the center of their social life. Angie and Angelo sang in the church choir, and Angelo was also an Altar Boy. The choir loft was in the balcony, where the kids could look over the congregation. In between the vocal parts of the *Amen* and the *Allelulia*, the boys and girls whispered jokes to each other as Aggie followed the liturgy. "Number seven," Aggie would say, and the kids would turn the page of the hymnal and begin singing without missing a beat. On Holy Thursday, the Gospel was so long that some of the older kids would sneak out of the loft and down the back steps to Sheffel's down the street, where they would buy a piece of pizza, enjoy it, and make it back in time for the next hymn.

    While the kids went to church every Sunday, Olga attended on holidays. Angie's favorite church holiday was Easter, and the week preceding it, when the church was decorated with flowers, and the women were busy baking *koulourakia* – the braid-like butter cookies, or sweet Easter Bread, its thick dough twisted around bright red hard-boiled eggs which had been dyed and baked into the bread. On the Wednesday before Easter, Angie joined members of the congregation in the Holy Unction service, the sacrament for healing ills and preparing for communion. Angie would walk up to the priest and bow her head. Dipping his fingers in blessed oil, the priest would make a sign of the cross on her head. On the Friday night before Easter, the *epitaphio*, which represented the symbolic coffin of Christ, was decorated by the ladies of the Philoptohos, who had twisted and tied into place thousands of fragrant flowers, and sprinkled them with rose petals. The epitaphio was placed in the front of the church, between the altar and the congregation who, one by one, would approach the epitaphio, make the sign of the cross, and kiss it. As children, Angie and the other kids had crawled under the epitaphio and come out on the other side. Once in the choir, she watched the children from the loft. The epitaphio was hoisted up by the Deacons of the church, and then carried through the middle of the congregation and around the back of the church as if they were pallbearers, while the choir sang lamentations of sadness and hope which Aggie had written.

The Saturday night before Easter was magic. Angie, her mother, and her brothers were given candles as they entered the church, which began its service around eleven o'clock. Towards midnight, the lights of the church were turned off, and the congregation grew silent in the darkness. The priest lit his candle from the lone altar candle still burning. He then used his candle to light some of the candles that people in the front pew were holding, with white cardboard around the middle of the candles to keep them from dripping on their hands. These parishioners turned to the people to their left and right, and behind them, lighting their candles. Within several minutes, everyone's candles had been lit from the single candle on the altar. At midnight the chant of *"Christos Anesti!* Christ has risen!" echoed throughout the pews. *"Alithos Anesti,* Truly He has risen!" came the replies.

After the service, Angie and her brothers were torn between walking slowly from the church, hands cupped around their still-lit candles, or rushing home to eat. After fasting for the last forty days, with no meat and no dairy products, they were anxious to sit down to a late supper of *mageritsa*, a thick egg-lemon soup with the chopped lungs and liver from the lamb they bought from the butcher's shop and would be roasting for Sunday's dinner.

The Sunday afternoon church service was the *Emera tis Agape*, or the "Day of Love." Young ladies donned their white straw Easter bonnets, and the women wore their hats and gloves.

Angie wore her red and gray church dress, along with her oxford shoes and white cotton gloves. When the service ended, she and her brothers shouted *"Christos Anesti!"* once more on the concrete front steps of the church, then ran around to the back of the church to Utica Place. The entire street smelled of lamb and garlic, as some of the mothers had left the lamb to warm in the oven during the services. Others, like Olga, had stayed home to roast the leg of lamb with lemon potatoes and string beans. The kids ran across the alley to #12, and in the back door. "Christos Anesti!" Angie said.

"Change your clothes!" Olga replied. She poured bowls of *avgolemono* - egg lemon - soup as the kids took off their only Sunday clothes and hung them up until the next church service. They came back and eyed the bowl of bright red dyed eggs, trying to select the best one for the ceremonial cracking of the eggs. Whoever managed to emerge with their egg intact after cracking it around the table would have good luck for the next year. The boys grabbed their eggs, leaving the smallest for Angie. They set them on their plates, and sat down to dinner.

"I have something for you," Olga said to Angelo, with a grin on her face. She held a small round item between her thumb and forefinger.

"What is it?" Angelo asked. "A marble?"

"*Eivai to mati*, it's the eye," she said, and held it towards Angelo. "*Pare* – take it!" Between her fingers, Olga held the eye of the lamb. "Eat it!" she told Angelo. He shrunk away from the object, his eyes large while the other kids watched on in suspense.

"Go ahead, eat it!" Pete said.

"I'll give you a dollar!" Olga said.

"A dollar!" The kids could not believe it. Oh, the things a dollar could buy. Licorice, a yo-yo, a pizza, movie tickets. The possibilities were endless. Angelo took the eyeball, and in one quick movement, swallowed it whole.

"Euuwwww," said Angie, but she was silently impressed with her brother.

"Where's my dollar?" Angelo asked.

"I'll get it for you later," Olga said. "Now we eat."

They devoured their special Easter dinner with relish, tasting the subtle oregano and heavy garlic in the roast lamb, the lemony soup, the buttery potatoes. After dinner Angelo asked again for his dollar, but it was time to crack eggs. He may have realized at this point that he wasn't going to get a dollar for his courageous feat. Angie picked up her egg, and, holding the larger end in her palm, pointed the other end at Pete's egg, which he had cupped in his hand. *Smack!* She brought the egg down with force, and watched as Pete's egg cracked. "No fair," he whined. Nick and Angelo had also emerged from Round One victorious, and Angelo, after cracking Nick's egg, smiled at Angie. "Ok," she said, holding her egg up to strike.

"Nope," said Angelo. "I'm hitting yours." They sat at the table, squared off, eggs held high, until Angie said, "Okay, Angelo. I'm still going to win." With a sly smile on her face, she cupped her egg tightly in her palm, face up, poised for defense. Angelo came down hard with his egg, and they heard a loud *crack*. They examined their eggs, and Angie shouted, "I'm the lucky one!"

The Nefopoulas family could have used a little luck. With no source of income besides the government Mother's Assistance, and five kids too young to work, the family had to be resourceful. Olga decided that there must be a way to make some money. She took the streetcar downtown to the Strip District on the outskirts of the city, where wholesalers offered fruits, vegetables, and fresh fish. On both sides of Penn Avenue were stores: the "Italian Store," the "Polish Store," and the "Greek Store" - Stamoolis Brothers, where one could find pure virgin olive oil from Greece, dried chickpeas, hunks of kasseri and feta cheeses, kalamata olives, phyllo dough for baking *tiropitas,* and barrels filled with ziti or orzo. Olga, however, was looking for something else . She went to the barrel in the back of Stamoolis Brothers and filled a large burlap bag with peanuts in their shells. She brought these back to Utica Place and had all the kids scoop them into paper bags which they placed in large tan baskets with handles on either side. Then Nick, Angie, and Stanley walked over to Forbes Field where the Pittsburgh Pirates were playing. They stood outside of the ballpark, calling, "Fresh peanuts, ten cents on the inside, five cents on the outside." The kids decided to spread out, and as the National Anthem signaled the start of the game, they reconvened outside of the turnstiles. Nick approached, beaming, holding his empty basket.

"Where are your peanuts?" Angie asked.

"I sold them!" Nick replied, opening his palm to reveal a dollar bill. "A man gave me this and bought them all!"

"Oh, Nick," Angie said. The amount of peanuts in his basket should have brought twice as much money. She began to scold him, but after seeing the pride on Nick's face, Angie said, "That's wonderful!"

Nick was schooled in the finer points of peanut vending and taught to look out for the unscrupulous characters who might try to take advantage of him. But the job of selling peanuts was not without its other perils. One summer afternoon eleven-year old Angelo and nine-year-old Peter carried their heavy straw baskets filled with bags of fresh peanuts to the ballpark. They stopped outside of the arched block entrance of the stadium and looked for a spot to set up shop. A man and his son, a young black teenage boy a few years older than Angelo, also scouted the area. The father situated the boy, then walked around the outside of the stadium, along the curve of the concrete walls. Fans streamed in by the hundreds – the capacity crowd of 40,000 meant good potential business. Angelo began to call, "Get your fresh peanuts. Ten cents on the inside – five cents on the outside!" when the boy approached him.

"Hey," the young man said, "this is our territory. Go somewhere else."

Angelo ignored him, and continued to vend his peanuts.

"Hey! I said get outta here, or I'm gonna make you get outta here," the boy threatened, moving closer to Angelo.

Angelo turned away from the boy, who then dropped his basket of peanuts, and pushed Angelo. Angelo dropped his basket and pushed back, and they began to punch each other. A small group of fans paused to watch, but no one intervened. All of sudden, young Pete burst through the group and jumped on the boy, shouting, "get away from my brother!" and began to punch him on the back. The force of the nine-year old was too much for the boy, and he shook Pete off, grabbed his basket, and fled around the curve of the stadium. The small crowd of onlookers who had formed quickly disbursed. Angelo, a little shaken, began his sales pitch again, when a policeman walked over to him.

"Hey kid," the policeman addressed him, "you got a license for selling those peanuts?" Angelo looked at him quizzically.
"You can't sell outside the stadium without a license." Angelo shrugged.
"Let's go, kid," the policeman said, and guided Angelo through the crowd. The policeman walked him up Forbes to the police station, where Angelo, already unnerved by the earlier events of the afternoon, was made to sit out the duration of the game in the holding area.

The trip to the police station holding room repeated itself throughout the summer, sometimes for Stanley, sometimes for Angelo, sometimes for the two of them. But, despite the brushes with the law and territorial disputes, the Nefopoulas kids continued to sell peanuts at the ballpark all summer long. They never made it into the stadium to see a baseball game; the cost to get into a Pirate's game was a dollar – the equivalent of 20 bags of peanuts and much hard work. Mr. Anastasi, who owned the hot dog cart outside of the main entrance was impressed with the family's entrepreneurship, and offered Angie a job selling hotdogs. Before every game, Angie worked behind the raised counter, handing steaming hotdogs down to the fans before they entered the ballpark. The money the kids made from their work was always turned over to Olga for household expenses and trips to the market.

Occasionally Angie accompanied Olga downtown on her shopping trips. Sometimes they took the streetcar to Donohoe's at the end of Forbes Avenue in Market Square to buy meat, vegetables, and butter. Then they went to the fish market on Diamond Street, where Olga examined the eyes of the fish to see if it was fresh. A big treat was getting four or five pennies to spend on penny candy at Murphy's 5 & 10. A bigger treat was having lunch at the counter, where Angie would sit on the silver stools with the deep red tufted seats and order a grilled cheese sandwich.

When it came time for Angie to get a new pair of shoes for school, she and Olga took the streetcar downtown to shop at the shoe stores on Fifth Avenue. By the age of thirteen, Angie was starting to realize that her plain cotton dress and brown oxfords were not what the other girls wore to school. They went into Baker's Shoe Store, and Olga pointed to a pair of brown oxfords similar to the worn pair on Angie's feet.

"I don't want those," Angie said. She pointed to a shiny pair of black patent leather shoes with straps that buckled instead of shoes that laced. "I want those." Olga insisted that she try on the shoes, and despite Angie's insistence that she didn't want "old lady shoes," Olga bought the oxfords.

As they crossed Fifth Avenue, the bag with her new shoes in hand, Angie continued to whine. "I don't want these," she insisted, and with that, Olga took her large black purse and whacked Angie across the shoulders.

It must have upset Olga not to be able to provide for her children the way she could when Archie was alive and times were better. One thing that she was able to do was treat the kids to the movies. Almost every Saturday, Angie and her brothers walked down Forbes to either the Schenley Theater or the Strand, where for ten cents they could buy themselves an afternoon of entertainment. They might see previously released films like *Frankenstein* and *Dracula*, or if they were lucky, a new release would be playing.

One Saturday afternoon, the marquis outside of the Strand Theater read, "Stella Dallas, starring Barbara Stanwyck and John Boles." The kids arrived early, so that Stanley could participate in the paddleball contest on the stage. Angie and her brothers watched from the plush auditorium seats as Stanley and several other boys each hit a blue rubber ball attached by a thin elastic rope to a wooden paddle, to see who could keep the ball going the longest. This kept the kids in the audience entertained until the show was about to begin. The lights dimmed as the heavy maroon curtains parted on the stage, revealing the black and white cartoon image of *Popeye the Sailor Man* on the large screen. The audience was full of kids whose parents had given themselves a quiet Saturday afternoon. They applauded as Popeye strutted down the street in his sailor cap, waving his overly muscular forearms, and with his raspy voice sang:

I'm Popeye the Sailor Man
I'm Popeye the Sailor Man
I'm strong to the finish, 'cuz I eats my spinach!
I'm Popeye the Sailor Man.

The giggling and chatter which accompanied the cartoon immediately subsided as the feature presentation, came on. Angie was mesmerized by the story of Stella Dallas, the young woman from the wrong side of the tracks who managed to marry a rich society man. By the end of the movie, when poor Stella had been abandoned by her husband and given up her daughter, Angie was sobbing uncontrollably. Pete, undaunted by the movie plot, laughed at his older sister's silly reaction to the movie.

On a Saturday afternoon a few months later, the tables turned. Angie, Stanley, and Pete went to the matinee at the Strand to see the new release of *Lost Horizon*. They heard the click click of the projector reel, and settled in to their seats just in time to see the face of Mickey Mouse on the screen, announcing the cartoon. Pete and Stanley laughed as Donald Duck tried to be a one-duck circus, and the balls that he tried to juggle hit him on the head. The feature began, and Angie and Stanley were silent as the main character, Robert Conway, led a team of soldiers to rescue a group of Westerners from an unfriendly city in China. Pete stopped fidgeting in his seat, entranced when the plane crashed in the Himalayan Mountains, and the team was rescued and taken to Shangri-la, an idyllic utopia sheltered from the bitter cold. The kids watched intently as Conway's brother George fell in love with Maria, one of the residents of Shangri-la, and asked her to depart with them, heedless of the warnings that Maria must not leave Shangri-la. The soundtrack played its funereal music as they traveled the dangerous snow-covered mountain paths, and Pete felt his heart beat a little faster. Poor Maria had become exhausted, and George had to carry her on his back. But George too was exhausted: his grip on Maria loosened, and she fell, face down in the snow. As Conway turned her over, to George's horror, he realized that Maria had, upon leaving Shangri-la, become an old woman, and was now dead. Her features were wrinkled and distorted, and as George screamed in terror and jumped over the cliff to his death, Peter screamed in terror and ran out of the theater.

  Every once in a while Olga accompanied the children to the movies, but more often than not, she used the peace and quiet to prepare food for the weekend. It was not unusual for Angie to come home from the movies to find her mother in her bedroom, covering a clean bedsheet with unprinted paper, preparing to make *trahana*. Back in the kitchen, Olga mixed sour milk and coarse flour in a bowl with her hands, and kneaded it into a thick dough. Angie washed her hands, and joined Olga in shaping the dough into two-inch balls, which they then spread over the sheet on the bed until they dried. Once the balls were dry, Angie and Olga crumbled them into small pea-sized pieces, and stored them in the cupboard in glass jars. The kids hated the bland trahana, which was eaten in a bowl with a little warm milk, hot water, or some chicken broth, depending on what was available. Often though, it was either this meal, or nothing, so they ate it.

In front of the University of Pittsburgh
Left to right: Nick (back), Pete, Angelo,
Olga, Angie, Stanley

CHICKEN EVERY SUNDAY - *Kotopoulo Kathe Kuriaki*: ΚΟΤΟΠΟΥΛΟ ΚΑΘΕ ΚΥΡΙΑΚΗ

The children often accompanied Olga on her trips to the market. On one of these trips, Nick and Angelo went with Olga on the streetcar which let them off at the bottom of the hill to Logan Street. They walked up the hill to the produce area, and Olga eyed the stands to see what she might want to buy for their evening meal. While the boys looked around at the tables full of fresh eggplants and melons, Olga found what she had been hunting for. Looking over the live poultry, she selected a plump tan chicken for Sunday dinner. The vendor bound the squawking chicken's spindly red legs with thick twine to keep it from running away, and put it in a large paper shopping bag. With the chicken in tow, Olga called to Nick and Angelo, and they walked back down the hill and crossed the street. The chicken began to fidget as they waited for their ride, but it was only a few minutes before they heard the rumble of the faded red streetcar on the metal tracks. They boarded the car, and the conductor paid no heed to the large paper bag in Olga's hand which held the fidgety chicken. Nick and Angelo ran towards the back and sat down on one side of the car; Olga sat down across the aisle from them. The streetcar chugged away from the stop and headed east toward Oakland. Without warning, the chicken burst through the paper bag and onto the streetcar floor. Slowly, awkwardly, and desperately, the chicken scooted itself forward, its legs still bound, wings flapping frantically, propelling itself towards the front of the car.

"Vaggeli, Niko!" Olga shouted, "*Piase ti kota*! Catch the chicken!"

Angelo and Nick looked on in dismay as their mother attempted to chase a chicken down the aisle in the middle of the streetcar.

"Vaggeli! *Voithia*, Help me!" she yelled at the kids, who had slunk into their seats like pupils who don't want to be called on in class, ignorant of the value of the chicken to the family. Olga knew that she could not afford to let the chicken get away under any circumstance. She made her way up the aisle, holding tightly onto each vinyl seat back as the car bumped along on the tracks, until she reached the front, where the chicken flapped helplessly. The conductor stopped the streetcar while Olga cornered the frantic chicken. She put her hands around it and picked it up as it squawked. At this point, the boys disavowed any knowledge they had of Olga or the chicken, avoiding her glare as she returned to her seat with the captured chicken. They rode the rest of the way home in silence, as Olga glowered at them from across the aisle, the chicken firmly in place on her lap. The streetcar slowly screeched to a stop in front of Utica Way, and Olga got off, the boys trailing behind, fearing the wrath they knew they deserved. But, once home, Olga had work to do. Her upbringing in the village had prepared her for the task at hand. She deftly grabbed the chicken's head, twisted it around, and snapped its neck. Once she killed the chicken, she plucked its feathers. After washing the carcass, Olga stuck her hand inside to take out the innards of the chicken. She then rinsed out the cavity, and singed the outside in the frying pan. While the chicken was searing, she put the liver and gizzards in another pan, and fried them in a little butter. Olga brushed the seared chicken with butter, and placed in the oven to roast, along with potatoes which she sprinkled with lemon, oil and oregano.

The smell of chicken in the oven lured the boys into the kitchen, but dinner was still a long way off. Olga boiled a pot of water, and dumped in fresh kale to make *lahana*. Once the greens had boiled, she strained them and squeezed a fresh lemon over them, letting them come to room temperature. She called Angie to set the table for dinner, and the meal was served, with no further mention of the incident on the streetcar. No matter how difficult times were, and how tight money was, Olga was determined to serve chicken dinner every Sunday.

One Sunday in December of 1941, the kids went to a dance at the church hall. All of the kids from Utica Place went to the dances "stag." The Greek boys didn't date the Greek girls – at least not at age fifteen. Some of this had to do with the fact that they were all friends, but most of it had to do with the fact that the fathers of the girls were quite protective. Yet, everyone danced together to the boogie-woogie and jitterbug tunes played by the live band on the stage at the far end of the church hall. Most of the kids had never had a dance lesson but somehow, intuitively, had picked up the moves. Angie loved to dance, and especially liked to cut the rug with Louie D, a rather homely, slim, short older man who specialized in the tango and the rhumba. All of the girls, young and older, wanted to dance with Louie, who they marveled danced just like Fred Astaire. Angie and Louie had just finished dancing a rhumba when Angie noticed a few of her friends clustered in the corner. She left Louie to entertain another young lady, and walked over to investigate. "What's going on?" she asked.
    "The Japanese bombed Pearl Harbor."
    "What's Pearl Harbor?" asked another friend.
    The news spread throughout the church hall, the kids in disbelief that America had been attacked. They returned to their dancing, unaware of the impact that the seemingly random act would have on all of their lives and families.

For the immediate future, life went on as it had been. Nick found work at Harris Brother's Florist, Stanley took the streetcar downtown to his part-time job at Philadelphia Florist, and Angie, Stanley, and Angelo continued to attend Greek School. But the fact that the boys were getting older didn't make them any better behaved at Greek School, and they continued to get into trouble. Daydreaming at Greek school brought Stanley not only a slap from "Cedar Chest," but a second slap from Olga when he got home.
    The real mischief-makers were Angelo and his friends, Harry and Gus. The boys continually passed notes and made

noises behind Cedar Chest's back to the delight of the other boys in the class, and the chagrin of Mr. Sidirigos. Their most elaborate stunt was when they spread the rumor that their friend, Jimmy Pantasis, who had been absent from school, had passed away. The news quickly spread from Greek school to Schenley High School, but they were not content to stop there. Their ultimate demise was when they decided to place his obituary into the Pittsburgh newspaper. Jimmy, of course, was alive and well, but the repercussions from angry relatives and the law ultimately suppressed the boys' antics. When Olga found that the police had questioned Angelo at school, she scolded him and hit him with a broom.

Stanley began his senior year at Schenley High School in September of 1942. He would walk up Bellefield Street with his friend Jim Bombouras, while Angie chatted with Virginia a few paces behind. As they crossed the street at Fifth Avenue, the smog from the nearby steel mills lay heavy in the air, and by the time the kids got to school, they blew their noses into clean white handkerchiefs to clear their nostrils of the black dust which they had inhaled.

Angie, now in her junior year, embraced learning and consistently excelled in her classes. She was especially good at English, in spite of the fact that her first language was Greek. She and her brothers spoke only Greek in their home – it wasn't until they began going to school that they became fluent in English. It wasn't just the academic subjects that she enjoyed – having grown up with four brothers, she found that she was good at physical education. She was taught how to swim in the large pool at Schenley High School, learning how to float on her back in case, as the instructor said, they were ever in a "situation." She liked running the relay races in the gym, despite having to wear the red one-piece bloomers with elastic at the legs, but she preferred the high school library, where she volunteered whenever she had a free period. Angie knew the location of every book in the library. She stacked books during her lunch period, checked books out for students after school, updated the card catalog, and typed memos for the librarian, Mrs. Kirkland during study halls. "You're my Angel," Mrs. Kirkland told Angie. "I don't know what I would do without you."

One afternoon, Angie sat in the small room across from the library at the typewriter which faced the door. She looked up briefly from her typing to see blond, blue-eyed Bill Robinette in the door frame. She had seen him in the halls with his girlfriend, but had never had a conversation with him. *I wonder what he's doing here*, she thought to herself, but continued to type. Bill walked around behind the desk, and paused by Angie's chair. He bent down, turned Angie away from her typing, and kissed her, slowly and decisively. Stunned and confused, Angie felt her face flush crimson as she watched Bill leave the room. Still perplexed, she wondered, "What would Peggy Bailey think if she knew her boyfriend kissed me!" The rest of her junior year passed without further incident, but also without any insight as to why she had received her first kiss from Bill.

Despite their mother's lack of English, Angie and her brothers encouraged Olga to become a naturalized citizen. Angie quizzed her about random facts as they sat at the kitchen table.

"Mamma', who was the first president?"

"Washeengton."

"How many stars and stripes in the American flag?"

"*Vre, then to ksero* - I don't know," she said.

"Forty-eight stars and thirteen stripes, Mother. *Entdaksi* - Ok?" Angie said.

"*Entdaksi.*"

"Ok," Angie said. "Where do you live?"

"Peetsiborg," Olga replied.

After weeks of quizzing, Olga felt she was ready. Angie and Olga took the streetcar down Fifth Avenue and got off at Grant Street. They walked up the grey slab steps and through the heavy revolving doors of the Allegheny County Courthouse, the clicking of their heels echoing on the marble floors as they crossed a large hall to the steps. They waited in the anteroom for the Deputy Clerk who escorted them into the courtroom.

"I'm going to ask you a few questions, Mrs. Nefopoulas," he said.

"My mother doesn't speak English," Angie said. The clerk allowed her to translate the questions for Olga.

"What are the colors of our flag?" he began, continuing the process with only a few simple questions, until Angie was given the last one to translate.

"Who is the president of the United States?"

Olga didn't wait for the translation. "Roosivel!" she announced.

"Do you promise to uphold the constitution of the United States," the clerk began, and as Angie finished the translation she said, "*Pes tou yes*, tell him 'yes.'"

"Yes," Olga replied.

"Congratulations, Mrs. Nefopoulas," smiled the clerk.

On May 19, 1943 at the age of forty seven, Olga Nefopoulas officially became a U.S. Citizen.

WAR YEARS - *Hronia Tou Polemou*: ΧΡΟΝΙΑ ΤΟΥ ΠΟΛΕΜΟΥ

Later that year the Nefopoulas family moved uptown into a larger house on Fifth Avenue. While this meant that the kids could no longer walk to school, they didn't mind taking the streetcar – especially if it meant a two-story house with a real bathroom and a basement. Angie now worked as a clerk at Autenrite's Five and Ten on Forbes, near the Strand Theater, and Angelo found work at Miller's Drug Store working the 6 p.m. to 2 a.m. shift for $18 a week. Stanley graduated and found a job at Reich's Ice Cream Store on Fifth Avenue. Like Angelo, he worked a night shift, and shortly after starting the job, which initially entailed moving and stacking milk crates, he was given the responsibility of mixing ingredients in a large aluminum vat to make 500 pounds of ice-cream. One night about two weeks into the job, Stanley poured in the sugar, milk, and flavoring which he combined in a large vat and then released into the cooling lines which carried the mixture into another container that stored the cold concoction. Stanley finished up his mixing, checked the lines, took off his gloves and apron, and left for the night. The next evening, his boss met him at the door. "Did you mix the ice cream?" he interrogated Stanley.

"Yes," Stanley replied, wondering at his boss's tone.
"Oh yeah?" His boss said. "Have a look at this."
He took Stanley into the cooler where the mixture traveled through the lines. Gooey melted ice cream covered the floor, having spilled from a split in the line which Stanley had not noticed. After cleaning up the mess with a bucket and a mop, Stanley was demoted on the spot, relegated to emptying and stacking the milk crates.

The wages earned by the children helped the family to afford the home on Fifth Avenue. To supplement the children's earnings, Olga rented the upstairs out to Sam and Maria Solomotis. With the bigger house came bigger chores, and Angie and Stanley were in charge of keeping the home fires burning. A large coal truck pulled up to the house and dumped a large pile of coal outside of the basement. Angie and Stanley shoveled the lumps of coal into the coal chute which led to the cellar basement. The coal whizzed down the chute and landed with a thud onto the basement floor. Down in the basement they opened the cast iron door and shoveled coal into the furnace, sending up a cloud of black soot which lingered in the musty air, coating their hands and nostrils. The coal burned hot white as it spread warmth through the heating pipes, before it turned to ash, dropping through the grate and onto the bottom of the furnace. The kids swept the gray ashes out with a dustpan into a bucket and shoveled more coal into the furnace.

    The house, warm at night, was chilly in the morning, and Angie quickly put on her robe and slippers to go into the basement to stoke the embers and shovel more coal into the furnace. She came back upstairs and opened the front door to bring the glass milk bottles by the front door inside. Her breath was clear and white in the early morning air, and she wrapped her robe closely around her as she left the old bottles, which she had rinsed out, for the milkman to take back to the dairy. The tops of the fresh bottles had popped off from ice that had formed on the caps. Angie waited for the caps to thaw so that she could put them back on the bottles, and put the bottles into the icebox. The Iceman had come the day before. With his huge metal tongs, he had grasped a large block of ice and placed it in the top of the icebox in the kitchen. Angie checked the pan underneath the icebox to make sure that the water from the melting ice had not overflowed the pan and spilled onto the linoleum floor. Olga was pouring farina into a pot of scalded milk on the stove. As she stirred the cereal it became smooth and thick. She ladled a bowl for herself and one for Angie, while Angie poured them each a cup of coffee from the percolator. She added a teaspoon of sugar and a little milk, and had a quick breakfast. Then she changed into her housedress and gathered up the laundry from the hamper and went into the basement for the next chore.

    Another perk of the furnace was the hot water which allowed Angie to wash the clothes in the washtub in the basement, rather than in the kitchen sink. In the winter months, clothes were hung to dry on rope lines in the basement. In warm, dry weather, Angie hung the clothes outside on the clothesline which was stretched between two metal poles on each side of the yard. From the backyard she heard the hucksters who came around to the neighborhood yelling, "Tomatoes, peppers, cucumbers!" Olga went outside to where the truck was parked in the middle of the street to pick out tomatoes and peppers to make *yemisted domates kai pipieryes*, stuffed tomatoes and peppers with rice and ground meat for dinner. Sometimes a man drove down Fifth Avenue in his flatbed truck which was loaded with ripe watermelons. Lifting one of the large green watermelons off of the bed, he would take his pocketknife and cut a small triangle in the side of the melon, handing it to Olga for a taste of the sweet pink fruit.

On warm summer days, Olga would often visit with a friend who was known as *Alekina* - 'wife of Aleko,' as Greek tradition dictated for women of that generation. Olga's friends called her *Ahila'ana* - 'wife of Achilles,' even though her husband had passed away. Now that the family was living on Fifth Avenue, Olga could walk to Alekina's house near Logan Street, to visit with her friend, who was also a widow. They would have a cup of coffee and some *glykes* or sweets that they had made, or perhaps bought from the Greek store in the Strip District.

     Nick's English had improved, and he had started a job at Harris Brothers Florist, taking orders and arranging flowers. But with World War II intensifying, he enlisted in the army and was deployed overseas. Some of their friends had already been drafted, and the family took it in stride, not really understanding the situations that Nick would be facing in Europe. Stanley had a job at Philadelphia Florist making corsages and delivering flowers to the funeral homes. Angelo was working at Miller's Drug Store at night. Pete had just started high school and Angie was entering her senior year.

     The annual talent show, 'Stunt Day,' was coming up, and although singing in the church choir was Angie's forte, serendipity sent her in a different direction. She had stayed after school to work at the library, and as she passed by the auditorium she heard her friend, Sarah, practicing a boogie-woogie song on the piano for the upcoming show. Angie ran up the steps of the stage and started prancing around to the beat. The girls laughed and decided that adding a dance would enhance the act. This would be their only practice. On the day of the talent show, Angie stood in the wings of the stage, dressed in a circle skirt, white blouse, black and white saddle shoes, and ankle socks, her long dark brown hair pulled back into a low ponytail. The first chords of the boogie-woogie rang out from the piano, and Angie emerged from the side of the stage, rocking to the boogie beat. She boogied her way to the center of the stage, pointing her right index finger down while shuffling to the beat, and shaking her shoulders from side to side. As she boogied her way around to face the audience, she caught a glimpse of Angelo and his friends sitting near the front. Angelo, a look of utter horror on his face, slunk down low in his seat. His friends on either side of him sat forward, laughing and clapping. Angie continued to dance forward and back, side to side, all over the stage, ending the dance to raucous applause.

Angie maintained her celebrity status for a day, as her friends greeted her in school with, "Great job, Angie," and "My gosh! Who knew!" But when she got into her English class, her favorite teacher, Miss MacDonald, raised her eyebrows and greeted her with, "Well! I guess you can't tell a book from its cover!"

During lunch the students were permitted to go outside for some fresh air, and Angelo and his friends made the best of it. Undeterred by the cold weather, they took advantage of the winter snow to have snowball fights. During one of these fights, one of Angelo's throws went errant, hitting Miss MacDonald in the back. Mortified, he ran into the building, but realized that she had most likely seen him. He decided that it was in his best interest to apologize to the English teacher, and approached her as he went into the classroom. "Miss MacDonald," he began, "I'm sorry that..." but she cut him off.

"How could you have done that?" she demanded. "You don't pay attention outside. You don't pay attention in class. I can't believe that you're Angeline's brother!"

No longer repentant, Angelo was now only annoyed at Miss MacDonald for comparing him to his sister.

Perhaps inspired by her musical foray, Angie became interested in playing the piano. A neighbor down the street was moving away and offered his old upright piano to the family if they were willing to move it. It took three of them – Stanley and Angelo to do the pushing and pulling, and Pete to navigate down the brick street and direct traffic away from them, as the piano wheels got caught in the cracks and the passing cars slowed down to watch the spectacle on the street. The boys rolled the heavy piece down Fifth Avenue and straight into the front door to the living room on the left. They set the piano bench down next to the piano, and Angie opened the smooth dark hinged top to find pieces of sheet music, and a few piano books. She read the cover of the first one: *John W. Schaum Piano Course Pre-A, the Green Book, Leading to Mastery of the Instrument*. Delighted, Angie opened the cover and soon taught herself how to play simple pieces, starting with *Little Steamboat*, which called for three notes played with the right hand. Within a few weeks she had added the left hand and the black keys, and continued to work her way through the beginning book, adding *The Happy Halibut* with its eighth notes and *the Detective* with its sharps and flats. It wasn't long before she had progressed to *Book C*, and felt that she had mastered *Gertrude and Elizabeth*, the Schaum arrangement of Beethoven's *Fur Elise*. Sam and Maria came downstairs as Angie sat down to play the piano. Angie adjusted her skirt, placed her fingers on the keys, and began to play the piece she had been practicing. She heard snickers and giggles to her left and realized that Pete and Angelo had come in and were standing in the doorway. Angie slowly turned her head to glare at her brothers, all the while continuing to play the melodic strains of *Fur Elise*.

    Angie received her yearbook towards the end of the school year, and found that her musical talent had not been forgotten. Her friend's comments in the yearbook ranged from, "To a girl who appreciates boogie woogie as I do," to, "Talk about nuts. Wow!" Angie wondered what the editorial committee meant when their caption for her picture in the yearbook read *the wisdom of one, the wit of many*. She agreed with their choice for her friend, Virginia – *so likeable*, and she smiled as she read the caption for Bill Robinette – *a madcap sprite* – which shed some light on the clandestine kiss.

On the last day of school, Miss MacDonald asked Angie to come to see her.

    "Angie," she said. "I wanted to talk to you about something. I have a friend who has a law office in Pittsburgh. I'd like to recommend you for a job there."

    "Oh, thank you, Mrs. MacDonald, but I have a job already."

    The high school counselor had called Angie and Margaret Bruno, and told them about jobs at the purchasing department of the Pittsburgh Board of Education. The jobs would begin immediately at a salary of $90 a month. Angie figured it would be better than her stenographer teacher's suggestion: *You have a nice voice, Angie. You might want to consider being a telephone operator.* And it was more realistic than accepting the scholarship she had been offered to the University of Pittsburgh for graduating first in her class at Schenley High. How would she be able to earn money to help pay the bills if she were attending college?

"I think that you would enjoy working for the law office, Angie," Mrs. MacDonald continued. "It's a very good job."

But with no counsel from the guidance department, and no guidance from her family, Angie began working as a clerk for the purchasing department of the Pittsburgh Board of Education the following day.

Graduating from high school also meant graduating from the bobby socks and saddle shoes that she wore to school every day. Angie struggled to line up the seams as she drew her nylon stockings up over her knees. As she walked to the closet to get her new pumps, the stockings started to slide down her legs. She pulled them back up again, but again they slid down. She didn't know what to do. She couldn't wear bobby socks to work, but she couldn't go to work with her nylons down around her ankles! She solved the problem by pulling rubber bands up over her knees and securing the tops of the stockings to her thighs. She discussed her dilemma with Virginia after work, and they consulted Yvonne, who introduced them to the idea of a garter belt. Angie walked up Fifth Avenue to Autenrite's and purchased the piece of elastic with the strange round snaps that would secure the stockings and keep them from falling down her legs – and would no longer cut off her circulation.

Stanley had received his draft notice, and as he prepared to leave for paratrooper training, Olga handed him five dollars so that he would have some money for the trip. He thanked her, and then made the mistake of telling her that the Ladies' Auxiliary organization had also given him five dollars. When she learned this, Olga took the money back.

Stanley's training did not last long; he hurt his ankle in a night jump, and was promoted to Staff Sergeant, stateside, because he knew how to type. Nick was now stationed overseas. There was little word from him, except for the occasional V-mail, which allowed the soldiers to send word home to their families. Angelo and Pete were still in high school, but Pete was determined to join the war effort, so he volunteered with the National Guard in Pittsburgh. During mandatory blackouts, a siren went off, signaling that all power was to be turned off. Drapes were closed and lights were turned off. It was Pete's job to go out with a flashlight and make sure that no one was out on the streets.

It was the summer of 1944, and Angie was cleaning the kitchen. She had emptied the pan of water from underneath the icebox into the sink, and got down on her knees to scrub the floor. She dipped the scrub brush into the soapy bucket and began to rub the yellow linoleum when a movement caught her attention. She looked up and saw Nick in his uniform standing in the doorway. She dropped her brush into the bucket, and stood up, wiping her hands on her apron as she smiled at Nick. Once again she found herself thinking, *my, how handsome he is.* Later that night, Nick told Angie and Olga that he had been wounded at Normandy Beach when he was hit with shrapnel. He did not elaborate. He showed them the Purple Heart that he had received for his valor in combat. It was hard for Angie to imagine her gentle brother in combat, but seeing the Purple Heart brought her a dose of reality.

Nick and Olga

Nick spoke little of his experiences overseas. During that summer, he began to teach himself to play the old upright piano in the living room. When he wasn't at the piano, he spent time sketching, and began to take art lessons in Squirrel Hill. Some days he would sit in the sun on the steep wooden back steps, and once in a while the little girl who lived next door would come over to talk to him. One afternoon as Nick chatted with the little girl, he noticed that her legs had strange marks on them, and motioned her to come nearer so that he could take a closer look at them. That evening, the police came to the door to question Nick. A neighbor had spotted him examining the girl's legs and had reported him to the police. After Nick explained what he had seen to the police, they thanked him, and left. The girl's legs were covered with cigarette burns. Her parents were arrested.

Nick decided to use the G.I. Bill to go to the Art Institute of Pittsburgh in the fall. In the meantime, he continued with his art lessons. Angelo was impressed with Nick's artistic ability, but even more impressed that he was drawing from nude models. "You're drawing naked women!" he said. "Take me with you!" Nick refused, but Angelo persisted. Nick finally broke down.

"Okay, okay. You can come with me. But you have to be quiet." Angelo took the bus with Nick, chatting all the way to Squirrel Hill, while Nick sat calmly, looking out the window. As they walked up to the house, Nick again cautioned Angelo to be quiet. They walked into the studio, and Nick set up his easel next to the other students. The model walked in and took off *his* robe. Angelo walked out.

Angelo enlisted in the Air Force and left for St. Louis. The days of Greek school were over for all of them, but Angie was still involved with the church choir and with the Maids of Athens, a Greek social group for young ladies. She discovered that she was good at organizing, forming committees, and coordinating shows and dances. Together with her friends in the Maids, they formed the unofficial GAVVAS: Georgia, Angie, Virginia, Vicki, Angeline, and Stella. The GAVVAS would meet each other at the movies, or get together at each other's houses to play the piano and sing. Sometimes they played board games like Parcheesi or Monopoly, or put together variety shows, where they performed for their friends. Angie and Virginia sang a Greek song, "*To yelekaki pou forees*..., the vest that you are wearing, I knitted myself," with a country twang in one of these shows, exploding into a fit of giggles.

    The GAVVAS decided to sponsor a Halloween dance. A few days before the dance, they drove out to a farm not too far out of town to collect cornstalks to decorate the church hall. They loaded the car with as many cornstalks as they could fit into the trunk and on the floor, and crammed back into the car, Georgia and Angie in the back seat. As they pulled out onto the parkway, Georgia took a pack of cigarettes out of her handbag. She shook out a cigarette, put it in her mouth, and pulled out a matchbook. The girls watched her as she struck the match on the book and lit her cigarette nonchalantly.

    "Georgia!" Angie said.

    "What?" said Georgia. She took a puff of her cigarette and offered it to Angie, her red lipstick rimming the tip.

    Angie giggled. She put the cigarette between her fingers, as she had seen in the movies, and hesitantly took her first puff. For a split second she felt like a glamourous actress as she slowly inhaled. She was anything but glamourous when she tasted the bitter tar and coughed on the smoke, deciding then and there that it was her first and last cigarette.

At the Halloween dance, as with all of the dances sponsored by the Maids of Athens, most of their friends arrived "stag." Greek boys didn't want to date the Greek girls, because people would expect them to get married. Virginia's mother not only encouraged her daughter to go to the dances, she insisted that she go, saying, "Who knows, you might meet somebody!" Some of the mothers would sit around keeping a watchful eye on their daughters, so boys were careful about dancing with the Greek girls at all.

    One evening Angie went to a show at Mellon Institute, and found herself sitting next to a handsome blond man who struck up a conversation with her. At the end of the evening, he asked her out for a date. She felt herself blushing, flustered at his interest in her. She also knew that she wouldn't be permitted to go out with him, and said "No, thank you."

    Since the Greek boys didn't date the Greek girls, and the Greek girls were not allowed to date non-Greeks - if they were allowed to date at all - there was only one way to get married.

Angie returned home from work one evening to find the Greek Orthodox priest, dressed in his black suit and white collar, sitting in the living room with Olga. The priest was visiting on behalf of Mr. Bombouras, the father of Stanley's friend Jim, who owned the University Grill on Forbes and Craig Street. Mr. Bombouras' older son, Pete, had recently started going out with an American waitress from the restaurant. His mother was quite upset about this, and told her husband to do something about it. He spoke to the priest, who agreed to pay a call on Olga to attempt to arrange a marriage between Pete Bombouras and Angie. Although Olga was amenable to the idea, especially coming from the priest, she also did not want to lose Angie, who did the majority of the laundry, ironing, and cleaning. Angie listened in disbelief as the priest spoke. When he finished his proposal, Angie politely said, "No, thank you."

Angie was shocked to find out that her friend Georgia suddenly married a much older man, Gus. This was followed by the news that her long-time friend, Mary, had married the accordion player who played at the church dances – a widower with a little girl - and Angie had known nothing about it. She discovered that the marriages had been arranged.

Fresh from the shock of this news, she was only slightly prepared when a man from the church spoke to her on behalf of his well-to-do friend from Burgettstown who was looking for a Greek bride. "This man has money, and you would have a nice house," the man told Angie.

"No, no, no!" was her reply.

Angie quickly made friends with her coworkers at the Board of Education, Dorothy and Myrna. When her brother Pete offered to lend her his car, the girls planned a trip to Florida. But first, they needed to get their drivers' licenses. Even though they were all twenty-one, none had bothered to get their license, since none of them owned a car. Their boss, Mr. Berardi, allowed them all to leave work early to go for their driver's tests. They returned to work the next day, embarrassed; none of them had passed the test. Eventually they each did, and they put together plans to drive to St. Petersburg.

Pete pulled up to the house where the girls were waiting with their suitcases. Angie looked skeptically at the old gray Ford sedan. "Is the car alright?" she asked.

"Angeline," Pete said. "Would I let you go to Florida in my car without checking it first? I just had everything looked at. New tires, new filter. It's in perfect shape." The girls were barely out of Pittsburgh when they noticed black smoke pouring out from under the hood. They pulled off of the parkway, popped the hood, and peered into the engine compartment, furrowing their brows.

"Maybe we should go back," Dorothy said. An older gentleman pulled up, diagnosed the problem, and took out a jug of water from his trunk, which he poured into the radiator. The girls thanked him and pulled back onto the parkway. A few miles later they went through the toll booth, and cruised onto the turnpike. As they neared Washington D.C., they noticed smoke pouring out of the hood again. They pulled off the turnpike and found a gas station. As the attendant flushed the radiator, the girls sat on a curb waiting. "Maybe we should just go home," Dorothy said again.

"We are not going home," Angie said. "We're going to Florida!"

The girls noticed a group of serviceman across from them, and one of the men approached them. "Hey! I know you gals. You work with my wife at the Board! What are you doing here?" He chatted with the girls until the car was ready. As they got into Pete's car, he called, "Good Luck!"

"We're going to need it," Dorothy said.
They were Florida-bound, windows down, in good spirits, hair blowing in the wind. "Angie!" Dorothy said. "How fast are you going?" Angie glanced at the speedometer. With no posted speed limit on the new turnpike, she hadn't realized that she was cruising along at ninety miles per hour. Although giddy at the realization that she was driving at such a high speed, her sense of responsibility took over. She eased up on the gas pedal, and Dorothy let out an audible sigh.

They found a motel in North Carolina to spend the night, all three of them sharing a room. Early the next morning they took off, and by the time the sun was baking the concrete of the turnpike, they had crossed the Florida state line. They traveled ocean route A1A, eager to arrive at the beach, when the right rear tire blew. Fortune was in their favor; they coasted to a stop right in front of a gas station.

"You ladies are lucky," the attendant said, shaking his head as he looked over the tire. "That tire is bald."

"Can you fix it?"

"Nope. You're gonna need a new one."

The girls continued on to Miami, cursing Pete for about ten miles, but the warm air and sunshine brightened their moods, and as they flew down the A1A, a sedan full of young men pulled up even with them in the passing lane.

"Hey girls, where ya headed?" one of the men shouted from the passenger side.

"Miami!" Angie shouted back.

"Angie!" Myrna said. "What are you doing? What if they follow us?"

Away from home, and spurred on by her first taste of independence, Angie kept the conversation going. As the boy in the back seat rolled down his window to get a closer look at the girls in the car, Dorothy slunk down in her back seat and rolled her window up. "Angie! Stop talking to them. You don't even know them!"

"We'll never see them again!" Angie said, but she reluctantly slowed down and let the boys pass. As evening approached they pulled up to a motel a few blocks from the beach. They ordered some burgers at the coffee shop down the street and turned in for the night.

The next day dawned hot and bright, and Dorothy and Myrna couldn't wait to get to the beach to work on their tans. Angie had never been one to lay out in the sun, but joined them at the beach. After several hours, Angie looked down to see that her thighs were bright red. She went in to shower, her thighs feeling like thousands of pins and needles were pricking them. The shower turned her legs a bright shade of crimson, and Dorothy went out in search of something to help. She brought back a thick salve which Angie spread on her thighs, and then covered them with gauze to ease the pain. The next few days were spent with her legs covered. By the end of the week, she was back on the beach.

On the way back to Pittsburgh, the girls stopped in North Carolina for breakfast at a roadside truck stop. They perused the laminated menus, as the waitress approached the table. "What'll it be?" she asked.

"I'll have the grits and scrambled eggs," Angie decided. *Why not try something new?*

The girls sipped steaming coffee from the thick white china mugs, as they chatted about the trip – the beach, the good company, and their adventures on the trip down. The waitress brought over their breakfasts and set the plate of grits and eggs down on the placemat in front of Angie. *They look like farina*, she thought. She picked up a forkful of the white cereal drizzled with butter and took a bite.

"How are the grits?" Dorothy asked.

"They're awful!" said Angie. The medicinal aftertaste of the bite of grits lingered in her mouth. "I don't understand why they're so popular here. I swear, I will never eat grits again!"

She also swore silently never to borrow a car from her brother again.

Working at the Board of Education expanded Angie's world beyond the culture of the Greek community, but most of her time was still spent with her family and Greek friends. Although in her twenties, she had yet to go on a date, and still looked forward to the monthly dances at the Greek Church, where live bands played a mixture of traditional Greek dance music, swing, and boogie woogie. Not much had changed in the past decade; the dances were still a place where the boys and girls, now young men and young ladies, could dance together without fear of commitment. (It would be much the same a generation later.)

Angie chatted with her friends in the low light of the church hall as Mike Theo's band finished a Greek *kalamatiano* and played the first notes of Glenn Miller's *Moonlight Serenade*. She was surprised to see Angelo Caloyeras, a handsome boy from a prominent family, walking towards her. "Do you want to dance?" he asked.

Why is he asking me to dance? She thought. Looking at his dress shirt, tailored pants, and new leather shoes, she was keenly aware of the difference in social standing. Angelo led her out to the dance floor, one arm behind her shoulder, his left hand clasping her right as they began to slow dance. She felt herself tingle with excitement as he brought her closer to him. The song ended, and he looked down at her, smiling. "Angie," he said, "Do you feel what I feel?"

    Poor Angie, ignorant in matters of dating, had no idea how to react. Her face flushed. The words refused to come out. She said nothing. He let go of her hand and walked away.

SECRETS AND GOSSIP - *Mystica kai Kouventoli*: ΜΥΣΤΙΚΆ ΚΑΙ ΚΟΥΒΕΝΤΟΛΉ

The war ended. With Angie working at the Board of Education, and all of her brothers in Pittsburgh, things eased up financially for the family. Stanley now worked at Sparks and Spanish Kitchen and Restaurant supply, and Angelo worked at the train station. Nick was using the G.I. Bill to attend classes at the Art Institute of Pittsburgh to pursue a career in commercial art. Pete's money was made or lost gambling at cards or on the horses, and he dreamed of going out to Hollywood and "making it big." The family had outgrown the house on Fifth Avenue, and by 1948 they decided that it was time to find a larger residence. Angie and Olga purchased a three-story red brick duplex with large rooms and high-ceilings on the Boulevard of the Allies, a few minutes away from their small house in Oakland. The boys would pay rent to help cover the cost of the mortgage. And, at the age of 22, Angie finally had her own room.

    Stanley had met Irene, the sister of Angie's friend Mary, at a Valentine's Day dance at the church. Irene's mother's expectations that Stanley would become her son-in-law were realized when Stanley and Irene announced their engagement shortly after the house on the Boulevard was purchased. The siblings and Olga pitched in together to buy a refrigerator to give to the couple for their wedding in November, even as they realized that their disposable income would be significantly reduced since Stanley would no longer be paying rent. Shortly after their wedding, on a late winter afternoon, Irene came over to the house on the Boulevard. She went upstairs to see Angie who was in her bedroom, and the two sat on her bed, side by side. Irene lowered her voice.

    "I have a secret to tell you, Angie," she said. "Promise you won't tell?"

    "I promise," Angie replied, and leaned in, lowering her voice to match Irene's. "What is it?"

    "Stanley and I got married in July."

    Angie looked at Irene, not comprehending.

    Irene revealed that she and Stanley had been secretly married in a civil ceremony by a Justice of the Peace in July, when

Irene's mother had gone to visit relatives in Detroit, but they were afraid to tell their parents. As Angie listened to Irene, she realized that when her brother had agreed to help with the mortgage, he was already married and planning to move to an apartment in Sheridan, close to his mother-in-law, and knew that he would not be able to help with the house payments. They sat together on the bed as the day turned to dusk. Angie's mood mirrored the grey late winter afternoon as she realized that her brother, whom she loved and had trusted, had not been honest with his family.

The house on the Boulevard was convenient for everyone. Nick and Angelo caught buses to Pittsburgh right down the street, and Olga could take a bus into Market Square for her produce shopping, or walk to the market on Ward Street. She could also walk around the corner to visit her friends, and often did so to play cards or sit and chat on the porch when the weather was warm. Pete found his way to Renziehausen Park for Pittsburgh Pirate baseball tryouts. Donning the uniform from his community league, he loaded his bat and glove into his car and drove out the parkway to McKeesport, hoping that this was the time he would strike it big. He had thoughts of heading to California to try his hand at acting after his friend, Charlie Buchinsky, went to Hollywood, took acting classes, changed his name to Charles Bronson, and landed a role in *You're in the Navy Now*. But Pete didn't have the resources to get to Hollywood, and after a hot, humid day of batting and fielding, he didn't get the call to join the Pirates organization either. He swore that someday he would make it big.

Angie walked to work at the Board of Education, down the Boulevard, up Bates Street past the yellow brick houses to Atwood, and across Forbes Avenue to the business district. She passed the Betsy Ross restaurant on the corner of Forbes and Oakland Avenue, and continued down Forbes past the Clock Restaurant, brother Pete's hangout, and under the huge Coca Cola Billboard claiming "Thirst Stops Here." On her way home, she noticed a young man with dark, deep-set eyes and curly black hair smoking a cigarette in front of the Clock. *He's handsome*, she thought, wondering who he was. She soon noticed him in front of the Clock every day on her way home from work. Their eyes met, but they said nothing. On payday, Angie, Dorothy, and Myrna walked to the Betsy Ross for lunch, and the handsome man would be sitting at the restaurant counter, cigarette in hand, drinking a cup of coffee and talking in Greek to the manager, Bill, a friend of Angie's from church.

One Saturday morning that summer, Bill called. "Angie," he said, "I'm driving over to see the new airport – would you like to go?" Although she was a working woman in her mid-twenties, Angie asked Olga's permission, which was granted since Bill was Greek Orthodox, of "means," and eligible. When Bill pulled up to pick up Angie, the handsome man was sitting in the back seat of the sedan. Angie smiled shyly, surprised and speechless. Bill introduced his friend, George Langas, who had moved to Pittsburgh from Greece to live with his father. The ride out to the suburbs was awkwardly quiet. They parked the car outside of the airport and walked towards the new terminal, admiring the fountain at the entrance, the large mobile suspended from the ceiling, and the large green and yellow compass embedded in the striking terrazzo floor of the lobby. They were astonished by the movie theater and the meeting rooms, and marveled over the modern exposed concrete and steel, while drinking coffee at the coffee shop which looked out over the rotunda. As the conversation about the airport waned, George and Angie discovered a mutual interest – opera.

Angie continued to notice George on her way home from work and at the Betsy Ross, but they had little conversation. While George was known to be a quiet man, Angie had never had trouble finding things to say, until now. She got up the nerve to ask George to go to the opera, *Manon*, at the Syria Mosque. Although she didn't think of it in these terms, it was her first date. She was twenty five years old.

At the restaurant with her friends one evening after choir practice, Angie noticed George on a stepladder painting the wall of the restaurant. At first she couldn't understand why he kept glancing at her booth with his dark eyebrows furrowed and a scowl on his face. Eventually it dawned on her that he was jealous of the men she was sitting with. George began to show up after church dances, and one evening fell into step with her as she walked to the

Betsy Ross with her friends. George and Angie slowed their pace and were soon walking alone. As they continued down Forbes Street, George hesitated, and steered Angie into the sheltered entryway of a closed store. He leaned into her and kissed her gently on the lips.

George, who had been somewhat of a loner, began going with Angie to picnics and outdoor concerts at Flagstaff Hill in Schenley Park where Angie gathered with her Greek friends. The men reminisced about Greece and sang Greek songs, and Angie noticed that George had a beautiful tenor voice. He told Angie that he had been offered the opportunity to take voice lessons to sing opera, but he perceived that the instructor was "making advances" towards him, so any singing career he might have had was left in that studio. George began coming to Angie's home where they would lie around in the living room with her brother Nick and other friends, listening to classical music. Olga never seemed to mind, and would drink her coffee in the kitchen, listening to the music and chatter of the group, and eventually go to bed. But then, the rumors began. "Tell me, Olga," the ladies would say to Angie's mother, "is your daughter seeing Langas? You know he has a reputation." Her brother Pete became protective of Angie when he realized that the man with whom he gambled, played cards, and chased women was interested in his older sister. One night at the dinner table, Pete asked Angie, "Are you seeing Langas?"

"Yes," Angie replied, "we like each other."

Pete spoke of how George was no-good, about his terrible reputation, and his gambling. "He's been nothing but kind and considerate with me," Angie said.

Pete continued to rant.

"Stop it!" Angie said.

"I'm telling you, Koula, he's no good....."

Angie stood up, picked up her plate of spaghetti, and dumped it upside down on Pete's head.

Angie silenced her brother, but Olga, even after meeting George and seeing him at the house, trusted her friends' gossip. While the stories of his gambling and card playing had some merit, it was not uncommon to find most of the Greek men gathering at night to playing *barbudi* - a dice game popular in the Greek community, outside in one of the back alleys behind the restaurants. George liked to play cards, shoot dice, and bet on "the ponies." Once he met Angie, his female-chasing days were over. Olga, however, remained firmly set against him.

George cut through the back alley, and ran up the steps to knock on the door at the house on the boulevard, only to be met by an angry Olga. "*Fiye apo etho!*' she scolded, waving her hand at him as if he were a stray cat looking for food. "Get out of here!"

But shooing George away did not keep him from seeing Angie. They made plans to meet at the park down the boulevard and across the street from the Isaly's ice cream store.

"*Pou pas?*" Olga called downstairs to Angie, who was putting on her cardigan. "Where are you going?"

Angie had never been a liar. "I'm going to meet George."

"*Putana,*" Olga spat out.

Angie was not deterred. And as she and George sat and talked on the park bench, she knew that what she felt for him was more than a simple friendship. They made plans to meet again.

"Where are you going?" Olga asked, a few days later.

"I'm going to meet George."

As Angie turned the doorknob, she heard Olga at the top of the stairs. Clutching her heart with one hand, and the wooden banister with the other, Olga groaned softly as she looked at Angie.

Angie sighed. "Bye, mother."

Eventually, the attempts at preventing the romance passed, but the gossip continued. Angie implored Olga to get to know George, but Olga refused to give him a chance. George was not permitted to come to the house.

George with his father, William Langas

GEORGE - *Yiorgos*: ΓΕΩΡΓΙΟΣ

The couple continued to meet at the park and go to the church dances or for a drive. On one of these occasions, George borrowed a car to drive to Zelienople, an hour north of Oakland, to visit his father who, after owning his own restaurants, had fallen on hard times and was now working for another restaurant owner. George and Angie entered through the glass doors of the restaurant, and George looked toward the register, where he expected to see his father greeting customers and ringing up checks. He glanced toward the counter where William, not yet aware that his son was there, was wiping up the restaurant counter after the last customer. George steered Angie over towards the counter.

"Yiorgo!" William said, and set down the rag to shake his son's hand. In the late afternoon, the restaurant counter was nearly empty. George and Angie sat down, and William poured them steaming coffee. "*Vasili*!" the manager called, and William excused himself. George sat in silence, staring at his coffee cup, his jaw clenched. After the visit, George and Angie got into the car. George put the key into the ignition, but he didn't turn it on. He began to weep, saddened to see his father who had been a proud restaurant owner, cleaning up someone else's restaurant counter.

It was on these weekend drives and meetings on the park bench that Angie began to learn who George Langas was.

George's parents, William and *Coula* (Vassiliki) Langas had emigrated to the U.S. in the 1910's. Coula, after years of discontent with the arranged marriage, left her husband and three of her four children in Pittsburgh to return to Greece to give birth to her youngest son, George. She went back to the states for her children, leaving George with her parents and her oldest daughter, Helen, who was already living with them in Greece. Coula didn't return until George was seven years old. He had never known his mother. George stayed with his grandparents. His mother divorced, remarried, and had another child.

George's tall, soft-spoken grandfather, who wore a monocle, would put candy under his pillow every night. His grandmother, Eleni, he told Angie, was "the loveliest woman I have met." Although he loved his grandparents, he no longer listened to them. When George became a teenager, he began to skip school. His grandfather began to drive him to school, dropping him off at the front door and watching to make sure George went in. When his grandfather drove away, George would walk out of the back door. He had been good at math, art, history and soccer, but he lost interest in learning, and was more concerned with life outside the walls of the school. His grandparents made the difficult decision to send him away to a boarding school on an island. "But," he said, "I broke out of the joint."

It was time for desperate measures. In 1936, at the age of sixteen, George was sent to America to live with his father in Pittsburgh. His grandfather hugged him, and, choking back tears, George boarded the ship. As he reached his hand into his pocket, he felt a pack of cigarettes that his grandfather had placed there. He hadn't known that he was escaping from a country that within five years would suffer *H Katochi*, the occupation of Greece by Fascist Italy and Nazi Germany. All he knew was that he was leaving his beloved grandparents to live with a father he had never met.

George's father, William, was a kind, soft-spoken, self-educated man with barely a trace of a Greek accent. He and his closest friend, Mr. Annis, drove to New York to meet George on a sweltering, humid July day. George recalled staying in a hot, sticky hotel room, and his father taking him to see the Rockettes as his first introduction to America. They drove to Pittsburgh the following day, and the open car windows did little to allay George's discomfort as rivulets of sweat poured down his back, soaking his dress shirt. As they neared Pittsburgh, the sky became dark. George realized that the grey haze that hung in the air was not from the weather, but from the steel mills that churned black smoke into the sky. He cursed himself for wearing white pants, which were dirty from the soot that permeated the car by the time they arrived in Pittsburgh. "It was so dirty," he said. "The streets, the sky. Everything was filthy."

George, who had never worked in Greece, was put to work at his father's restaurants – the *Athenian* and the *Buffet* on Wood Street. His older sister Anastasia, called "Sassa," worked the cash register, and George learned the restaurant trade – cooking, working the counter – whatever he was called upon to do. William watched as the young American waitress flirted with George. George later told Angie, "I didn't know what to do. I knew she liked me, but I didn't want to take advantage of her." And, at the time, he didn't speak English well enough to explain himself. It wasn't until he joined the service that he really picked up the language.

George was twenty-one when he and a friend got work on a freighter in order to travel to South America. When war broke out, the freighter was commandeered to Vancouver Island, and George found himself in British Columbia. Far from his intended destination, and far from home, he enlisted in the army. He boarded a ship in San Francisco for Australia. He spent six months in Perth, Australia, where he had two horses, and went horseback riding every day. He worked in the kitchen and peeled his share of potatoes, attaining the rank of Mess Sergeant. He told Angie of his different money-making "rackets," including becoming the base barber, even though he had no experience in cutting hair.

George played cards often, and he recounted a scheme that he and Blackie Papparousa concocted during a blackjack game after they won everyone's cigarettes. Orders had come in for New Guinea. George and Blackie bought all of the available cigarettes, knowing that they were scarce in New Guinea. They figured that when the cigarette supplies ran low, they would be able to get a good price for them. Sure enough, after three or four weeks in New Guinea, everyone ran out of cigarettes. Blackie and George unlocked the trunk, ready to reap the rewards of their clever plan.

The smell of mildew mingled with tobacco burst forth from the open trunk. "What the hell?" George said, looking at the moldy cigarettes. This was one of the few plans that backfired.

    In his thirty-nine months overseas, he had no choice but to learn English. He found himself in a 25-man first-aid battalion, where he built wells and worked for a portable hospital unit. There were no front lines in the jungle, but their unit was often strafed by Japanese planes. George was required to serve guard duty at night. Every rustle in the trees or cooing of a bird was a potential Japanese sniper. "I was really scared," he admitted. "I didn't know what was out there."

    George told Angie that he had been up for court-martial seven times, but was only busted once. It was hard for Angie to reconcile this kind, intense young man with the man who spent thirty days in the brig after getting into a fight with another staff sergeant who angered him to the point that he threw his cup and saucer at him and refused to work. He showed Angie a photo of himself in a black leather jacket which was taken after the fight. In the photo his lip was bruised, and he was looking directly at the camera, his eyes dark and his face calm. His jaw was square, and his hair short, dark, and curly. His mouth was partly open, as if he was saying, "You don't want to mess with me."

    After the war, George joined the United Nations Relief Association, an organization whose purpose was to provide relief of victims of war in U.N. countries by providing food, fuel, clothing, shelter, and other basic necessities. George joined a boat full of volunteers who were taking horses to Athens, and then picking up donkeys from Cyprus and delivering them to Salonika and Patras, Greece. He had not been back to Greece since he left at the age of sixteen, and knew that the boat would be docking in Piraeus for a few days, which would allow him to see his family in Athens. On the ship he met George Retos, a veterinarian from Pittsburgh. During one of the nightly poker games, George observed Retos dealing from the bottom of the deck. He waited for a break in the action to confront him privately. Retos stopped his cheating for the remainder of the trip, and he and George formed a lasting friendship.

George, bottom left. Retos, top right.

When George got to Athens, he went to his mother's apartment on Imvrou Street. He stayed only briefly – he had little affection for his mother, whom he felt had abandoned him. He met his nieces and his sisters and brother, and had a bittersweet reunion with his grandparents. He left for Pittsburgh with a lump in his throat.

"The only people I ever loved were my grandmother and my grandfather," George said to Angie. "Until now."

After returning to Pittsburgh, George continued to work for his father's restaurant. He also worked for a few months at a steel mill, at the Post Office during the Christmas rush, and as a painter. George had a knack for estimating and painting, and was soon painting buildings and bridges in Albany, Baltimore, Michigan, Iowa, and Kentucky. This, and gambling, were his main sources of income when he met Angie. George loved the racetrack, and often visited George Retos at the Meadows Racetrack, where he was now a veterinarian. Lucky at the horses, George was even luckier at cards, and often played poker in the back room of one of the clubs in East Liberty, or the restaurants in Oakland. Here he met Louie Xides, the bartender and Mike Kapsal, the barber, who would soon become his close friends.

East Liberty in the late 1940's was a cultural hub, boasting seven theaters and forty clubs within a three-block radius. The bars, by law, closed at midnight, but there were plenty of after-hour clubs with piano players, live dance music, or rooms in which to play blackjack and poker. Between here and the "colored district" on

Wylie Avenue, the nightlife was plentiful, as were the women. But, as George spent more time with Angie, he spent less time chasing women, until he realized that Angie was the only woman he wanted.

Coffee and poker with the men in the backroom of Mike's barber shop was one of George's favorite pastimes. The barbershop was on Oakland Avenue between Forbes and Fifth – a traditional shop with a red and white barber's pole, and "Barber Shop" stenciled on the window. Mike had three chairs in the shop, and cut hair in the chair closest to the window. If you came into the shop and he liked you, he would give you a haircut. If not, he would send you back to the other barbers. On a busy Saturday afternoon, if his friends were around to play cards, Mike would hang a "CLOSED" sign in the barbershop window. Louie, George, and other Greek friends smoked their cigarettes and dealt five card stud around the card table in the back, as Mike puffed on his ever-present cigar and watched his pile of quarters dwindle. The men teased Mike because they knew that they could always get a reaction from him, but one day they took it too far. Mike was a staunch democrat, and in 1952 he was supporting Adlai Stevenson for president. Stevenson was an underdog, despite the fact that democrats had held the presidency for the past twenty years. After a fair bit of razzing on a Saturday afternoon, Mike cut the poker game short and closed up the shop for the weekend. On Tuesday morning, Mike walked down to the shop to open up for the day. Spray painted across the windows, in large capital letters, were the words, "MIKE LIKES IKE." He was furious. No one fessed up to the deed, but he had his suspicions, and would get his vengeance in time.

In December of 1952, on Christmas Eve, Angie sat upstairs in the loft of the church with the rest of the choir waiting for their director, Mr. Agraphiotis to arrive. "Aggie" was never late. He was devoted to the church and to the choir. He had written and arranged the music that the choir sang at the church services, and played the organ to accompany the singers. The choir members heard footsteps on the stairs, and turned expectantly to greet Aggie. But it was Mr. Sidirigo, the canter, who approached them, his face ashen. "Aggie has had a heart attack," he said. "He passed away tonight." Angie was stunned. *How could that be? He was so young*, she thought. The men and women of the choir burst into tears and expressions of disbelief. Mr. Sidirigo paused, and looked at JoAnn Marinakis. "Joann, you know the music. You must play the organ." He turned to Angie. "Angie, you will direct the choir. I will tell you when to come in with the songs." Angie froze. *How can we sing without Aggie?* With sorrow in their voices on this holy day, they raised their voices to sing the songs that Aggie had lovingly composed for the church.

    Although only twenty-six years old, Angie remained the choir director. After choir practice, she continued to meet with George at the Betsy Ross. When the days got warmer, they went to Schenley Park, over 400 acres of green rolling hills adjacent to Forbes Field and Carnegie Tech. On Saturday afternoons, they spread a blanket out on Flagstaff Hill, which was dotted with hundreds of college students from Pitt, Chatham, and Carnegie Tech. Students and families came to listen to a jazz band play, or to Mary Martha Briney, the local classical singer who acted in musicals, and produced hit recordings with the Al Goodman Orchestra. Her duets with Donald Dame such as "I Want You to Marry Me" played on the radio. For her Schenley Park performances, she sang solo on the wood platform stage, and her clear soprano voice filled the air.

    Louie would accompany them to Schenley Park, and sometimes Angie's brother Nick came along. One Saturday, Angie was surprised to see Nick with JoAnn Psinakis, a mutual friend from Greece who often met up with the group at the Betsy Ross after the dances or came to the house to hang out and listen to records. Although JoAnn and Angie had become good friends, JoAnn had never mentioned anything to her about Nick.

    Then, one day, Nick announced that he was marrying JoAnn. Angie was stunned. She had never seen any chemistry between Nick and JoAnn. Whenever JoAnn was with the group, she chatted with Angie and the others, but Nick always seemed to be in the background. Angie didn't understand, but she didn't question Nick. As she spent more time with JoAnn, she learned that JoAnn's documentation was going to expire. JoAnn was not permitted to remain in the states - unless she was married to an American citizen. Angie liked JoAnn, and hoped that her suspicions were unfounded.

One summer evening, Angie met George at the Betsy Ross after choir practice. George nervously tapped a matchbox on the table as they ordered their coffee. Louie arrived, and sat down in the booth next to George. Angie didn't realize that he was there for moral support. George pushed the matchbox over to Angie. "What's this?" Angie asked.
George said nothing, but waved his hand toward the matchbox, motioning to her to open it. She slid the box open, revealing a white gold diamond engagement ring; her mouth fell open. She stared at the ring, and then at George. He nodded towards the ring, and Angie took it out of the box, but did not put it on right away. "You're asking me to marry you?" Angie asked, when no words came out of George's mouth. He nodded. In the growing silence, Louie discreetly moved to the counter. Angie hesitated before she spoke. "George," she said kindly. "I wasn't prepared for this. I need to think about it. I need some time."
With disappointment in his heart, he simply nodded.

    At work the next day, Angie confided in Myrna and Dorothy. Dorothy's boyfriend was also pressing for a deeper commitment. Myrna's was playing "hard to get," and she was not sure that she wanted to work that hard. As they discussed their situations over lunch, they determined that what they needed was a vacation to Florida. After the fiasco with Pete's car, they decided that they could afford to fly this time. A few weeks later, they headed to Miami.

    The three single ladies, in their new two-piece bathing suits, attracted several would-be suitors who came over to flirt with them at the beach, but the girls said no to all date requests, preferring instead to hash over the questions: *Should I break up with him? Is he right for me? Should I marry him?* By the end of the trip, each girl had decided that she was not ready to be tied down, and would make the difficult break when she returned home.

    The plane touched down in Pittsburgh, with each young lady certain of her decision. Angie walked down the runway and emerged, surprised to see George waiting for her at the gate. Her heart rate quickened, and she smiled at him, her resolve to end the relationship forgotten. She knew then that she was going to marry George Langas.

They announced their engagement to their friends and family. George's father and sister, Sassa, were delighted, and threw them an engagement party at the Conley Motel. By this time, Brother Pete had not only accepted George, but welcomed him. The neighbor ladies stopped their gossiping. One day as Angie sat at home at the kitchen table with her mother, the doorbell rang. The ladies, the same ones who had perpetuated the gossip, stopped by with a present for the engaged couple. But Olga refused to come around. And Cousin Gus, who had known Angie since she was a toddler, said, "Angie...do you have to get married?" She felt her face flush, hurt and angry because she suspected that her mother had put Gus up to asking the question.

On the morning of the wedding, Angie sat at her dressing table, holding a hand-mirror up to the back of her head to see the French twist that Nick's fiancé, JoAnn had combed into her hair. Although she had not participated in any of the planning or preparation for the wedding, Olga had bought a new silk dress for the occasion, and was dressed-up with a small black hat and white gloves. Angie had bought a plain white sleeveless satin tea length dress for $40. To transform the dress, she and JoAnn added lace to fashion short sleeves and trimmed the bottom of the skirt and the sweetheart neckline with lace and beads. They purchased a wreath, and attached a lace veil to the back of the wreath.

JoAnn was Angie's *koumpara*, her maid of honor. George's friend, George Mantzouros, was his *koumparos*. Angie had asked Irene if her young son, Archie, could be the ring bearer – but she did not ask Irene to be in the wedding party, nor did she ask her brother Stanley. Brother Pete, Louie Xides, and George's roommate, Louis Zappas rounded out the ushers. Sassa, Gloria Mantzouros, and Betty Athens, Angie's friend from the Maids of Athens, completed the bridal party. It did not occur to Angie to ask her American friends, Dorothy and Myrna, to be part of this Greek celebration of marriage.

As the man of the house, Nick walked Angie down the aisle of St. Nicholas Greek Orthodox Church. Father Demetrios Eliopoulis handed George and Angie lighted candles representing Jesus Christ, the Light of the world, who would light and bless the couple in their new life together. The priest held the *stephana* - wedding crowns, pearl-white wreaths decorated with beads and small pear-shaped pearls, over their heads, making the sign of the cross with them three times over George and Angie's heads. The crowns were linked together with a white satin ribbon to represent the joining of two souls, and George and Angie kissed the crowns before the priest placed them on their heads. The koumbara switched the stephana back and forth three times. After the priest spoke of the responsibilities and duties of marriage, George and Angie drank red wine from a gold cup, signifying their willingness to share happiness and sorrow together. Angie and George followed the priest around the altar three times, the circular dance representing the eternity of a marriage.

They held a reception in the church hall at St. Nicholas. Louie had already gone downstairs to set up a bar, and JoAnn and Olga had prepared Greek mezethes. Angie and George handed out *bombonieres* - almonds coated with sugar and colored pink, yellow, teal, and white, and wrapped in white netting, to symbolize that the couple could not be divided. American music piped over the speakers as the wedding party and close friends danced waltzes, rhumbas, and cha-chas, and toasted the couple with champagne. After a short celebration they headed back to the house on the boulevard, where JoAnn had prepared Greek fish with lemon and oregano for the wedding party and family.

After dinner, George and Angie changed out of their wedding clothes, got into the sedan they had borrowed from George Mantzouros, and started on their way to Florida. Angie thought with nervous anticipation about the sheer pink nightie that her girlfriends had given her for the wedding night. But as the hours passed, fatigue and hunger set in. At three a.m. they stopped in Virginia and rented a cottage for the night. Famished, they went to a 24-hour diner, and after eating, went back to the room. Exhausted, they fell asleep on the bed, too tired to be disappointed. They consummated their marriage the next day, but the nightie remained packed in the suitcase for the duration of the trip.

On the way back from St. Petersburg, George and Angie looked forward to moving into their apartment on Darragh Street in Oakland. George had worked out a deal to paint the apartment in lieu of their first month's rent, and they would still help with the mortgage for the house on the boulevard which was now occupied by Olga, Angelo, and Pete. They crossed the West Virginia border, nearing the Washington, Pa. exit, when they decided to stop at the harness races at the Meadows Racetrack to say hello to George Retos and watch a few races. Retos knew which horses were healthy, which horses were not, which horses were on medication, and which horses were likely to defy the odds. George and Angie stayed long enough to get a bite to eat with Retos, and bet on a few of the races. They left with $500 in winnings, which in 1954 was enough to pay several months' rent.

The honeymoon at Darragh Street did not last long. Angie's brother Angelo began working at the railroad station where he met Jane, a college student who worked there as a secretary for the summer. By late fall, Angelo told the family that he would be leaving the house on the boulevard. Jane was pregnant, and he had done the honorable thing - he married her quietly in front of a Justice of the Peace. Although Jane still lived with her family, Angelo had rented an apartment, and was looking ahead to taking care of Jane and the baby. Pete's income was sporadic at best, rising and falling with his winning or losing streaks at cards, as he shifted between bartending jobs. Nick had married JoAnn and moved out. Without their help with the rent, Olga would not be able to stay in the house. Rather than risk losing the house, in spite of Olga's continuing disapproval of George, he and Angie decided to move in with Olga. Angie was pregnant, and had to leave her job at the Board of Education. The house on the boulevard would be a good place to raise a child.

George and Angie, May 1, 1954

George on Honeymoon, 1954

Angie on Honeymoon

Rita with Uncle Nick (l), Daddy, and Uncle Pete (r) at the Boulevard House.

BOULEVARD - *Leoforos*: ΛΕΩΦΟΡΟΣ

George and Angie moved into the house on the Boulevard in the summer of 1954. They took over the second floor and the mortgage. The brothers had agreed to help financially, but faced with their own problems, they offered nothing. George confronted each of them. "At least give your mother $10 once in a while so that she has some of her own money to spend." They didn't, and George and Angie found themselves to be the sole financial contributors to Olga. Despite this, Olga, still wary of his reputation, refused to warm up to George. It bothered Angie that Olga would not take the time to sit down with George to get to know him. If it bothered George, he didn't let on.

    In October Angie quit working at the Board of Education. She resumed the household chores at the boulevard, and also made sweets for the coffee shop that George had rented. Tired of waiting to play cards in the back room of Mike's barbershop when it was convenient for Mike, George sometimes went to a *kafeneio*, a coffee house on Court Street in Pittsburgh. But often there was no coffee and no refreshments of any kind. George rented space above the Clock Restaurant on Bouquet Street. The room on the second floor was spacious, with plenty of daylight coming in the large windows that overlooked the street. Here the men, mostly Greek, convened to play cards or *tavli* - backgammon. George didn't have regular hours for the coffee shop. He worked in the hours between his painting jobs with Jimmy Tsouris, and somehow, through word-of-mouth, his patrons knew when he was open for business. He also wanted to avoid any problems with the law, since the men were gambling for money. He need not have worried - the police knew and liked George, and never bothered him or his clientele.

Angie would walk up the long flight of steps to the second floor to deliver the sweets that George sold at the kafeneio. Sometimes she brought homemade yogurt or *kourabedies* - Greek powdered sugar cookies. Every so often she brought *melomakarina* - moist Greek cookies dripping with honey and topped with chopped walnuts. She would drop off the baked goods, give George a kiss, and leave. Angie was the only woman who ever stepped foot inside the kafeneio.

As he did most afternoons, Louie sat at one of the tables with Jimmy Tsouris and a few others. At the table near the window, a couple of older Greek men sat drinking Greek coffee and playing with their colorful *koboloi,* the stone worry beads they had brought from Greece. *"Giorgo,"* called one of the men at the card table. *"Ena Turkiko cafe`*, a Turkish coffee!" Greek coffee, Turkish coffee – it was the same – thick, dark, bitter coffee served in a small demitasse cup.

George poured water into the *vriki*, the small metal pot with the long handle. He added two *coutalitses* - small spoonfuls of the finely ground dark Greek coffee and one teaspoon of sugar to counteract the bitterness of the coffee, and heated the vriki on the stovetop behind the counter. He watched until it came close to boiling and stirred it. Then he poured it into the small white demitasse cup, the thick syrupy grinds settling to the bottom, the rich frothy liquid filling the cup.

The telephone rang, and George picked it up. *"Nai*, yes?"

"Hello," a woman's voice answered. "Is Mike Pappas there?"

"Pappas?" George asked. *"Ena lepto*, one second." He left the receiver uncovered. "Is Pappas here?" he called out to the men.

Mike Pappas, holding his hand of poker in front of him, lifted his chin, ever so slightly, never taking his eyes off of the cards.

"No, sorry. Pappas isn't here today," said George. He placed the cup on a saucer, placed a cookie next to the cup, and took it over to Pappas.

In March, Angie went to see her obstetrician, Dr. Canter, for her check-up. "Well," he said, "You're ready to have this baby. How about coming in on Tuesday?"

"What?" Angie was dumbfounded.

"It'll be simple," Dr. Canter said. "Instead of waiting for contractions, we'll induce the labor."

Angie made an appointment for Tuesday, and went home to tell her mother. Olga's eyes widened. "You're going in on Tuesday to have the baby?" Olga had delivered all of her children as nature intended. She was frightened at this turn of events.

On Tuesday, March 8, George took Angie to Montefiore hospital. Then he walked down the street to the kafeneio to wait with Mike and Louie.

A few cups of coffee later, the telephone rang. "Mr. Langas?"

"Yes," George answered.

"This is the nurse from Montefiore Hospital. Your wife is out of labor. You have a baby boy. You may see them now."

George hung up the phone, ran down the steps and across the street to the drug store, and bought a dozen cigars wrapped with blue labels reading, "It's a Boy!" He ran back up the stairs to the kafeneio and handed out the cigars to his friends. Then he hurried down the street to the hospital.

In the course of Angie's appointments with Dr. Canter, she had discovered that he was also an opera fan. Now under the influence of the ether, she belted out "*La LA, la la LA, la la LA, la la LAAAA,*" in tune to an aria from *Il Trovatore* as Dr. Canter laughed. As he delivered the baby, Angie declared to the short, bald, pleasant man, "I love you, Dr. Canter!"

Once the baby was cleaned up, and the ether had worn off, Dr. Canter asked Angie, "Would you like to hold the baby and walk to your room?"

As George walked down the hall towards the maternity ward, he saw Angie walking towards him with a baby wrapped in a blanket. "Hi George," she smiled, looking down at the baby, and then back up at George. "We have a little girl."

George looked at Angie for a minute. "I know, I know," he said gently. He did not tell Angie about the trick that was played on him until much later, when he discovered that it was Mike Kapsal who masterminded it.

George embraced the responsibility of fatherhood, and his card-playing days dwindled. He kept the kafeneio for a while, but focused on his painting business. Angie did the accounting and signed the paychecks, and their life together formed a pleasant rhythm. Once in a while Olga watched the baby and George and Angie walked to the Black Angus restaurant where Louis was now bartending. Angie phoned her girlfriends occasionally, but was too busy with the baby and the business to get together with them.

On weekends they often saw Stanley and Irene and their young son, Archie, and Angelo, who was in the process of renting an apartment for his fiancé and their expected baby. Nick and JoAnn were living at the house on the Boulevard. JoAnn and Angie had become close friends, and Angie asked JoAnn to be the baby's godmother. But despite her affection for JoAnn, whose company and sense of humor she enjoyed, Angie was concerned. She noticed that whenever a group of friends were together, JoAnn paid no attention to her husband. JoAnn had begun studying at the University of Pittsburgh, and was in the process of completing the documentation to bring her mother and her brother, Steve, over from Greece. And in the back of her mind, a seed of doubt nagged at Angie.

In July of 1955, Jane went into the hospital to give birth to her baby, and Angelo went to see them. As he attempted to enter the hospital room to see his newborn son, Jane's uncle, a muscular veteran of many years in the steel mills, blocked his entrance. His eyes were filled with rage as he told Angelo to leave. Angelo tried to get into the room, and Jane's uncle grabbed him by the arms and threw him out the door. "Get out!" he cried. "Don't ever try to see her again."

He didn't. Perhaps it was pride, perhaps it was fear, or maybe even relief at escaping the responsibilities of fatherhood and marriage, but Angelo never saw Jane again. He took a job with Lustra, selling light bulbs and lighting equipment, which kept him on the road and away from Pittsburgh.

In 1956 George met Pete Kalomiris. He had come to Pittsburgh from Greece the previous year at the age of 14 to live with his brother. Pete was a handsome well-built young man with dark curly hair and dark eyes, and George took a liking to him. Maybe he saw a little of himself in Pete. George took Pete under his wing and showed him how to paint, and as the business grew over the next few years, George hired Pete to work with him on several jobs. George and Jimmy's specialty was bridges and buildings. Pete was not comfortable with heights, and preferred the jobs that kept him grounded. He watched one day as George painted the trusses of a bridge in Pittsburgh. George pulled on the ropes and lowered himself on the platform towards the river as Pete talked to him. George, usually careful, was paying attention to Pete, and not to what was below him. He went too far and landed in the water. "*Na pare O Diavolos*, the devil take you!" he swore, as yellow paint from the bucket swirled around him in the current, and his pants were soaked to the knees.

    A few months later George drove to Baltimore for a job with Jimmy and Pete. They had been contracted to paint a building under construction that rose several stories over the ocean. The steel beams, about one foot wide, had to be primed and painted. The men had rented an apartment for the duration of the job. To keep expenses down, they shared one bedroom with two beds. George lay down in one, and Jimmy in the other. Pete looked at Jimmy, who was already snoring in the middle of his bed, and then to George. "Move over, George," he said, but George didn't move.

    "George – move over!"

    "Hey!" George replied. "I don't sleep with nobody, and I'm not moving from this bed."

    "Come on, George."

    "*Vre poustareli*, motherfucker. You heard me!"

    They woke up in the morning to a fine mist from rain the previous night, Pete a little stiff from the night on the floor. They pulled up to the work site. Pete looked up at the several stories, and broke out in a cold sweat. "George, you can go up there, but I'm not going up there. I'm afraid."

    "What's the matter with you? Get up there." George said.

Pete took the elevator up several stories, and climbed tentatively out onto the steel beam. He looked down, and his leg slipped on the moist beam. He sat down, and froze. "George!" he called. "I'm going to land in the ocean and I don't know how to swim!"

"*Pas na pnigeis,* go drown yourself!" George answered.

"George!" Pete yelled.

"What?"

"My mother just called me and told me to go home!"

"*Pas ta diavolo, vre,* go to hell!" George said. But when he looked up at Pete, even at the distance, he saw the terror on his face.

"Okay," he said. "Get down here."

Pete slid over to the concrete floor, and rode the elevator down. "George, please take me to the bus."

"No, no, no," George said. He had promised to paint the garage doors of the apartment in lieu of rent. "You paint the doors, and we'll all go to Pittsburgh on Friday."

Although Pete felt gratitude and respect for George, with every painting job he did, he realized that he did not want to be a painter, but each time he was going to quit the painting business, George had another opportunity for him. After he painted the St. Nicholas Church in Oakland, Pete said, "George, I'll see you later." But George wasn't done with his protégé yet. Pete painted the mansions on Fifth Avenue, and Negley, and in East Liberty. He finally went into the restaurant business at the William Penn Hotel.

Despite the heights, the bridges, and the long hours away from home, Angie never worried about George, because he never showed a concern himself. The only things that mattered to George were his wife and daughter, and making a living to provide for them. And if that meant scaling a height or suspending from a bridge, then that's what he would do.

SEPARATION - *Horismos*: ΧΩΡΙΣΜΌΣ

In October of 1956, Angelo pulled into a bar in Charleston, West Virginia for a bite to eat and a beer. He sat at the bar, watching the World Series game on the small black and white TV on the shelf behind the bar. Mickey Mantle's homerun in the fourth inning broke the scoring impasse for the New York Yankees, but the Brooklyn Dodgers had yet to get a hit off of Yankee's pitcher Don Larson. Angelo watched the unlikely Larson in the familiar blue and white Yankee stripes throw strikeout after strikeout, and realized that he might be on his way to making history. The pretty waitress started talking to Angelo, and soon they were caught up in the excitement of the game, as Larson threw the final strikeout to seal the first no-hitter ever in a World Series contest. Angelo stayed and talked with Joyce until she got off work. He introduced himself as Tom, thinking in terms of a one-night stand, his recent experience apparently not serving as a lesson. At the end of Joyce's shift they left the bar and went to a private club where Joyce seemed to know everyone. They danced, then sat and talked. Joyce told Angelo that she was divorced and had three children – aged one, two, and three; her mother lived close by and took care of them when she worked. Angelo told Joyce about his situation with Jane. Before the night was over, he had fallen in love. He told Joyce that he wanted to marry her someday – and that his name was Angelo. He eventually found work in California, and in January of 1958, he drove Joyce and her three children out to Anaheim. He and Joyce drove to Mexico, where he got divorced and married on the same day.

    The family, which had been at the core of Angie's upbringing, began to splinter. JoAnn, after bringing her mother and brother over from Greece, and finishing her degree at Pitt, asked Nick for a divorce. If he was sad or regretful, he did not express this to his family. Perhaps in a way he expected it. Pete was often unaccounted for - bartending, playing cards, going to the racetrack, and showing up at the Boulevard occasionally for dinner, where he would dote on his sister and his niece. Stanley, Irene, and their now three children, moved to Charlottesville, Virginia. Angie was pregnant with her second child. The family decided to sell the house on the Boulevard. George and Angie needed privacy, and the money from the house would help to pay Olga's living expenses. George and Angie rented a small upstairs duplex apartment on Dawson Street. Nick and Olga moved into a small apartment on Ward Street, a ten-minute walk from the duplex.

Over the Christmas holiday, Nick and Pete went to visit Stanley and Irene in Charlottesville. When they returned, they told Angie that they couldn't wait to get out of there. Archie was sick and crying, and Irene was plagued with headaches, and short-tempered with Stanley. "Oh," Angie said, "Things must be very difficult for her." Irene was working in a hair salon while her mother watched the children. Angie wrote a letter to Irene. She described how the family had spent their time over Christmas. She asked after Stanley and the children, and wrote what she intended to be words of encouragement. *Nick and Pete were telling me how difficult things were for you with your long hours working, and Archie not being well. I hope by now that things have calmed down for you.*

A few weeks later, Nick came into the kitchen where Angie was visiting Olga, with an envelope in his hands. He dumped out the contents of the envelope: the letter that Angie had sent to Irene, torn into pieces. A letter from Irene accompanied the scraps: *How dare you all try to tell me how to run my life... Who does Angie think she is? She and her husband should look at their own life before making judgment on mine. Who thought that I would have a bunch of psychoanalysts coming down here to diagnose me? Stay away from my family. We want nothing to do with you.*

Angie and Nick took each piece of the torn up letter, fitted the pieces together, and taped it. They read it, looking for anything that could have been insulting or misinterpreted, and found nothing.

"Well," Nick said, and shrugged. "Consider the source."

But Angie was upset, and called Irene that evening. Her mother answered.

"Mrs. Ploomis, this is Angie. Is Irene..."

"You – you –you…Why don't you take care of your own business before meddling in other people's business!" She hung up the phone on Angie.

A few months later, Olga began to experience severe discomfort, and was diagnosed with gall bladder disease. Angie went to visit her in the hospital as she recuperated from surgery. Olga told her that Irene and Stanley had been in to see her, and had gone to get a cup of coffee. Angie went into the coffee shop, and saw Stanley and Irene sitting at a table in the corner. She approached them, and smiled. "Hi Stanley, hi Irene."

They did not respond.

"Irene," Angie said. "Surely you must not have meant all those word you said in...."

"Angeline!" Irene looked at Angie. "You're talking to me like a lawyer now. I never say anything I don't mean." Stanley stared at the table, never looking at his sister.

Angie turned and walked away.

George continued to paint with Jimmy, and also formed a partnership with another Greek painter, Bill Katsafanas. They got wind that a job at the William Penn Hotel downtown had become available because the men who had been painting the rooms that would be used as dormitories for Robert Morris College were non-union painters. Bill and George held union cards, and were given the contract. On the job, George met Jack McCartan, the President of Robert Morris. Jack took a liking immediately to this "ornery son of a gun" who spoke directly and worked honestly. He hired George to do several jobs at the RMC Pittsburgh Center.

"George, how much for this job?"

George flashed both hands open.

"Are you telling me $10,000?"

George nodded. Any job that Jack contracted with George was sealed by a verbal agreement.

Several months later, Jack approached George as he painted the walls of the cafeteria. "George," he asked. "Can I talk to you a minute?"

George wiped the excess paint from the brush on the rim of the can, and set the brush down on top of the can. He wiped his hands on his white painting pants, turned, and nodded to Jack.

"How would you like to run the cleaning and maintenance department for the college?" The job came with steady hours, health benefits, and housing. The family would live in Shadyside, next to Oakland, in the former servants' quarters of a stately mansion. Shadyside was the home of several manors of the descendants of Pittsburgh Steel magnates like Andrew Carnegie and Henry Clayton Frick. The mansion and house sat on a large corner lot, surrounded by a dark grey stone wall about three feet high. The mansion, with its marble floors, high ceilings, and large Corinthian columns, now served as a woman's dormitory for Robert Morris College, and was just a streetcar ride away from its downtown campus. The elementary school was only a few blocks away. George accepted the offer.

Rita and Yiayia Olga.

RITA

KIDS - Paidia: ΠΑΙΔΙΆ

My sister Ellen and I, at ages four and seven, were in heaven in Shadyside. We christened the entire yard our playground, free to imagine ourselves as secret agents, cheerleaders, or wild horses. The servants' quarters had a large rectangular room with hardwood floors and a chalkboard mounted on one end. On gloomy days, we drew on the chalkboard, and even roller skated in the room. Sometimes Daddy would draw sailboats for us in pink chalk. We were only a streetcar ride away from Yiayia Olga, and enjoyed holding on to the silver bar and feeling the rumble of the tracks as we rode the 76 Hamilton into Oakland, or all the way downtown to shop for shoes at Bakers. Once in a while mom treated us to a movie at the Fulton or Warner theater. Occasionally we accompanied Yiayia to Market Square to shop for vegetables and fruits. The market on Logan Street had closed, and Olga now bought her chicken packaged at the meat market. Often, we took the streetcar to the Carnegie Library, where mom would take us to the Children's Room. I was amazed at this area with its child-sized tables and chairs, and its floor-to-ceiling shelves of children's books. I discovered Maj Lindman's adventurous Swedish triplets *Snipp, Snapp, and Snurr*, and grew to love Beverly Cleary's characters: Ellen Tebbits, Beezus and Ramona, Henry and Ribsy. That we were permitted to borrow books from this library thrilled me, and I walked away after each visit with a stack of books cradled in my arms.

    Like I had done when we lived on Dawson Street, I walked to school. Unlike Holmes School, at Liberty Elementary School we were permitted to go home to eat lunch. The school was only two blocks away, but it seemed like a long way to go just to eat and then come back. My third grade teacher was Mrs. McKee, who may have only been in her fifties, but to me seemed ancient. After lunch we sometimes formed a large circle and Mrs. McKee would call on students to read aloud. I always volunteered. One day I read for a while, followed by a few other students. The mid-afternoon sun poured in through the high glass windows, and the dust motes floated in its path. Mrs. McKee asked for another volunteer. Of course, I put my hand up. "Reeda," she said, and I happily began to read. "Not you!" Mrs. McKee snarled. (She may not have snarled, but to my 7-year old self, she did). "You already had your turn!" I felt my face flush and my heart pound. I realized that she had been saying "Read…uh…" as she pondered over the students, and not "Rita." I never volunteered to read in her class again.

    We were not far from Oakland – we could get the streetcar out in front of our house which took us directly to Saint Nicholas Greek Orthodox Church. Mom continued to sing in the choir, and Ellen and I attended Sunday school. We met in the basement of the church, the teachers schooling us on stories from the Old Testament, and teaching us the Lord's Prayer in Greek. Ellen was in a pre-school class, and had the misfortune of having to learn a Greek poem, and perform it on the stage in the church hall at the tender age of four. My class also learned some sort of poem, but I honestly don't remember this as much as I recall my sister's performance. I don't remember the occasion for the celebration, but I do remember watching Ellen line up, her brown dark eyes even bigger as they peered uneasily from under her dark bangs. She and the other children walked reluctantly onto the stage, each dragging with him or her a large doll.
On cue from the teacher, in the timid chorus of uncertain voices, they chanted:

> *Eho mia oraia koukla,*   (I have a lovely doll)
> *Ellinitha pera pera*   (She is Greek through and through)
> *To proi otan ksipnisi*   (In the morning when she wakes)
> *Mou fonazei kalimera*   (She calls to me good morning)

    The congregations broke out into "Oohs, aahs, and of course "Bravos," as the kids dragged their dolls off the stage and down the steps, and the children rushed to the protective arms of their proud parents.

    Mom enrolled us in a summer church camp at the Presbyterian Church because it was across the street from our house in Shadyside. It was so different from the Greek Orthodox Church. There were no floor-to-ceiling stained glass windows depicting the story of Christ and the disciples. There were no priests walking around in black robes and black hats, with their long grey hair tied back in a small bun below the cap. There was no lingering scent of incense permeating the hallways. Somehow, it didn't feel like church.

At the end of our second summer in Shadyside, Daddy told us that we were going to take a drive out to the airport. We passed the entrance to the airport, made a right turn, and headed down the four-lane road for about two miles. The farther we got from the airport, the sparser the amount of businesses we saw on the road. We passed a couple fast food restaurants, Floyd's Grocery Store, and Mel's Texaco Gas Station and Tony's Sunoco Gas Station, oddly right next to each other, and took the next right onto a deeply rutted dirt road.

We pulled up in front of a magnificent tree – its trunk so massive that we could not form a ring around it holding hands. Thin branches bent from the tree like a large umbrella whose spines formed the structure of the protective canopy. Long thin leaves drooped from the branches, creating mottled shadows on the soft ground underneath. The huge weeping willow obstructed the view of an old farmhouse whose pale olive shade blended with the scenery. We had never seen so much green.

    Jack McCartan had offered Daddy the position of Superintendent of Grounds and Maintenance for Robert Morris College. They were building a new campus in Moon Township, and my father, despite his lack of a college education, had impressed Jack with his work ethic, his honesty, and his willingness to take on challenges. We had the opportunity to rent one of the two servants' quarters of the former Kaufman Estate which were now part of the RMC campus. Over the hill lay the former Kaufman mansion which now housed the faculty offices. Construction was underway for a new dormitory to accompany the recently erected cafeteria building, library, and classroom buildings. Mom joked, "You mean we're going to leave the cultural center of Pittsburgh and move to this hick town?" She smiled, but I wondered the same thing. Still, there was a draw to this bucolic place.

Daddy negotiated rent of $100 per month for as long as he remained at Robert Morris. The move meant fresh air, no traffic sounds, the chirping of cicadas at night, kickball with the kids in the housing plan until nightfall, riding our bikes on huge dirt piles, picking wild black raspberries, climbing trees and catching tadpoles in the stream. But it also meant distance from the church, movie theaters, department stores, sidewalks, Yiayia and Uncle Nicky.

SUBURBAN LIFE - *Zois Sta Proasteia*: ΖΩΗΣ ΣΤΑ ΠΡΟΆΣΤΕΙΑ

We moved out to Moon Township at the end of the summer in time to register for school. Since we didn't live in a housing plan, there was no bus service to take us to school. Rather than walk down the dirt road and along the highway, we chose to cut through the housing plan, ironically walking past the kids who were waiting for their buses, across the churchyard on a well-worn footpath, and down a narrow path in the woods. Carnot Elementary School was being renovated, and my fourth grade class was held at the "tin can," a temporary metal structure that acted as a magnifier for whatever the temperature was outside.

    I was the only girl in my class with short, dark, curly hair. My mother, having gotten weary of combing out the knots, pouring crème rinse in my hair, and setting me under the bonnet hair dryer, to my dismay had my hair cut short. But, no matter how awkward or out-of-place I felt, how hot (or cold) the classroom was, or how long the walk to school was, none of it mattered, because I absolutely adored my classroom teacher and my art teacher. I looked forward to the days that Mr. Miller would teach us to create with paints, crayons, and oil pastels. I began to sketch constantly, and now when we would visit Yiayia and Uncle Nicky in Oakland, I would sit at his art desk with giant sheets of tracing paper, and trace over the models that he had drawn for the Gimbel's ads in the newspaper. My classroom teacher Mrs. Eberle, after the critical sharpness of Mrs. McKee, was light and joy. I brought her bunches of fragrant pale purple lilacs from the tree in our yard and wrote her poetry. She encouraged me to write and greeted me every day with a smile.

    On November 23, 1963, that smile turned to tears. One of the other teachers came in to the classroom and whispered something to Mrs. Eberle. She burst out crying, and the teachers left the room. The students sat stunned. The anxiety that plagued us for those few minutes as we waited and wondered was no match for the degree of horror that we would come to know. President Kennedy had been assassinated.

    The students were sent home, and I walked into the house to find my mother watching the news on the television. I sat down on the couch next to her, and we watched for hours, as the comprehension of the crime set in. I did not know at the time that it would be the first of those moments in life in which time is suspended, and the memory becomes frozen forever in your mind. The following week I created a scrapbook in memory of John Kennedy. I also did not realize at the time that the seeds of creativity were being sown during this integral fourth grade year. It was all downhill after fourth grade. I wasn't one of the pretty girls, I did not like my fifth or sixth grade teachers, and I believed that they didn't care much for me. School was to be tolerated, and except for Mr. Miller's art class, much of my time at Carnot Elementary was spent staring out of the windows of the old yellow brick building, waiting for summer vacation. Mom attempted to keep us involved in the church, but the forty-five minute trip to Oakland kept us away not only from church, but from Yiayia and Uncle Nicky. Summer vacation provided more opportunity, and Mom would occasionally take me and Ellen to see our grandmother when she could get the car from Daddy.

    We parked in front of the four-story faded yellow brick apartment building on Ward Street and ran up the steps. Ellen and I skipped down the hallway, which was permeated with the odor of cabbage or some other boiled green, and knocked on the first large wooden door to the right. We didn't hear Yiayia's footsteps, so Mom entered using the key.

    We walked down the long windowless hallway, and found Yiayia sitting heavily in her easy chair, her cotton housedress tightly buttoned around her ample body, her short sleeves revealing dimpled arms resting on the arms of the overstuffed chair. Her housedress dipped between her legs which were bowed slightly as her feet soaked in a metal washtub filled with water and Epsom salts.

    Ellen and I went over to our grandmother, hugged her, and kissed her on her check. Yiayia's skin was soft and plump; her white hair was tinged with yellowed streaks and drawn loosely back into a bun at the base of her neck, a few tendrils escaping to frame her round face. We sat on the itchy couch listening to Mom talk to her mother in Greek. Mom and Daddy only talked in Greek at home once in a while, mostly when they didn't want us to understand what they were saying Yiayia turned to smile at us, and the water sloshed while she lifted her legs out of the pan.

While mom got to work cutting Yiayia's toenails for her, Ellen and I went out the kitchen door onto the black iron fire escape. We were fascinated by the wooden-handled mop with thick twisted white ropes which rested on the grimy metal, in contrast to the yellow spongy mop that we had at home. We hung out on the fire escape in the sunshine until we smelled hot dogs boiling in the kitchen, and scrunched up our noses in distaste. Unable to devise an acceptable excuse not to eat lunch, we went in and nibbled at the hot dogs. Yiayia disappeared down the hall, and returned from her room, smiling at us. "Here dime, go get icee-creamy," she said, as she handed each of us a dime. We ran down the hall, as she called behind us, "Watch crossa street!"

When we returned from our trek to Reiser's Drug Store, Mom was still chatting with Yiayia, so we went past Uncle Nicky's room and through the French doors which opened up into a small art studio, whose big sunny windows overlooked Ward Street. We took turns tracing models on the large sheets of tracing paper from the fashion ads that Nick sketched on his art desk until it was time to go.

When we got home, I looked at the photographs of Yiayia and Papou that my mother displayed in the burnished gold double frame on the mantel. The pictures were taken shortly after Yiayia arrived in the states: Papou with large droopy eyes like Mom's and a thick dark handlebar moustache, and Yiayia with short dark wavy hair and a soft, subtle smile. It was hard to recognize my grandmother as the serene young woman in the photograph.

ADVENTURE - *Peripetia*: ΠΕΡΙΠΕΤΕΙΑ

The summer after sixth grade my mother, sister, and I went to visit our relatives in Greece. My father could not take the time off from work, but he wanted his family in Greece to meet his wife and children. It is just as well that he didn't go because the turn of events would have tried his patience to the maximum.

Ellen and I dressed up in our new two-piece sailor outfits and shiny new patent leather dress shoes for our first airplane trip. We kissed Daddy goodbye and boarded the plane with my mother for Kennedy Airport, to connect with a charter flight to Athens. When we arrived in New York, we were shuttled to the North Terminal, where we began a wait that would come to span several hours. Olympic Airlines, the former TAE Airlines which had been started in part by my great-uncle Mike Savellos, was now owned by Aristotle Onassis. Olympic had initiated its first Boeing 707 service with the inauguration of a non-stop route between Athens and New York earlier that summer. In a competitive move that would eventually be determined to be outside of the law and overturned, Onassis used his political clout to prevent all charter flights originating in the U.S. from taking off or landing in Greece. The news spread quickly through the terminal, whose metal walls and high ceilings echoed with the shrill complaints of hundreds of angry Greeks. The trip to Greece, which should have been a nine-hour flight, became a three-day adventure. We finally departed at midnight, but not for Athens. We flew to Rome, and then boarded a bus to Ancona, Italy. The bus driver serenaded the weary passengers with *O Solo Mio* and *Come Back Sorrento* as we left the Rome airport and looked out the window at the fields of grape vines and groves of olive trees. I was surprised that the cars were so small, and for some reason also surprised that they still drove on the right side of the road. Cows, horses, and goats grazed by the dusty roadside as we began our ascent through the mountains, past crumbling castles and old stone houses with clothes hanging outside of the windows to dry. Eight hours later we found ourselves in Ancona, boarding a ship in the dark to take us to Greece. Somehow, we ended up on a cruise ship, complete with swimming pool, and passengers who spoke French, Greek, German, English, and Italian. By the time we found our luggage, which had been dumped together with everyone else's luggage in a heap, and got to our cabin it was past midnight. We wanted to fall into the bunk beds in the tiny cabin, but we hadn't eaten for several hours. We were ravenous, and a little overwhelmed by the events of the last 24 hours. Mom didn't seem to be the least worried, so we relaxed as we sat down to a late night snack of ham, cheese, and rolls. The next morning we slept through breakfast, waking past noon. After a second night on the ship, we pulled in the port of Patras, but our trip was not over yet. Ahead of us was another bus ride to Athens.

We were exhausted when, three days after leaving Pittsburgh, we finally arrived by taxi at Yiayia Coula's apartment. We rang the buzzer, and walked up the marble stairs. Yiayia Coula was already at the door. She hugged my mother, then me and Ellen. She grabbed my shoulders and held me away from her to look at me. "*Koukla mou*, my doll!" she said, as she pinched my cheeks painfully between her thumb and forefinger, and then pulled me in for another hug. Ellen's eyes grew large as Yiayia Coula turned to her and repeated the process.

My father's sister Loula and brother Dino joined us for dinner that night. We sat around the formal dining room table as Yiayia's maid served soup, followed by a large platter of baked fish – complete with the head! After dinner, fresh fruit was passed around the table, and we all took peaches off of the platter. I brought my peach to my mouth and took a juicy, delicious bite, as the sticky nectar of the peach dripped down my chin. Aunt Loula looked at me, picked up her knife, sliced her peach with her fork, and nodded. As Loula nodded instructions to me, my mother was also nodding – but her eyes were closed. The last few days of travel and responsibility had taken their toll on her. With the pleasant lullabye of conversation, my mother had fallen fast asleep at the table, sitting up.

The trip was a whirlwind of relatives and activity. We met mom's friend and maid of honor, my Godmother JoAnn, who had moved back to Greece along with her brother and his family, after divorcing my Uncle Nick. We met Aunt Loula's lovely daughters, my cousins Aliki and Helen. We saw my father's other sister, Helen, her husband Bill, and her youngest daughter, Rena. They were kind, generous, and affectionate, and we were delighted to come to know these Greek relatives. But our hearts were in the suburbs of Psihiko, with mom's uncle, Mike Savellos, his wife Zorka, and her son Thanos. The house in Psihiko was hidden by large shade trees, earthy-smelling holly bushes, and a large stone fence which surrounded the perimeter of the property and kept the noise of the city, which was stretching out its tentacles to the suburbs, at bay. A concrete path led to a set of steps which took us to a large front porch, where we spent much of our time playing with their two miniature dachshunds, Kiki and Lizzie, and their Dalmatian, Dick. Uncle Mike was a fit, handsome man in his late fifties who used his eyes and eyebrows to punctuate the endless stories that he told. Aunt Zorka was an attractive woman with wild auburn hair, a deep, throaty voice and boundless energy. She kept two dust rags on the hardwood floor in the hallway. When she walked into the hallway, she would step on the dust rags and drag them along with her feet to keep the floor clean. Thanos, her son, was an artist. He was tall, dark, and handsome, and showed me how to draw noses correctly and how to shade faces. They took us snorkeling and bought us masks for underwater. They took us out to dinner and up an incline to the top of Mt. Lycabetus, where we saw the thousands of apartments that made up Athens, and a huge forest fire in the distance. They took us souvenir shopping and sightseeing, and Zorka made a cake for Ellen's birthday. But mostly we enjoyed staying at the house in Psihiko, which began to feel like home.

Aunt Zorka's niece Helen, who was about my age, came with us for an overnight trip to the nearby island of Poros. On the short ferry ride to the island, Zorka told us about a young woman who worked at the small hotel where she had stayed before.

"Ah," she said. "The woman thought I was Alekah Katselis. She is a famous actress in Greece. No matter how much I told her that I wasn't Alekah, she wouldn't believe me."

We disembarked from the ferry boat on Poros and walked to the same small hotel to check in. The same woman was there. She smiled broadly as she saw Aunt Zorka approach.

"Alekah!" she cried. "You have come back!"

"No, no, no, no, no! I am not Alekah Katselis. How many times do I have to tell you this?"

"That is okay," the woman smiled. She brought her voice to a whisper. "Your secret is safe with me."

The woman showed us to our rooms, where we deposited our bags, and then went out for the afternoon. After a day of sightseeing, shopping, and eating, we trudged back to the hotel.

The woman nodded to us as we entered the hotel. Aunt Zorka and Helen turned right to go to their room and we turned left to go to ours. Suddenly my mother stopped, and turned around. "Alekah, Alekah! Uhhhhhh…..Zorka!" she called.

The hotel clerk's eyes grew wide. "*Se piasa*! I caught you!" she cried.

Zorka glared at my mother, who had put her hand over her mouth as if she had gotten caught. But her hand was hiding her laughter as we turned and unlocked our hotel door.

On our last night in Greece, as Aunt Zorka assembled the dinner to bring out onto the porch, Uncle Mike approached me where I sat sketching outside at the table.

"*Ela etho*, come here," Mike whispered to me, raising his eyebrows and looking around as if we were about to embark on a secret mission. We walked down the outside stairs and around the front of the house. Uncle Mike lifted the large wooden doors which led to the cellar, and the air was suddenly cool and moist. We walked down a set of concrete steps into the dank cellar which smelled of must and something pungent that I could not identify. Uncle Mike handed me a glass pitcher, and told me to place it under the spout of a large wooden barrel. He pushed the spout, and pale yellow liquid poured from the faded barrel into the pitcher. I carried the pitcher up the steps, both hands closed tightly around it. We would be having Uncle Mike's homemade Retsina wine at dinner that night. I was even allowed to taste it, but at age eleven, the wine did not roll off my tongue easily. Nor did Uncle Mike's homemade yogurt, although he tried several times to encourage us to develop a taste for it.

Our return trip was even more eventful than the trip to Greece had been. Onassis was still on his power play, and we learned that we would be taking a bus through what was then the country of Yugoslavia, and departing from the Belgrade airport. Joseph Tito had unified the six republics that made up Yugoslavia into a communist dictatorship. After the communist attempt to take over Greece in the late 1940's on the heels of the German Occupation during World War II, it was not unreasonable that many of the people on our charter flight were concerned about traveling through Yugoslavia.

We approached the northern border of Greece, where we had to pass through a government checkpoint before entering Yugoslavia.

"We are entering enemy territory," said the bus driver. "Do not talk to the soldiers. Hand them your passports. Do not attract attention to yourself. Do not say a word."

The busload of usually garrulous Greeks was silent as we stopped at the border. Two young soldiers boarded the bus and stopped at each seat, inspecting every traveler's passport. A soldier stopped at our seats. My mother was across the aisle from me and Ellen. She handed him all of our passports. "Hello," she said, and smiled. "These are my children." She pointed towards us. We looked up at the handsome soldier. He looked back and smiled at us as he handed the passports back to my mother. "Good day," he said, and moved on.

It felt like everyone on the bus had held their collective breaths until the soldiers left the bus. At that point, the man directly behind my mother poked her on the shoulder.

"You must always remember this day," he said with a Greek accent. "The enemy, he smiled at you!"

It was 3:00 a.m. before we arrived at our hotel in Belgrade. Once again, we were ravenous. The small hotel was unprepared for 183 guests, and those of us that chose to stay up to get something to eat were squeezed into a small dining room. Only one harried young man was available to serve all of the tables, and he did so as efficiently as possible, reacting to the impatient guests with an anxious smile and an apology in broken English. The next morning, the same dark-haired young man was serving breakfast. He approached our table, and my mother smiled and said, "You are very pleasant."

The waiter's eyes narrowed and he took in an angry breath. "Nyet!" he said, and pointed to himself, tapping his finger on his chest. "I student!"

My mother realized the miscommunication immediately. "No, no, no!" she said. "Not peasant...*pleasant*! It means you are very nice and we like you very much."

The tenseness left the young man's body and he smiled broadly. "Oh! For that I am very happy!"

It never occurred to me or Ellen to be concerned about anything that was happening on the trip. While other passengers shouted or cried, my mother smiled and encouraged. Her calm was pervasive, and whether it was this, or that she was traveling alone with two young children, or perhaps her striking smile and no-nonsense attitude, we were never without a fellow passenger to help us with luggage or with navigating the transportation, passport, and paperwork issues. Mom's humor and composure enabled us to experience what was surely an unsettling expedition as an exciting journey.

THE GREEK PICNICS - *Elleniki Peekneek*: ΕΛΛHNIKʹH ΠIKNIK

When I wasn't playing kickball or riding bikes with the neighborhood kids, I was playing tennis, drawing, or reading on the large covered patio that my father and mother built a few steps away from the house. At sixteen, I was an avid reader, and the patio provided a haven for my summer days with a book. It took Mom and Daddy the better part of a month to erect the structure with its inlaid flagstone floor and built-in wooden benches and cabinets. At the far end they constructed a charcoal grill from a steel drum which they cut in half and covered with a metal grate. They ran electricity out to the patio and put a refrigerator outside. They planted pink and red zinnias and bright yellow-orange marigolds around the perimeter of the patio. The patio was large enough to hold a few picnic tables and my Aunt Sassa's old glass-top white wrought iron dining room table and chairs. A patio that size begged for people, and my parents began to have yearly Greek picnics. Ellen and I loved those picnics, and we looked forward to seeing Dad's friends. Louie Xides, the bartender who told such funny jokes, would get a ride out to the suburbs with tall, handsome Pete Kalomiris with his dark curly hair and dimpled smile. They would pick up Mike the barber on the way, since he also did not drive. Jimmy Tsouris, the charming artist and painting contractor, came with his wife Virginia, and the whole Retos clan would come – George, the veterinarian and his wife, Irene, along with their four children: George Jr., Gregory, Gary, and Karen. Uncle Pete would drive up late in his old white Cadillac El Dorado convertible, cigarette burns dotting its red leather seats. As the years went by the parties grew, and often mom and dad would invite some of their American friends, but it was always that core of Greek friends from their Oakland days that formed the basis for every party.

    The portable cassette player on the counter played music from our new "Sounds of Greece" cassette as Daddy and Louie "discussed" how they would be cooking the lamb. Louie had come out early on the bus to help Daddy with the lamb, which had to be started ahead of time if they were going to cook it on the spit.

"*Pas ta diavolo*! It's not going to work that way," my dad shouted at Louie, who was trying to rig a spit over the charcoal grill. Finally they decided that the spit was not going to work, and they calmed down as they decided to simply butcher the lamb into pieces.

"*Vre, vlaka*! Why you cutting those pieces so big? Cut them this way!" And the discussion continued until the cooks reached a compromise. With the lamb on the grill, and the company starting to arrive, I followed Louie to the garage for picnic supplies. The garage was an old painted wood structure with a packed dirt floor. We didn't park the car there - instead, we used it for storage. The cabinets in the garage held our paper plates, utensils, and other picnic paraphernalia. For reasons that I can't recall, a large jug of red wine sat on the counter in the garage. "Psst," Louie said. He pointed to the wine, and held an empty plastic cup out. He lifted the jug and poured a half glass for me, smiled, and put his index finger to his lip. I had not tasted wine since Uncle Mike's retsina five years before. I liked this wine much better.

The men gathered on the patio, smoking cigarettes and drinking whiskey or ouzo, as the women congregated in the small kitchen and Ellen and I delivered appetizers to the patio. The lamb sizzled on the grill, delicious smoke teasing our stomachs as we nibbled garlicky Greek meatballs and cheeses. I was getting thirsty, and Louie nodded towards the garage. The second glass of wine proved too much, and my father caught on. I didn't get in trouble, but for the second time that day, Louie was in the doghouse.

As the sun set and the heat subsided, the women finished cleaning up after the meal. The ladies chatted over coffee and sweets on the patio and the men moved inside to the massive Mediterranean dining room table that my parents had acquired at an estate sale. Ash trays lined the table as the poker game began. Mike Kapsal smoked his fat stogie and my father puffed on his Winston's. Uncle Pete smashed his cigarette out with almost half of it left, and immediately lit another. A cloud of smoke hung over the table upon which was mounded a pile of ones and fives. Ellen stood behind Uncle Pete and I stood behind Jimmy. Daddy was in his usual spot at the head of the table, across the table from us; we never stood behind him. Pete put his cigarette down for a few seconds to shuffle and deal the cards, and the room was silent except for the flapping of the cards as he dealt them around the table for five card stud, deuces wild. We stayed for a few hands. If we were lucky, the player we stood behind would win, and give us a few quarters for being his good luck charms. The novelty wore off after a few rounds, and we went outside to see what was happening.

Up by the garage, the Retos boys were unpacking fireworks that they had bought across the border in West Virginia. It was illegal to set these off in Pennsylvania, but that didn't stop the boys. They lit the fireworks which went off with a streaming sizzle, a loud bang, and a sparkle of light. After about ten minutes of this, we saw the headlights of a car at the end of our long driveway. I wondered who could be coming to the picnic this late. As the police car pulled up, my mother jumped up from the patio, ran into the dining room, and started pulling the drapes shut. The men continued on with their poker game, paying no heed to the warning about the cops. My dad got up, opened the door, and met the policeman outside.

Mrs. Retos also met them at the front door, taking full responsibility for the misdemeanor, and offering to pay any fine that her sons incurred, while her husband continued on with the poker game inside. But the policeman let them off with a warning, and all was well as the men played on.

Our Greek picnics always went long into the night, and Ellen and I usually stayed up until the last guest left. We nibbled on leftover Greek meatballs and cheeses and sat with the ladies on the patio, listening to the conversation – sometimes in Greek, sometimes in English, as our eyelids got heavy.

In addition to the Greek picnics, our family enjoyed having friends over to the house. Sometimes Greek friends would take a ride out to the suburbs to visit Mom and Daddy, and once in a while Daddy's friends would come to play cards. Sometimes Daddy's work friends came to the house, and often they brought their children. Ellen and I always enjoyed these visits. Once in a while Pete would drive Yiayia out for a visit. She would go out into the yard with a scissors, and cut dandelion leaves to make boiled greens. In the winter, however, we rarely saw them. If Pete was around in December, he might come over on Christmas Day. Then again, he might not - he was never very reliable.

Our Christmases in the suburbs were far removed from a traditional Greek Orthodox Christmas. We did not go to church. If mom missed singing in the choir, we never knew it. We always got a live tree a few days before Christmas that Daddy recycled from the college dorms. It was usually short, so he would set it on top of the corner coffee table, and we would string large multi-colored lights through branches still clad in left-over tinsel. On Christmas morning we opened the stockings, which were always filled with a large orange in the toe, and some of the *koulourakia* that Mom had baked that week, along with a few *Archie* comics. Then Mr. Bassett, one of Daddy's friends from Robert Morris, came over for brunch. Mom prepared eggs, bacon, and toast, and we all sat around the large dining room table, chatting with Mr. Bassett until it became clear to our parents that we could no longer wait to open presents. After opening our gifts, we set the table – sometimes for only the four of us, but sometimes for more if Uncle Pete was bringing family out. On Christmas Day in 1969, we set the table for seven.

Yiayia had died of a heart attack on the steps of her apartment building in September of 1968. I did not go to the funeral home, nor to the funeral. I remember being home watching mom put on her red lipstick, which she applied bright from the tube, then blotted with a Kleenex. She was wearing a dress and her good pumps. I was surprised to see Daddy come home in the middle of the day. Mom called a babysitter to watch me and Ellen, but no one told us yet that Yiayia had died. Perhaps mom's experience as a child with the coffin made her decide that we were too young for a funeral.

Uncle Nick was now living in the apartment alone, but this December he had a visitor. Her name was Anneliese. He had met her the past summer during a trip to Greece with Pete. Anneliese, a Swiss German, had traveled to Greece to visit her friends, Mike and Zorka Savellos, whom she had met through her brother, who was also a pilot. "You're so lucky," Zorka told her. "Our two nephews from Pittsburgh are here visiting." At first Anneliese was unimpressed with Nick, who she mistakenly believed to be an actor, not an artist. As the week progressed, they found themselves together at a party, at the beach, at a luncheon, and at a casino in Athens, where Pete was losing at the poker table.

"*Fige*, Go – you're bringing me bad luck," Pete said, motioning them away without looking up from the cards.

"Shall we sit on a bench and have a cigarette?" Nick asked Anneliese.

Anneliese agreed, and the two left the casino. They walked together in the warm night, and found *Prasino Kokkoras*, the Green Rooster. Breathing in the heady scent of fragrant lemon trees, they climbed the steps to the second floor which opened out into a veranda with grape vines forming a roof over the patio. The waiter served them fresh figs which they peeled to get the sweet flesh, and they drank dry white wine and talked into the night.

Anneliese stayed in Greece for a week after Nick and Pete returned to the states. When she arrived in Switzerland, she opened her mailbox to find an elongated envelope with the familiar red, white, and blue airmail stripes. It was from Nick. He had written it on the airplane.

Ellen and I were anxious to meet Uncle Nick's friend, and could barely contain our excitement when Pete drove up in his Cadillac. We watched Anneliese walk down the path in her black patent leather pumps and her wool skirt and fur jacket. Uncle Nick looked dapper in a wool dress coat, and we hugged him when he came in. "This is Anneliese," he said, and she opened her arms to hug us. Her hair was a short, wavy reddish brown, and her complexion was creamy white, her cheeks flushed with the cold. She wore a sweet perfume, and a bright red lipstick which she hadn't blotted, like my mother did whenever she put on her lipstick. Her dark fur coat was cold and soft as she hugged me tightly. "Ooh, it is *so* good to meet you."

She turned toward Uncle Nick. "Oh, *Schatzeli*, it is so good to meet your family."

Mom had hung the red curtains in the dining room, and decorated the windows with plastic poinsettias. She had opened the leaves on either end of the long table and we congregated around it, Ellen and I across from Daddy. To our right sat Nick in his wool vest and salt and pepper mustache and Anna in her pearls. Pete, who looked dapper as always in a crisp white shirt and deep tan from his many visits to Florida, sat next to Mom, who at forty-

three, already had a full head of stunning silver hair. Looking around the table I knew that there was no place that I would have rather been.
 Anna returned to Switzerland after the holidays. The following September, Nick went to Switzerland to visit her. When he returned, he brought her back with him, as his wife.

RETURN TO GREECE - *Epistrophe Sthn Ellatha*: ΕΠΙΣΤΡΟΦΗ ΣΤΗΝ ΕΛΛΆΔΑ

In July, following my high school graduation, we returned to Greece – this time with both my father and my mother. Although we were not descendants of the island of Ikaria, we hooked onto a charter trip for the Ikarian Convention. This allowed my parents to visit with relatives while Ellen and I took part in some of the tours associated with the trip. This also allowed us to meet kids closer to our age, more specifically, a boy - a good-looking Greek boy with dark hair and dark eyes, named George, from Baltimore, Maryland. George's buddy Angelo kept my sister company while I sat with George on the bus, swam with him in the Mediterranean, shared a few kisses at the temple of Piraeus, and a few more at the Ikarian Dance, to which I wore a flower print mini-dress that would barely pass a "wrist-length test," let alone a "fingertip test." But it was 1972, and miniskirts were the fashion of the times. That my father would allow me to wear something this short in public is a mystery. He never criticized my choice of clothing; whether it was a super-short skirt, frayed bell-bottom hip-hugger jeans, or a midriff top, I was free to dress in the fashion of the times. Daddy never forbade me from wearing make-up, and though I never wore too much, I was up-to-date with my frosted pink lipstick and baby blue eye shadow. But when it came to boys, it was another story altogether. To say that my father was strict was an understatement. I wasn't permitted to date, and the few boys I had gone out with were under the guise of hanging out with friends. Any boys who might have been interested in going out with me with realized that dating me meant answering to my father, and quickly moved on.

    The Icarian conventioneers moved on to Icaria, and we flew to Thessaloniki to visit Aunt Helen and Uncle Bill, their children – our cousins Rena and Roi - and their husbands. They were all involved with the business aspect of a resort in nearby Marmara that John Karas, Aunt Rita's husband, owned. At dinner that night, I sat next to Roi and her husband, Niko at the restaurant. It was the beginning of a love affair with my cousins that would span decades. Niko was handsome and charming, and Roi was polished, professional, and lovely. I was enamored by their jobs (he was an engineer and she was an architectural designer), their kindness, and their obvious affection for one another.

The next morning we drove to Marmara to spend a few days. The village was small, but lively. We stayed at a cozy whitewashed house – the *kaliva*, or cottage, owned by John Karas. The home was surrounded by geraniums and wildflowers. It sat high on a hill which jutted out on a point that was surrounded by water. I had never seen a view like this, and I was overwhelmed at the beauty of this place. We swam in the mornings, napped in the afternoons, and went out to dinner at night. I became friends with Roi's son, Vasili. He was seven years old and talked to me in Greek – very soft, and very fast, although I understood little of what he said.

One afternoon we drove over to see John Karas's multi-million dollar house which was under construction. The house sat on top of a mountain, and looked down upon the ocean and the resort– the hotels, golf course, vineyards, wineries, olive factories, and the harbor which was under construction. The ceramic tile floors and white walls gave the house a coolness, along with the breeze that blew gently into the copious open windows. I imagined what it must be like to live here, on top of a mountain in Greece, where the view from your kitchen window is the ocean.

When we returned to Athens, Ellen and I stayed for several days with Uncle Mike and Aunt Zorka. We were overjoyed to stay at their home in Psihiko, where rose bushes and shade trees grew in abundance, and we also had the company of Kiki, Lizzie, Dick, and of course, Thanos. On our last night in Greece, we were sitting on the porch when I heard Alex pulling up on his motorcycle, and I broke into a smile. Alex was a friend of the family whom we had met earlier in the week. I was enamored by this twenty-four year old dark eyed man with long hair and a short beard who treated me as an adult. He had stopped to say goodbye before leaving for his mandatory one-year stint in the army, and I walked him to the gate when the visit ended. I admired his motorcycle, and he asked me if I wanted to go for a ride. Of course I did, but I also knew that my father would never let me.

"You ask him," I said, and we climbed back up the steps to the porch. Alex spoke to my father in Greek. My father spoke back. I could only imagine what he was saying, and I knew the answer was no, but when they finished their conversation, Alex said, "*Ela*, come on," and we were off. The evening air was cool, and I held tightly onto Alex as he drove me around the city. I was happy and excited at this unexpected freedom granted to me by my father.

Reflecting later on my trip to Greece I realized that part of my joy in the country stemmed from my delight in our family's relationship there. I looked at photographs of my father and me – in them he was relaxed, his arm was around me, and we were smiling. There was no furrow around his eyebrows and no frown on his lips. In Greece Ellen and I took bus tours with other teenagers. We went shopping and took taxis to dinner by ourselves. We went to dances until 3 a.m., and met boys at the beach. In Greece I rode a motorcycle. There was a lightness as though a weight had been lifted from my father's shoulders. When I returned to the states, George and I sent three or four letters to each other, but the spark ignited by the Greek sun fizzled upon touching American soil. In the fall, I began a two-year degree program in Office Administration. Because my father worked at the college, my education was free. I yearned to go to art school, or take an entry-level job in the art department of Gimbel's department store in Pittsburgh, where my Uncle Nick was an artist. But my father told me that unless I was 100 percent sure of what I wanted to do with my life, I would go to Robert Morris College to earn my Associates Degree, so that I could get a good job and become financially stable.

     I celebrated my college graduation by going once again to Greece, this time with just my sister. After spending two weeks with my relatives, we returned, and more than ever I felt Greece pulling at me. I found a secretarial position. The pay was decent and the people were nice, but something was lacking. I obtained the application for a foreign service job in Greece. I begin filling out the paperwork, and was in the process of assembling the necessary documentation. And then, I met John – my future husband. With the spark of a new romance, my life began its altered course. The application was forgotten. It would be twenty-three years before I returned to Greece.

COLLEGE - Panepistimio: ΠΑΝΕΠΙΣΤΗΜΙΟ

John and I dated for two years before becoming engaged. He outlasted my father's glowering stares and gruff countenance. Others whom I dated did not fare as well; they did not value me enough to put up with cross examinations and curfews. I had dated only one boy during my senior year of high school – Mike, a college freshman. But we stayed out past my eleven o'clock curfew one night, and Mike was not up for confrontation. "Sorry, but I don't need that shit. I'm in college." I wanted to date a Greek boy, and yet it was funny that my mother, raised so traditionally, and my father, as strict as he was, did not expect me to marry a Greek man. Perhaps my mother recalled the matchmaking attempts by her parents. As for my father, I'm guessing he didn't trust Greek men with his daughters any more than he trusted American men.

At Robert Morris College, I walked to class. The classroom buildings were a twenty minute walk up over the hill from our house. My father's maintenance men were everywhere. If I even said hello to a boy, chances were I'd be spotted. One day at dinner I could tell by my father's expression that I had done something wrong – but I had no clue as to what it was.

"How was school today?" he began. I knew he didn't want to know how school was. It was another version of, "Do you have anything you want to tell me?" which had busted me more than once.

"It was fine," I said.
"How was lunch?"
Lunch? I had eaten lunch with Janet and JoAnn in the cafeteria. What could I possibly have done at lunch?
"It was fine?"
"Stay away from the basketball players."
"What?" I had stopped by the table to say hello to Billy Odom, one of the nicest boys I'd met on campus. He was black. The other boys at the table were also black.
"Why?" I said.
"Just stay away from them."
"Because they're black?" I said.
"I don't want people talking about my daughter," he said.

I had never thought of my father as racist. In retrospect, it may have been less prejudice on his part and more discrimination based upon what his co-workers might think. Which was still racism to me. I thought back to my first-grade friend, Mildred, on Dawson Street with whom I walked to school. My parents never told me to stay away from her, and she was black. Yet, there was the first time I asked my friend Candy to come to my house in fourth grade. After we had played for a few hours, my mother drove her back to the housing project. As we rode home in the car, my mother asked, "Rita, why didn't you tell me she was black?" It hadn't occurred to me that she was anything other than my friend. We remained friends through junior high, frequently hanging out at each other's houses on the weekends. My dad never told me to stay away from her. But when we went to high school she began to date Horace, an older militant black student, and I lost Candy. Under Horace's grip, she no longer hung out with her white friends. I lost my naiveté about prejudice. Suddenly I understood that this was about being seen with a black *man*. I had always winced when my father had used the term *jigaboo*, as in *that jigaboo can really run* when he was watching a football game. I had written it off as ignorance, perhaps coming from the fact that there were few blacks in Greece. But there were plenty in Pittsburgh, and I saw my dad's armor crack a little.

I didn't stay away from the boys on the basketball team, but I didn't make a public display of my friendship either. It was best to stay on Daddy's good side. It was hard enough sneaking to a fraternity party here and there. I didn't understand why I wasn't permitted to go to dorm parties or fraternity parties.

"Daddy," I'd say. "I'm not going to drink. I know how to behave."

"It's not you I'm worried about."

"I'll come home early. I just want to go with my friends."

"NO! I know what goes on at these parties."

Unfortunately, he did.

I met one Greek-American boy in college. His name was Gus. Although he was my age, he wore a fedora, a trench coat, black framed glasses, dress pants and shiny black shoes. He looked about thirty-five. In class, he would lean over and whisper in an awkward mixture of Greek and English, "*Theleis na pas exo* (do you want to go out)....Thursday night?" He would raise his eyebrows, waiting for a reply.

I pressed my lips together to hold back my laughter at his covert approach. "*Ohi, efharisto* - no thank you."

I met John the summer of 1975, when he and I were both on dates with other people. We ran into each other before a movie, and I laughed when he told a story about a fraternity party that summer, as his eyebrows rose up with enthusiasm, and his hands did as much talking as his mouth. I didn't see him again until that fall, when we both had night classes at RMC. The college had set up a large coffee carafe on a table in Hale Center, where we met and talked during the break. As the semester drew to an end, I knew that I wanted to see John again.

"What are you doing over break?" I asked.

"My family is going to Acapulco. We haven't been on a family vacation for years."

The gears turned quickly. "Acapulco? Oh, I love Mexican jewelry!" I came dangerously close to gushing. "Could you buy me a piece? I'll pay you for it."

"Sure," he said.

John's mother later told me that she wondered who this girl was that he was buying jewelry for. "He spent his whole vacation trying to find just the right piece of jewelry!"

John called when he returned from Mexico and gave me a leather choker with small brass bolts on it. It was perfect. We started dating. A month later, we were officially a couple.

John did not make an immediate positive impression on my father. He had long brown hair and a mustache, wore a drab green army jacket, and drove a faded red 1967 Dodge half-ton pick-up truck, which he affectionately called "the Mongoose." Having served in Vietnam and come to college as a veteran, he was five years older than I was. My mother liked him immediately. She found him to be respectful, kind, and humorous. We had been dating for several months and were hanging out at John's apartment, a place that was positively off limits for the daughter of George Langas. We were watching TV in the living room when John got up to get a beer out of the refrigerator. He glanced out the window as he walked into the kitchen, only to catch the taillights of my father's dark grey Plymouth sedan as he drove down the road. When we returned to my house, Daddy was waiting under the chestnut tree in the driveway with his arms folded, an angry grimace on his face. John and I got out of the car.

"Go in the house," Daddy told me. He and John rose to their full heights, shoulders squared, eyes blazing. Although John was six foot one, and my dad was only five foot ten inches, he was strong and his arms were muscular.

"Where were you?" George demanded.

"At my apartment."

"No you weren't, you were at the fraternity house."

"No we weren't. I know why you think we were. I saw your car pulling away. But we weren't there. I just parked there."

George mulled this over, then spoke again. "What are your feelings for my daughter?"

"Mr. Langas, I love your daughter. My intentions are honorable."

George relaxed his stance. John watched him cautiously. George extended his hand to John. "Okay," he said, shaking John's hand and added, "You can call me George."

After John's confrontation with my father, things changed. Daddy began to affectionately refer to John as *Yianni*, Greek for John. He found John to be honest and hard-working. He even hired him to work on the painting crew in the summer. My curfew was extended – but as a 21-year old Greek girl living at home, I still had a curfew. And I was still not allowed to go to John's apartment.

In February of 1978, John asked me to marry him. We went to spend the weekend with Uncle Nick and Aunt Annaleise who had moved to Akron, Ohio. Nick was working in the art department of a jewelry store, and Anna had gotten certified as a gemologist. We wanted their help to pick out a ring and make our engagement official. We arrived at their home in Akron to be greeted enthusiastically by their schnauzer, Winston (who was named after Winston Churchill), and almost as enthusiastically by Nick and Anna. They took us on a tour of their home, and stopped at the entrance to one of the bedrooms. "Here is your bedroom," Anna said. I was astonished. After the protective blanket of my parents, even as someone who was engaged, I never expected to actually be allowed to sleep with John. "This is *our* room?" I asked, to make sure.

"Of course," Nick said.

On Sunday evening we arrived home from Akron to find my father in his usual Sunday position, laying on the built-in couch, elbow bent, leaning his head on his hand, and watching football on television. My mom sat on the opposite couch working on a crossword puzzle. We made our announcement. My dad sat up and smiled. "Congratulations," he said, as he got up to shake John's hand. I looked at my mom. Her face was blank. She hugged us both, but I could tell something was wrong.

    I asked her after John left. "Mom, aren't you happy for me?"

"Of course I am, Rita" she said.

"But?"

"Rita, you're so young. There are so many things that you haven't done yet. You'll meet people in the workplace. Don't you want to travel with your friends?"

"But mom," I said. "If I travel, I want to travel with John!"

She said nothing more. At 22, I didn't understand what she was telling me.

We planned the wedding for that August. My father put himself in charge of the reception. We agreed that the wedding would be outdoors, the dinner at Jefferson Center (the cafeteria), and the dancing back at Pine Hill Manor, where Daddy's men would set up the bandstand, the tables, and colored lights.

"What if it rains?" I asked.

"Don't worry about it."

"But, Daddy, what are we going to do if it rains?"

"Don't worry about it!"

So I didn't.

On a Saturday morning in early August, I sat having coffee with my father on the patio after breakfast.

"Does it bother you that I'm getting married?" I asked.

"No," Daddy said, and thought for a moment. "It would bother me if you moved away, but it doesn't bother me that you're getting married. Yianni is a good boy."

The wedding venue was Pine Hill Manor, the old Kaufman mansion at Robert Morris College. Outside of the majestic mansion, which now served as staff offices, were rose gardens. My father had his maintenance men spruce up the gardens – the white lattice trellises were painted, the pink roses pruned, and the grass freshly mowed.

Our intention was to have a Greek wedding. Although we had not been faithful church-goers since living in the suburbs, it was my family's heritage, and the only religion that I knew. I wanted the traditional Greek ceremony, and I wanted to wear my parents' *stefana* – wedding crowns. Daddy asked the Orthodox priest to officiate, but was told that he would not officiate a wedding that was not held "in God's house" (for a fee to use God's house, of course). My fiancé's parents brought their Methodist minister, Reverend Hawke, to meet our family. As we sat on the patio drinking coffee, my father said, "I hope you understand, I don't want this Jesus-Christ, God-Almighty stuff. I just want a simple wedding."

Reverend Hawke smiled and replied, "George, I know exactly what you want."

A week before the wedding, George Retos Jr. drove up to the house in his red Mercedes convertible. He was now a lawyer, and he was picking up Ellen for a date. He gave me a hug and a kiss on the cheek, and I watched them pull out of the driveway. I felt a sense of panic. It was not that I had feelings for George. We had gone on one uneventful dinner date. He caught me off guard when he tried to kiss me in the living room during one of our Greek picnics, and I had not kissed him back. It was not that I wanted to date George, so why, I wondered, was a lump forming in my throat? I called Susan, a close friend and bridesmaid. Twenty minutes later, she got out of her baby blue Camaro and parked herself next to me on the front porch step, where I sat in the evening sun. I poured out a long string of what if's, trying to analyze why seeing my sister and George drive away would prick the balloon of happiness that I had been floating in for months. *Was I ready for this? Was I too young? Was John right for me? Did I still want the possibility of a Greek man?* There was something about them – their curly hair, their dark eyes and skin, their charming arrogance. I always associated Greek men with the

culture – the music, food, language, and passion. Was I going to lose my heritage? Of course I loved John. But, what if this was the spot where the road diverged, and I was taking the wrong path? Susan pondered for a moment.
"It's just cold feet," she said.
I hoped that she was right.

The day of the wedding was hot and so humid that my short dark curly hair had wound itself tightly around the hair comb that secured the wreath and veil to my head. My mom and Ellen had gone up to the cafeteria to make some final changes to the place cards on the tables. Daddy had gone up early to survey the grounds and make sure that they were wedding-ready. I waited at the house – the realization dawning on me that the only person who wasn't at the venue was the bride. Relief flooded me when I heard tires on the driveway, and I pushed the dining room curtain aside in time to see Uncle Pete, looking like Dean Martin in his white suit and slicked back hair, cigarette in hand, getting out of his latest Cadillac.
"Thank God you're here!" I hugged him.
"You look beautiful, honey," he said. "Where's the wedding?"
I gladly directed him, and he delivered me to the old Kaufman mansion, where my father and I were to wait until the wedding got underway. The photographer wanted to get a picture of me and my father before he walked me down the aisle. "Look at each other," the photographer directed, and as Daddy looked at me his dark eyes were bright. I felt my heart pound as my eyes welled up with tears. I broke the gaze and hugged Daddy tightly. We composed ourselves and prepared to walk down the path to the altar. True to his word, Reverend Hawke delivered a brief, engaging ceremony, after which we met our guests in the courtyard for champagne. Uncle Nick and Aunt Anneliese had flown in from a trip to Greece to arrive in time for the wedding. Nick's blue and white polka dot shirt and white pants hung loosely on his thin frame; his grey hair was whiter than it had been only six months ago. My dear uncle had been diagnosed with stomach cancer. I did not realize at the time that the trip to Greece was a "farewell" trip. I was simply overjoyed that he was at my wedding.

We managed to fit the wedding in outside, but as we had our photos taken the wind picked up, and grey storm clouds rolled in. The guests hurried down the path to the cafeteria, and we were not far behind. The storm clouds released heavy rains, thunder, and lightning, the circuit breaker sizzled and popped, and the room went dark. Luckily, my father's maintenance men were at the wedding and quickly shed their sport coats and rolled up their sleeves. In no time they engaged the generator, and the reception was underway again. My father had arranged fresh shrimp cocktails, prime rib, salad, and a bottle of Mateus Rose at every table. I ate about two bites of steak, my salad, and a piece of wedding cake. I never even saw the shrimp.

  We hired a friend's band for the reception. In with the mix of popular dance music, they played Greek tunes. My mom had taught my wedding party and shower guests how to dance the *kalamatiano,* a Greek line dance, at my bridal shower. We had danced around the patio while the static crackled on the old Greek records playing on the stereo system which was now part of the growing assortment of furniture on the patio. The wedding reception took a lively turn as the dancing circle got larger, faster, and rowdier, and the American guests joined the Greeks, kicking their feet and trying to keep up with the steps.

  Louie slow-danced with me and told me how he remembered carrying me out of the hospital when I was born. I looked around the dance floor and saw my mother and father dancing cheek to cheek. My mother was radiant with her silver hair and her light blue gown. My father was light on his feet, and dashing in his tan suit. My sister was lovely in her sundress, and I realized that somewhere along the way she had lost the gawkiness of her young teen years. The Greek tables were joyful and raucous, and I watched the familiar faces – Uncle Pete, Mike the barber, and the rest of the gang from the Greek picnics - talking and laughing. Uncle Nick was no longer at the table. He was not able to last for the reception. I felt a pang of apprehension.

Rita and John, August 19, 1978

NEWLYWEDS - *Neonoumos*: ΝΕΟΝΟΥΜΟΣ

John and I moved into a red brick duplex in Carnegie, about twenty minutes away from my parents' house. John worked night shift for an air freight forwarder and I worked downtown as a financial analyst for a bank. When I took the bus after work, I came home to an empty house. It was a strange feeling to know that nobody was keeping track of my whereabouts.
I was bored and discontented with my job at the bank. It was demanding and busy for only a few days a month. On the other days, there were often hours with little to do. John's employer had reneged on the promise to switch him to day shift. We both began to look for work. It was not long before I was offered a management training position with a division of Westinghouse. The company flew me to Minneapolis for an interview, and a month later they flew both me and John there to look at houses. My friends warned me that winters in Minnesota were harsh, but when we visited the last weekend of October the temperature was in the seventies and skies were clear and blue. We failed to recognize that this was Indian summer, and did not heed our friends' warnings. We were taken in by the lure of a large salary increase for me, opportunities for John, the lakes, and the sunshine. We made plans to move to Minnesota. We were excited about this adventure, but in the back of my mind were my father's words: *It*

doesn't bother me that you're getting married, but it would bother me if you moved away.

Before moving I traveled to Ohio to visit Uncle Nick who was now at the Cleveland Clinic. The daily trips back and forth between Akron and Cleveland had exhausted Annaliese. She was worn and thin from worry and long hours at the hospital. I went to visit Uncle Nick by myself. He looked so frail in the hospital bed, but his eyes were clear and his smile warm. I pulled the chair closer to Uncle Nick and held his hand, with its familiar softness. He was too weak to talk, but wanted to listen, so I chatted about John, the new job, and moving to the Midwest. Uncle Nick said that he hoped to be able to visit me in Minnesota, and I felt my heart catch in my throat. I realized that this would be the last time that I would see my beloved uncle. This wonderful man, who had been through so much – arriving to this country as a stranger, earning a purple heart, learning a new language and forging a successful career – was not going to enjoy a deserved retirement with the woman he loved – would not see my children grow up or spend another Christmas with me. When I got up to leave I kissed Uncle Nick on the cheek. He held my hand and looked closely at me. I reached the door and turned around to wave. His eyes watched me intently and I wonder if he fixed my image into his mind as strongly as I fixed his memory into my heart.

Two weeks before we moved to Minnesota the headlines in *The Pittsburgh Press* read, "Minneapolis Buried Under Two Feet of Snow," and I wondered what we had gotten ourselves into. That same week, Uncle Nick passed away. He was only 54 years old. At the memorial service in Akron, my mother chatted with the people around us, introducing herself, exchanging pleasantries. I didn't understand how she could be so cheerful when I could not even speak because of the lump in my throat, and I could not hold back my tears. A man approached us and my mother stopped talking.

"Hello, Angie," he said.
"Hello, Stanley."
The woman next to him said nothing, then walked away.
"Rita," my mother said. "This is your Uncle Stanley."

They spoke for only a moment, expressing their sorrow over the loss of their brother. Then Stanley joined his wife, Irene, and we did not speak with them again.

When John and I arrived in the Twin Cities, we were unable to get to our duplex – no one had shoveled the walk or the driveway, and the snow had drifted about four feet high in front of the door. We spent two weeks in a hotel, along with our black cat, Gus, waiting for our furniture, and digging out the path. I was terribly homesick. My father understood, and flew us home to Pittsburgh for the Christmas holidays, only a month after we had moved away.

John and I spent almost four years in Minnesota. We enjoyed our new friends, new jobs, and new home. John landed a sales job within a week of moving to the twin cities. I went to night school and earned my MBA from the College of St. Thomas. We bought a rambler, the mid-western term for a ranch home, in the suburb of Apple Valley. We enjoyed our independence as newlyweds, our new friends, and our new home. After the hills and valleys of Western Pennsylvania, we were amazed at the expansive horizon line and the clear blue skies that surrounded us. But the winters were every bit as cold as we had been warned, and the summers were short and mosquito-laden. After the novelty of a new life in a new place, we longed to be home. There was a different culture in Minnesota. I'd not met one Greek person, nor had I seen one Greek Church or eaten at a Greek restaurant. Minnesotans pronounced John as *Jahn* and God as *Gahd*, and asked us if we were from the south. In December of 1981 we flew to Pittsburgh for the holidays, and explored the possibility of moving back within the next year by going on a few informational interviews. By the time we returned to Minnesota, I had an offer from Mellon Bank waiting for me. In February, we moved back home.

It took us awhile to find a house. I did not want to buy one in Moon Township – I was afraid that I would feel like I never left. But, after searching in vain for something with a decent-sized yard in our price range, our realtor, Ron, convinced us to just look at a few in Moon. One had come back on the market because the initial offer fell through – a two-story red brick with a fireplace, a covered porch, and a good sized yard on a cul-de-sac. We put an offer on it, and Ron called me the next day at work.

"I'm sorry, Rita, but the house is off the market."

"What do you mean? It just went back on the market!"

"Well," he said. "Apparently it's owned by U.S. Steel. They won't let the original buyers out of the deal. They can't sell their house, but they didn't sign a contingency. U.S. Steel is enforcing the contract."

"Wait a minute...." I took a minute to process this. "So, you're saying, that even though we are willing to buy the house, they're going to try to enforce the deal with people that can't afford to honor their contract?"

"That's right."

I knew that U.S. Steel had offices in the skyscraper where I worked. I looked at the directory. U.S. Steel Realty was housed on the top floor. I moved into action while my adrenalin was still high. I marched into the elevator, and got off at the top floor. The doors opened onto a quiet lobby where a middle-aged receptionist sat behind a large oval wood reception desk. I peered behind her into a large office where a silver-haired gentleman sat at his desk. I walked around the receptionist's desk and headed towards the office.

"Excuse me," the receptionist said. "What are you doing? You can't go back there!"

I reached the open door, rapped twice, and walked in. My face was flushed and my heart was pounding, but I said, "Excuse me."

The man wore a bemused expression. "Can I help you?" He asked.

I explained the situation, voicing my frustration, and my inability to understand why U.S. Steel Realty would turn down a bona fide offer to try to enforce an offer by people who weren't able to buy. He listened intently. "Please have a seat," he said, as he reached for the telephone.

After a brief conversation, he hung up the phone. "Okay," he said.

"Okay?"

"The house is yours. $89,900, right?" It was the price that we had offered.

Astonished, incredulous at what I had accomplished, and relieved, I figured that I now had nothing to lose. "Would you take $85,000?" I asked.

The house in Moon was only five minutes from my parents' house. Our happy reunion was short-lived. Within a year of our return to Pittsburgh, my sister moved to Philadelphia, and our best friends Kenny and Jamie moved to the middle of the state. The following year our son Nick was born, and my father retired. My parents decided to move to Florida.

"How can you leave when we just got back?" I asked my mother.

"You left," she replied.

"But we came back!"

"Ellen left."

"But mom," I said. "How can you leave your grandson?"

"Rita, you can visit us. You and John left. And now you're telling us not to go?"

The powers that be at Robert Morris decided that once my parents left they would tear down their home in order to build a parking lot for the new athletic center. My parents decided to have a garage sale. This particular sale actually included the garage, the house, and anything that could be carried away. John and I bought the dining room set. The large Mediterranean table was the source of too many memories for me to let it go. My dad's maintenance men loaded it into a truck and delivered it to our house. We returned to my parents' house to see if we could help with anything in time to see a man loading the doors from the house onto a truck. A woman was carrying the bathroom faucets to her car. The man returned to the kitchen where my father was detaching the sink from the wall.

My mother joked, "We would say we sold everything but the kitchen sink. But we sold the kitchen sink, too!"

Three years later, our daughter Alexandra was born. My parents had embraced having grandchildren, but had not embraced the job-title. My father refused to be called *Papou* or Grandpa. My kids were the only toddlers I knew who called their grandparents by their first names – Georgie and Angie. Over the next decade we were busy raising children, changing careers, and maintaining a home. Since we married in the Methodist Church, we baptized our children in the Methodist Church, but I heard that there was a Greek church in Aliquippa, about twenty minutes away from us, and I wanted for us to try it out.

The service was still ancient Greek, and none of us understood a word of it. To me it was familiar – the melodious incantations of the priest and the cantor, the clang of the metal container as the priest spread sweet incense through the church, the harmony of the choir as their voices resonated with ancient hymns. But the incense got to John. His eyes watered and his head pounded. We tried again – this time sitting in the loft, but the results were the same, and we did not return.

TEACHER - *Daskala*: ΔΑΣΚΆΛΑ

Motherhood brought with it an intense desire to spend more time with my children, and less time on an airplane, bus, or car. I was also increasingly disillusioned with my marketing job. I cut back to part-time, and to supplement the loss of income, I began to teach a few night classes in Marketing at Robert Morris. I realized that I was challenged, inspired, and effective in the classroom. In 1993 I made a major decision. I returned to school on a full-time basis to get my teaching certification. We calculated that we could afford this if we were very conservative with our budget. When I had finished only one semester, John was laid off. He had always wanted to start his own business. He now had the opportunity to do so. We borrowed money from both sets of parents, and lived under the poverty line for the next year. We were not used to counting dollars, let alone pennies, but we kept a positive attitude. Our kids were enrolled in the free school lunch program, and we made do with what we had. (Years later my daughter told me that she wondered why she had to go to a different line in the cafeteria.) As difficult as this time was for us, at least we had support from our family. I could not imagine how difficult life must have been for Yiayia, trying to raise five children as a single parent with no family support and no education.

    I was nearing the end of my program. I continued to teach several classes at RMC while taking a full course load. In the spring of '94 I learned that there was to be a cohort of Greek graduate students attending Robert Morris for six months as part of a joint venture with a university in Athens. I applied to teach the marketing class, but I was told by Dr. Corea who was in charge of the program, that I did not have the proper credentials.

    "But, Dr. Corea, I've taught the graduate level marketing class before. How can you say that I'm not qualified?"

    "They will not respect you."

    "But I speak Greek. I would think that it would be helpful for them to have someone who knows the language. Why would they not respect me?"

    "You do not have a doctorate," he said, and dismissed me.

I was disappointed, but as it turned out, no one in the fulltime faculty wanted to teach the graduate marketing class on summer mornings at 8:00 a.m. By default, I was selected.

I was anxious to meet the 21 graduate students from Athens. I arrived at the classroom about ten minutes early the first Monday of class. Eight o'clock came, but no students had arrived. At 8:15 the classroom was still empty, and I placed a call to the graduate office to make sure that I was in the correct classroom. At about 8:40 the first of the students entered the room. By 9:00 all 21 of them had arrived. We made introductions, and then I said, "You know that this class starts at 8:00?" They nodded.

"I know you just got in last night, but in the future, you need to be here on time."

One young man raised his hand.

"Yes?"

"We cannot do that," he said.

"Excuse me?"

"We are Greek. We cannot get up for an eight o'clock class. We don't sleep until two, sometimes three. Can you move it to nine o'clock?"

I started to laugh, but then I realized that he was serious. "If I move it to nine," I explained, "you will not have time for lunch between your classes. You won't get done until eleven forty-five instead of ten forty-five."

"We don't need lunch," he replied, and the others nodded their agreement.

I went to see Dr. Corea, who thought the idea was preposterous. "You have to give them lunch," he said. "It's part of the program."

"But they don't want lunch!" I said. "They don't eat lunch until three or four."

Once again, he dismissed me.

Wednesday morning was a repetition of Monday. I began teaching to a third of my students at about 8:15. By nine o'clock they had all arrived. "If you keep coming in late, you're going to miss important subject matter," I said.

A few students nodded. The rest leaned back in their chairs, arms crossed, frowning. I knew I was at an impasse.

"Okay," I said. "Here is what we'll do. I'll start class at nine. But you will promise to be here on time. If you agree to this, then I will move back the start time. But if you come even a minute late, I'll move the start time back to 8."

No one was late for the rest of the summer session.

The students, most of whom hailed from the megalopolis of Athens, did not take well to being stuck on a suburban campus with no form of public transportation. The administration's idea of having a bingo night as a social event did not impress these young adults who were used to the nightlife of Athens. Only one of the students had a car which he had borrowed from a sister who lived in Pittsburgh. My husband and I took the students out a couple of times to a restaurant and a club downtown to hear music. I took the three girls under my wing, and occasionally we went for ice-cream or coffee.

My parents made their bi-annual trip to Pittsburgh for a week-long visit in early August. During that week, one of the Greek boys approached me with an offer. Several of the students had gotten tickets to see the Greek national basketball team play against Croatia in Toronto the upcoming weekend, but they needed a way to get there. If I would drive a few of them to Toronto, they would pay for my gas, my hotel room and a ticket to the game. One of the girls was going, and I could room with her. It was tempting. Between my schedule and John's, we had not had any type of break for a year. I needed a change of pace, and I really wanted to go to Toronto. I discussed it with John who said, "Go. Have a good time. I'll watch the kids." There was only one problem. The students were leaving early on Saturday morning, but my parents weren't planning to depart until Sunday morning.

On Thursday evening we invited my friend and colleague, Jim, to join us for dinner at the house. We chatted about the Greek students, and how pleasant they were to teach, and I told my parents about the offer to go to Toronto. "The only problem is," I said, "that we would have to leave Saturday morning, and I know you weren't planning to go until Sunday morning. But John and the kids will still be here, and I know you also wanted to spend time with the Morgan's."

My father spoke. "No."

"What?" I said to him. "I wasn't asking your permission, Daddy. I was just telling you...."

"No." He cut me off. "You're not going."

I was almost forty years old, and my father was still telling me what to do. I was furious. Jim switched the subject, but John could see that I was seething. After Jim went home and my parents went to bed, John and I sat on the on the porch-swing, sipping wine.

"I can't believe he is *still* trying to tell me what to do. I'm not a little girl anymore," I whined like a little girl.

"Rita, if you want to go, go," John said. "I'll handle your parents."

I woke up early on Saturday morning and left a note for my mom and dad, thanking them for visiting and apologizing for leaving early. I attempted to explain again why I wanted to take advantage of the opportunity to go to Toronto, and hoped that they would understand. When we checked into the hotel before the game, I called John. "How did they take it?" I asked.

"They left."

"What do you mean, they left?"

"Your dad told your mom to go pack their suitcases, and they left."

"But the kids were still there!" I said.

"I know," John said. "That's what I told them. But they left."

Outside of the Skydome in downtown Toronto, the students wildly waved the familiar blue and white Greek flag as we waited to enter the arena along with hundreds of Croatia fans waving fans and carrying banners. The 28,000 seat stadium was filled to capacity, and we climbed....and climbed....until we reached the top section of the venue. The basketball court was barely discernible from our seats, but it didn't matter to the kids who were soaking in the atmosphere. Shouts of "*Ellatha*! Greece!" mingled with the equally ebullient Croatia fans, and the cacophony of the stadium was delightfully deafening.

Despite the lopsided 81 – 55 loss to Croatia, the Greek students were intent on enjoying the evening. Our two-car motorcade headed east on Danforth Avenue to our destination: - Greektown. I didn't know what to expect – a few Greek restaurants? But as we got to the business district, I heard the mingling of Greek bouzouki music and Greek conversations coming out of the open doorways. Street signs were no longer in English. Now after dark, the restaurant signs glowed neon with Greek names like Pappas Grill, Maras Gyros, Zorba's Mezedes, and Asteria Souvlaki House. We scanned the area for parking spots, and met up at Astoria Shishkebab House where the proprietors greeted us in Greek. We ordered creamy, garlicky *tsatsiki*, tender *dolmathes*, and grilled lamb souvlaki, the specialty of the house. For the first time in a long time, I felt myself relax, listening to bouzouki music and Greek conversation late into the night.

On the way back to Pittsburgh the next evening after a long day of sightseeing in Toronto, one of the boys asked if we could stop to see his uncle. I calculated that stopping for an hour would bring us home around midnight. "Okay," I said, "but we can't really stay long." I was anxious to get home to the children after being away all weekend.

We pulled up to a pretty red brick home in the suburbs, and our entourage walked to the front door. Uncle opened the door. "*Vre paidi mou*, my child, *ti kaneis*, how are you!" He hugged his nephew, then peered past him. "Where is the teacher?" He asked. The students parted to let me through. "*Ah, H Daskala*, the teacher. *Ela*, come in," he smiled. The uncle put his hand on my back and ushered me into the foyer which opened into a long living room, in which he had set up an oblong of several chairs. The smell of onions and garlic drifted in from the kitchen. A long table was set up in the other room with stacks of china plates and silverware, and I had the feeling that it was going to be well past midnight by the time we got home. "*Katse ekei*, sit here," Uncle said, and pointed me towards the chair at the top of the circle. "The teacher must sit here," he said, and bowed slightly. I smiled, wondering what Dr. Corea would think of this unexpected veneration.

I called my parents a few days after I got home. My mother answered and we chatted for a while about my trip to Toronto, and their trip home. I asked to talk to my father, but Mom told me that he couldn't come to the phone. I knew that she was making excuses for him. I had seen this silent treatment used on my

mother before – sometimes for a few days when Daddy was angry or upset about something. This was the first time I was the recipient. The next few times that I called, only my mother spoke to me. Then, a few weeks after my trip, I called them. My father answered in his deep voice. "Hello."
    "Hi Daddy," I said.
    "Hi honey," he replied. "How are you?" The silent treatment was over.

In August of 1995 I landed a full-time job teaching high school English. John sold his business to a freight-forwarding company and took a full-time position with them. Finally, the financial handcuffs were loosened. We paid off both sets of parents, remodeled our kitchen, took a family vacation, and splurged a little at Christmas. When the opportunity to coach the girl's tennis team at school came up, I grabbed it. Not only would it be a good opportunity to expand my career and get back into the game of tennis; this would be my travel money. I began to plan for a trip to Greece.

    I was determined to improve my Greek. I knew that many of my cousins spoke English, but was also aware of the limitations that my lack of proficiency in Greek might have on conversations with my aunts and uncles. I contacted local colleges and churches and discovered that *Kimisis Tis Theotokou* - Assumption of the Virgin, the Greek Church in nearby Aliquippa, offered adult Greek lessons. For the next few years, every Tuesday night, together with Maria, Stavroula, Lee, and Helen, I learned under the tutelage of Christina Travlos.

    Helen was a pediatrician - Polish, Romanian, and Jewish by heritage, and a *filellinas* - a friend of Greeks - who had visited Greece several times. On a trip to Athens in 1984 she met Panos. The following Labor Day he came to visit her in Pittsburgh. That New Year's Eve they married. Lee was from the island of Rhodes and, though he spoke Greek, wanted to improve his grammar. He was short, slim, and balding, with a sweet disposition and an easy smile. Maria and Stavroula were teenage sisters with long, dark hair and large dark eyes. Their parents demanded that they attend Greek school. Together we became a community. Led by *Kuria* Travlos, we traveled through the fourth and fifth grade readers, analyzed word origins, learned deviations and pronunciations, read, conversed, and socialized. We shared stories and sweets, and once in a while Alexandra would come to Greek lessons with me. My seven-year-old daughter adored Lee. While the students were conjugating verbs and reading about the gods, Alexandra would crawl under the table and tie Lee's shoes together. On the ride home one night, she said, "Mommy, if anything ever happens to Daddy, could you please marry Lee?"

On the last lesson night of the school year, Christina invited us to her home for a celebration. She prepared a feast of *souzoukakia* in tomato sauce, grilled vegetables, baked chicken, and Greek salad, and served a dry Greek red wine. We finished the evening with homemade *kourabiedes* and Greek tea brewed with cinnamon and sweetened with the perfect amount of honey and cream. We had passed the fifth grade.

Santorini Sunset, oil painting by Rita Wilson

SUNSETS and SEA URCHINS - *Iliovasilemata kai Ahinous*:
ΗΛΙΟΒΑΣΙΛΈΜΑΤΑ ΚΑΙ ΑΧΙΝΟΎΣ

I had saved up enough money through my coaching to take a trip to Greece, and in June of 1997 I packed my bags with hopeful confidence that I would be able to better communicate with my relatives. I hugged my 13-year old son Nick and kissed him goodbye, then loaded my suitcases into John's car. We drove Alexandra to her softball game at Moon Park, and I stayed to watch her hit a hard single down the third base line and catch a high fly ball in right field before we left for the airport where I met up with my friend Jean. I had come to know Jean through colleagues at Robert Morris. We had gotten to be close friends, and she was traveling to Greece with me.
     Jean and I boarded the American Eagle propeller jet bound for JFK, where we were meeting my sister to travel to Athens together. I looked out of the window and saw John in the cloudy window of the terminal waving. I knew that he couldn't see me through the small windows on the plane, and I wondered what he could be waving at. Then I realized that he was waving his arms back and forth in a furious motion. I looked down on the airstrip and realized that the baggage handlers were taking bags *off* the plane – including one of mine and both of Jean's.

"It will be okay," said the young flight attendant when I told her what was happening. "They'll check them through to your final destination."

"No, they won't!" I pleaded. "Our bags are only checked through to New York. They don't even know where our final destination is. They're going to get stuck in New York."

The flight attendant rolled her eyes and told me to sit down. The bags got stuck in New York.

Cousin Helen and her husband Alexander greeted us at the Athens airport holding a "Langas" sign, but there was no need. I would have easily recognized Helen's smile. We left the airport with only of my suitcases and neither of Jean's, and drove to Voula, a suburb of Athens, where Helen and Alexander now owned a four story building close to the town square, only a ten-minute walk from the ocean. Their son Constandino lived on the first floor, Aunt Loula on the second, and Helen and Alexander on the third. The top floor was an efficiency apartment, with an expansive balcony that looked out over the sea, that their daughter Beatrice used when she was in town.

I tested out my Greek skills at lunch with Aunt Loula, and found that I was able to maintain at least a simple conversation. After lunch we put together a care package for Jean, who was leaving to take a four-day tour of the mainland, and would meet up with us to go to the island of Santorini. Luckily we were all fairly close in size. So with my skirt, Ellen's tee-shirt and underwear, and one of Helen's blouses, Jean was off for Athens.

Ellen and I spent the next few days reconnecting with our relatives. Helen's son Constandino, now 25, had been only a toddler when we last met. Aunt Loula had fallen recently and had suffered a head injury. Her head had been shaved for the operation, and her hair was closely cropped and white. Uncle Mike had passed away. His house in Psihiko had been sold to make way for commercial building, and Aunt Zorka and Thanos now lived across the hall from each other in a modern apartment building in New Psihiko with large balconies on either end. Thanos had not changed, save for his silver-grey hair. Much of his time was spent taking care of his mother, Zorka who had been hit by a car a few years back, and had become reclusive.

Cousin Helen had changed little. The years had added a few pounds, but to me she was lovely. A kindness radiated from her and although she was concerned about her mother, she wanted to make sure that we were content. She arranged visits to the relatives or drove us to the beach and showed us where to get a bus or taxi back to the apartment. When we returned after swimming or sunning, she had a homemade meal waiting – one day *bifsteaki* and *fassolathes* - green beans with tomato sauce, another day stuffed eggplant and potatoes.

"Stay at the beach with us, Helen. Even for an hour," we asked. But she did not want to leave her mother, although there was a nurse on duty. "Let us take you and Alexander to dinner," we begged.

She smiled sweetly and refused. "We will eat here. The important thing is that we are together."

On our last day in Athens before heading to Santorini, Ellen and I lay in canvas lounge chairs on Voula beach. At mid-morning the sand was already radiating the intense heat of the sun's rays. I surveyed the shoreline – a couple of middle aged women walked by clad only in black bikini bottoms, their stomachs protruding over the tops of the low cut briefs, their breasts sagging. Nearby a young woman and young man lay close together on one towel, their arms around each other, their faces close. I slathered on some Coppertone, inhaled the coconut scent, closed my eyes, and leaned back in the chair, absorbing the sunshine.

Sometime later I opened my eyes, and slowly turned my head to the left. Ellen was sitting up, writing in a notebook.

"What are you writing?" I asked.

"My goals," she replied.

"Your goals?" I raised my eyebrows. We were at the beach. In Greece! And Ellen, my dear, hard-working sister, was writing down her goals.

"Yes. My goals. You know – what I want to accomplish in the next five years, where I hope to be."

"Hmm," I said, and closed my eyes again.

"What are *your* goals?" Ellen asked.

"I don't have any," I answered, my eyes still shut.

"You must have goals," I heard Ellen say, and reopened my eyes. I brought my chair up to the sitting position.

"Nope," I said.

"You have to have goals," she said. "Everyone should have goals."

I pondered this for a minute. "Well," I said. "My goals were to get a full-time teaching job and to go to Greece. I got a job, and I'm in Greece. I guess I'm good for the next five years!"

We reconnected with Jean at the Athens airport to travel to Santorini. Our bags had finally surfaced, and we were happy to have a choice of outfits to pack for our trip to the island. We arrived at the Santorini airport to find George (from his eponymous Pension George), waiting for us next to his old white van. We drove past brown sun-dried fields to the village of Karterados. Tucked into a side street, the small whitewashed hotel was accented with blue shutters and trim and surrounded by bright red and pink hibiscus. George's British wife, Helen, checked us in, and showed us a selection of rooms, giving us the choice between screens and a fan. The temperatures had been on an upward climb for the past week, with temperatures expected to hit over 100 degrees Fahrenheit that afternoon. The decision to opt for a fan seemed like a no-brainer.

We fell easily into an island routine: eggs and toast in the courtyard under the arbor, a walk into Thira for some sightseeing, a swim at the beach, a nap, and a late dinner. Thira, the capital of Santorini, was about a twenty minute walk uphill from Karterados. The bright white buildings with sunlit blue domes seemed to be stacked one upon the other. This was the spot where the whitewashed buildings, with winding stairways interspersed between them and the deep blue Mediterranean in the background, formed the backdrop for postcards and calendars. Here were the restaurants, bars, nightclubs, coffee shops, and tourist shops. And here is where Ellen found *the ring*. As the warm evening faded to a soft blue, we wound our way through the narrow streets of Thira, zigzagging into jewelry shops and souvenir shops. We rounded a corner on the top of the grey stone street, where outside of a small shop stood a most beautiful human being. He was of medium height and build, with dark hair and dark eyes, an expensive gold chain around his dark neck, his white shirt unbuttoned to form a low tanned V on his chest.

"Ladies," the deeply tanned Adonis greeted us, each accented word in his melodic voice drawn out like the last note of a love song. "Would you like to come into my jewelry shop?" Feeling a bit giddy, we walked into Antoniou's store. The shop was narrow, deep, and well lit. A long counter of gold jewelry lay to the left side. Perpendicular to that in the back of the shop stood a slightly taller counter. Antoniou walked around the back counter, reached underneath, smiled irresistibly, and pulled out a bottle of white wine. "Would you like some wine?" he asked. "It is from my family's vineyard." He poured three glasses and handed them to us. Ellen examined the rings in the counter. Antoniou sauntered over to Ellen and peered closely into her eyes. "Do you see anything you like?" he asked. Flustered, she managed to hold his gaze.

"Yes," she replied. Still locking eyes with him, she pointed down towards the counter and said, "That ring."

"Ah," said Antoniou, as he reached under the counter to pick up the ring. Holding her right hand in his left hand, he slid the ring on her finger without breaking eye contact. Jean and I watched the scene, mesmerized. "It is very lovely," he purred.

"I'll take it," she said. The ring was bright yellow gold with a midnight blue stone. We would need to return to pick it up, as it was a bit large and would need to be sized. At that point, Ellen's senses slowly returned as she realized that she did not know how much the ring cost. Luckily, the price was not unreasonable. She paid for the ring and made arrangements to pick it up the next day, we finished our wine, and we left the shop. Once into the warm evening air, the spell of Antoniou was broken. "What an idiot!" Ellen said.

"Antoniou?" I asked.

"No, me!" she said. "I didn't even try to dicker on the price. I don't even know what kind of stone is in the ring. I'm an idiot!"

"You *are* an idiot," I agreed, "but how gorgeous!"

"The ring?" Ellen asked.

"Antoniou!"

A heat wave had descended upon Greece with the intensity of Apollo's fire. At night the humid air brought mosquitoes in through the open, screenless windows, and the ceiling fan's circulation of ninety degree air did little to cool us. We arranged to take a tour of the caldera and volcano around Santorini, despite the prediction of one hundred plus temperatures. Cable cars took us down the mountain to the Old Port where we boarded the Belle Aurora for Nea Kameni, the sleeping volcano which stood high over the bay. We claimed three of the few seats that were located in the center of the boat, under protection from the unforgiving Aegean sun, as the captain took off for the volcano. We pulled up to the docks shortly, and the crewmen helped us to step out of the boat, while three old men sitting at the end of the dock dully watched our every move. As we climbed the smooth black lava rock of the volcano, our breathing became more difficult, and our steps slower. Our sunhats did little to allay the relentless beating of the sun, and by the time we returned from our climb, we were enervated and drenched with sweat. We boarded the boat and approached our seats. A tall short-cropped blonde man and a slim dark-haired woman were now sitting in the spot where our towels and bags had been. "Excuse me," I said, "those were our seats." The couple ignored me. "Excuse me," I said, a little louder now. "We were sitting there."

The woman looked up at me. "Well, we're sitting here now," she said.

"Our things were there!" Jean said.
The woman pointed to the end of the bench, where our items now lay baking in the sun.

"Why would you move our things?" I asked.
"So we could sit here," she said.

At this point Jean, who had no tolerance for injustice of any kind, began to loudly complain about the rudeness and ignorance of the couple. Some of the other tourists watched in amusement as the woman folded her arms and glared as us, while her companion blushed in embarrassment. Ellen politely leaned over to the man, smiled, and said, "So, where are you from?" The shocked woman glowered at her partner, forbidding him to enter into conversation with us, while Jean glowered at Ellen for daring to make contact with our adversaries. But he replied, "Dusseldorf." And as Ellen deftly drew him into conversation, she discovered that the woman and I had both worked for Mellon Bank at the same time, before she met this man and moved to Germany. Having established a connection with the enemy, Ellen announced, "You guys have something in common!" and forced us into polite communication. Jean would have none of it, and the onlookers continued to watch, still hopeful for some entertainment, but Ellen had successfully negotiated a truce. We turned our attention back to our sweltering discomfort, when the captain approached the group.

"Don't worry," he said. "Soon we will go for a swim!" We rode to a small cove on the island, our skin already slightly cooled by the ocean breeze, and dropped anchor. "You may jump off or climb down the ladder," the captain instructed. Splashes and plops sounded around the boat as some of the crew dove over the side of the vessel, followed by the tentative jumps of the tourists. We plunged into the sea and joined them. I tread water for several minutes, then made my way over to some shallow rocks to rest. As I did so, my foot slid on a slippery surface, and I put my palm down on a rock to brace myself. A stinging sensation shot through my right hand, and I gasped. I shook my hand in pain, and swam back to the boat. The captain, a glass of ouzo in one hand, leaned over to pull me aboard with the other. Holding back tears, I held my fingers out to him. My index finger had swollen up to twice its size, the middle finger not far behind it.

"Ohhh," he said, shaking his head. "Tst tst tst."

"What is it?" I panicked.

"Ah, how you say?" He looked at the other crewman. They discussed my situation between themselves, and informed me that I had been stung by an *achinos*, a sea urchin.

"What can I do for it?" I asked.

The short captain looked straight into my eyes. "Nothing. You are going to die." I looked for a twinkle in his eye, but none was forthcoming.

"Don't worry," said the crewman, who then admonished the laughing captain in a barrage of Greek. "It will be okay. Come with me," he said, and took me over to the table which had been set up with feta, olives, bread, and ouzo. "Here," he said, and handed me a glass of ouzo. Still reeling from my near-death experience, I downed the ouzo while the crewman disappeared below deck. He returned with a bottle of olive oil, from which he poured a capful onto my wounded fingers.

"What will that do?" I asked.

"I don't know," he shrugged. Maybe it will make it feel better?"

Perhaps it was the ouzo, maybe it was the olive oil or the crewman's kindness, but as we set sail for Oia to watch the famous Santorini sunset, I became less aware of the pain. I was in the Aegean Sea, with two of the people closest to me, experiencing the trip of a lifetime. I thought about John, and wondered what he and the kids might be doing. Allowing myself to miss them did not lessen the pleasure of the moment. As the scarlet sun descended through the warm haze into the sea, the chatter and laughter of the passengers turned to an awed silence. The last light of the sun dipped below the horizon, and we burst into applause as the curtain fell on the day's magnificent performance.

It was nine o'clock the next morning and already the heat of the day was making its presence known. Although the temperatures were predicted to reach 105 degrees, George assured us that it would be cooler down by the beach. Because Santorini is a volcanic island, its beaches vary throughout the island from brick red sand, to deep black, to the light brown that one might find on the east coast of Florida. After breakfast at the pension, George offered to drive us in the van down to the latter beach, as it was "just down the road."

"Is it in walking distance?" Ellen asked.

"Well, yes, but it is quite hot today," George said.

"How far is it?"

"Hmm. A kilometer. Maybe two. Not too far. But it is *very* hot today."

"We'll take the ride," I said. "Thank you for offering."

Ellen wanted to walk. Annoyed at us for our lack of adventure, she stubbornly grabbed her bag and began to trek down the hill. A few minutes later, we rumbled down the rocky road and waved at Ellen as we passed her. Bright poppies decorated the roadside, and dormant windmills stood hazily in the background as we wound our way down. We had been riding for almost ten minutes when Jean and I exchanged glances which wordlessly said *this is definitely more than a kilometer.*

Dust stirred under the wheels as George came to a stop on the side of the gravel road and said, "We are here!" A closed taverna stood alone across the road from Monolithos Beach which was dotted with bright blue umbrellas. We ran quickly across the warm sand and settled ourselves in canvas beach chairs under one of the beach umbrellas. Gazing contentedly at the water, we noticed a few young children splashing rather far from the shore. The sea beckoned and we responded, swishing through the lapping waves for several feet before we reached water deeper than our knees. We turned towards the shore now about fifty yards away, looking for a sign of Ellen approaching, but saw an empty road. The tepid water was doing little to cool us, and after several minutes we returned to the chairs. Off to our right, three rotund Greek women on lawn chairs loudly chattered away, their buxom bosoms unencumbered by bathing suit tops. After a few minutes, they rose heavily from their chairs and walked towards the water, bellies and bosoms sagging. Jean and I suppressed giggles, and I attempted to turn my attention to the June issue of *Glamour* that I had pulled from my beach bag. A few minutes later Jean whispered, "Rita! Psst," and nodded towards the sea. About a hundred feet away the women had formed a circle as the waves gently swooshed against their ample bodies. Their continuous chatter blew into the shore with each intermittent gust of wind and receded with each returning wave. And there, on the surface of the water, with each gentle ripple, bobbed their large breasts. After another fit of giggles, I returned to my magazine, as Jean gazed out towards the sea.

"Well," she said, "when in Rome...." I turned to see Jean unclasping the hook on the back of her bathing suit top. "Ahh," she said, and leaned back in the chair. My suit was feeling a little damp; I reasoned that I would probably be more comfortable without the top. I untied the strings around the back of my bikini, and lifted it over my head, smiling at the newly found freedom. Perhaps on a more crowded beach I would not have had the nerve to let it all hang out. But on that morning in Santorini, as the sun rose higher and the breeze blew softly up from the sea, going topless felt natural. The shuffle of footsteps in the sand signaled an approach from our left, and we looked up from under the umbrella to see Ellen, wilted, her face as red as the poppies that we had passed on the way to the beach. Her white t-shirt was wrapped awkwardly around her head, and sweat dripped from every pore. She plodded towards the umbrella, dropped her bag, dropped her towel, and stared at us.

"Oh my God, Ellen! Are you ok?" we asked with a mixture of pity and amusement.

Ellen's eyes moved from our faces to our unclad breasts. She took a deep breath, and blew it out slowly, shook her head, and said, "You have *got* to be kidding."

We had been told by the locals that although we had seen the sunset from Thira and from the water, we must not miss viewing it from the top of the mountain at Oia. "It is the most beautiful sunset in all the world," said our server at dinner one night. "You must go!"

    We had rented a small green Opel four-door five-speed, and over the past few days I had driven to the excavation at Akrotiri to see the ruins of the ancient Minoan civilization, to the red sand beach, Glaros' Restaurant for fried Santorini "tomato balls," and Antoniou's family winery. None of that driving had prepared us for the trip to Oia. The narrow two-lane road coiled up the mountain - mountainside on the left, steep cliff on the right. There were no barriers or guide rails, only occasional shrines erected to honor the memory of the people who had died at those spots. I felt confident as I navigated the curves in the road, as long as I did not look out the passenger window to the sea beyond the cliff. My passengers, presumably because their hands were not the ones on the wheel, were not as comfortable. With each car or truck that bore down upon us from the opposite direction, I heard the sharp intake of breath. A close call would beget an occasional scream, but all-in-all, the trip was without disaster.

    We arrived at Oia in the early evening, when the sun still lingered hazily over the sea. We had plenty of time to grab a souvlaki and patronize the myriad of souvenir shops. We meandered over the stone paths into the whitewashed shops, examining jewelry, embroidery, ceramics, and paintings. Ellen looked anxiously at the sun, which had slowly begun its descent and said, "I think we better get out to the point." Jean glanced in the direction of yet undiscovered treasure, and we reluctantly left the shops. We walked over the narrow path, Ellen striding purposefully in the lead, I attempting to keep up, and Jean, gazing longingly in the shop windows and bringing up the rear.

    "Why don't we just poke in here for a few minutes?" she said, veering towards an inviting doorway hung with colorful embroidered bags, as I grabbed her by the elbow and steered her back onto the path.

"Hurry up," Ellen said, "we're going to miss it!"

We arrived at the cliff side to find hundreds of people armed with blankets, chairs, and cameras. The three of us found a spot to sit on a large flat boulder. The crowd hushed as the sun, now bright crimson, sank towards the sea. I could almost imagine Helios, the Sun God, driving his flaming chariot from east to west across the sky. Shutters clicked and red record buttons were pressed on camcorders as tourists, in their haste to capture the event, missed the experience. I had seen more vibrant sunsets on the west coast of Florida, and more potent sunsets in Pittsburgh while driving home on the parkway on a mid-summer evening. The power of this sunset was its serenity. For at this point in time, the harrowing car ride was forgotten, petty differences were put aside, and the tranquility of the moment erased any cares or concerns. The sun settled behind the horizon, leaving behind a suffusion of pink. Tourists quietly put their cameras back in the cases, folded their blankets, and walked back towards the town. The three of us remained on the rock, content to watch as the sky deepened to midnight blue and stars blinked softly. A delicious chill diffused the warm night air, and we got up and walked together down the path into town.

A local shopkeeper recommended that we have dinner at the Neptune restaurant, a mile or so out of Oia. We ate dinner overlooking the sea which shone golden under the full moon. On the drive back to Karterados, I negotiated the curves more slowly in the dark. Back at the hotel we dropped off Jean. It was already midnight, but Ellen was leaving the next morning, and we weren't quite ready to call it a night, so we went into Thira. We had been given passes to the "Koo Club." The disco inside was loud and raucous, so we took seats at the outside bar. Ellen had been in high gear from the beginning of the trip, making sure that we saw everyone and everything that we needed to see, and it seemed that everything was crossed off of her "to do" list. Like a tight fist unfolding into an open palm, on her last night in Greece, Ellen slowly, visibly, finally relaxed.

Jean went on to Crete for a few days, and after stealing a day to myself in Santorini, I took a ferry back to the mainland, where the excitement was building. We were heading to Marathon to celebrate Uncle Bill and Aunt Helen's 60th anniversary. "You know, *my* father knew her first," Cousin Helen told me, referring to our Aunt Helen, her mother's sister. "But, he didn't like her at first. They worked at the bank together. But she wasn't serious enough. She was beautiful, you know? Very beautiful."

"Your mother was very beautiful also," I said, recalling photos of Aunt Loula as a young woman, tall and regal looking, with serious, dark eyes.

"Yes," Helen said. "Maybe she was more beautiful. But, there was something about Aunt Helen. I think it was the way she walked."

"The way she walked?"

"Yes. She was very attractive. But I think it was the way she walked. She liked to have fun. They all ran together. That was how he met my mother."

"But, then, how did Aunt Helen meet Uncle Bill?"

"I don't remember," she said. "You will have to ask Roi."

Helen's daughter Rena and her husband, John had built a home in Marathon, about ninety minutes from Voula. Niko and Roi built a smaller one next door – a country home with red tile floors and whitewashed walls, and a small guest house next to that. An oasis in this small old town, the entire complex was enclosed behind a brick wall. "You are lucky to be here now," Cousin Helen said, as we approached the gate. "Everyone will be here!" For the party, several large wooden tables covered with crisp white tablecloths and set with crystal wine glasses had been set up in the large yard which stretched between my cousins' houses. Soft lights twinkled in the grey dusk and the air was full of chatter, laughter, and the clinking of glasses from the bar, which was serving wine, champagne, and shots of flavored Schnapps. The buffet table was set with roast pork, Greek *horiatiki* - village salad, shrimp, home-baked breads, and grilled vegetables. The dessert table proffered cakes, ice cream, and a lemon crème custard served in the lemon skins. The pink bougainvillea was in full bloom, and the evening air held the sweet honeysuckle scent of the blossoms.

I hugged cousins whom I had met on previous trips to Greece, and I practiced my Greek with aunts and uncles who spoke no English. Helen took my arm and led me to a man who appeared to be about my father's age. "This is your Uncle Niko," she said. I looked at this smiling man, but Helen could see that nothing registered. "Your father's brother, Niko Saryas," she said. And this is your cousin Julia." My mind churned as I tried to keep my expression benign. *Why did he have a different last name? Why had I never heard of him? Was Helen mistaken?* Helen pulled me aside. "Your father did not tell you he had another brother?"

    I sat with Niko and Julia for a while, and they asked about my mother, my father, and my family. Julia was tall and slim, with dark hair and big dark eyes, and a wide smile. She told me that she was an English translator – she spoke more quickly in English than I did. We were joined by a handsome, outgoing man who I learned was her brother - my cousin Dionysis. He had lived in Texas for twelve years as a student, and said that he would go back there in a minute if he could find work. These cousins, new to me, were warm and congenial, and I regretted the years that I had not known of them.

    When we got back to Voula, Helen showed me a photograph of my Uncle Niko Saryas with all of his siblings, including my father. When I returned to the states and asked my father why he had never told me about Niko, he simply shrugged. I couldn't understand his apathy towards his brother, but then I had never been left behind by my parents. I realized that my father's gruffness masked deeper hurt.

    I also realized that I was wrong about something: Ellen had asked me what my goals were. At the time, I was satisfied with simply being in Greece. I now knew that wasn't enough. I wanted to return to spend time with my relatives. I wanted to learn more about who I was and where I came from. To do so, I would need to be able to communicate – through letters, phone calls, and when time and funds would allow, in person. I had a new goal: to return to Greece as a fluent speaker of the Greek language.

PART II

Meros II: ΜΕΡΟΣ II

ALEXANDRA

Port of Gytheio, oil painting, Wilson

BEACH SCENE - *Skini sthn Paralia*: ΣΚΗΝΉ ΣΤΗΝ ΠΑΡΑΛΊΑ

In the summer of 2006 I take Alexandra to Greece to celebrate her high school graduation. I am elated that she wants to go. Nick, until this point, has preferred the U.S. soil, and John, since 9/11, has become a nervous traveler. Alexandra is adventurous and outgoing, and the only potential misgiving I have of her as a travel partner is her propensity to stay up extremely late, and wake up accordingly.

We are biding our time during a layover at JFK Airport, and are standing outside so that Alexandra can smoke a cigarette before the ten-hour flight to Athens. It bothers me that she smokes, but she has long since quit hiding the fact from me.

We are leaning against a concrete post near the terminal. As she smokes her cigarette, I notice two young men in light blue work shirts, smoking in front of the terminal doors, about 20 feet away. The wind shifts, and the smoke from Alexandra's cigarette blows in my face.

"Corva!" I exclaim.
"Slut!" she returns.
"Harlot!"
She giggles. "Whore."
"Prostitute."
"Bitch!"

She puts out her cigarette on the concrete wall, and throws it in the trash can, and we turn towards the terminal. As we open the doors, we overhear one young man say to the other, "I told you they were sisters. No one talks to their mother like that!"

We both laugh. I am feeling lighthearted and adventurous. It has been nine years since my last trip to Greece. Since that time, Uncle Deno has passed away, and Aunt Loula has become reclusive. But I'm cautiously optimistic that all is well in Greece. My sister Ellen and her young teenage daughters will also be staying for a week, and I'm looking forward to having this time together.

Cousin Thanos has offered to pick us up from the airport and deliver us to Voula. Once we clear customs in Athens we spot him. He smiles broadly, cigarette in hand. He is slightly stooped and his dark hair is now a shock of white. I guess his age to be in the mid-sixties, though he looks more like a man in his seventies. After a cup of coffee to revive us, we depart for the Voula relatives. Thanos decides to take the "short-cut" through the narrow side streets of Athens suburbs, and my daughter's first impression of Greece is not sun and sea, but crumbling buildings and graffiti. An hour later we are buzzed in and welcomed to Helen and Alexander's spacious apartment. The sliding balcony doors are open on each side, allowing a warm cross-breeze. The smell of eggplant frying and something baking in the oven sets our stomachs growling. Helen has prepared a delicious lunch of *tiropita* – cheese pie, fried eggplant, and tomato salad. We finish lunch and the adrenaline of travel gives way to exhaustion. Helen shows us to our room in Loula's apartment so that we may take an afternoon "siesta." The drapes are already drawn, and Alexandra walks over to the window. She opens the drapes a crack and shouts, "Mom.....Mom, come here, quick!"

I walk over to the window to see what she could possibly find so exciting. She opens the drapes a little wider, and I look outside. I see lemon trees in the courtyard below, with their yellow fruit as large as grapefruits, and clothes and sheets hanging from lines strung across balconies of the apartment buildings on the hill leading up to the *platia*, the town square. "What?"

"Look!" She points to the square, and I laugh. There is a new establishment in the platia. I see the familiar green and white "Starbucks" sign, and I realize my daughter's cultural assimilation might take some time.

Ellen and the girls arrive that afternoon. She has a full itinerary planned, as they will only be in Greece for a week. I warn Alexandra that we might as well conform to it, since we will have another week to ourselves to relax and unwind. We have decided to start with a trip to the Parthenon the next day, and we ask Alexander the best way to get to Athens. He takes Ellen aside and shows her a map, painstakingly depicting the route to the Parthenon. I watch Alexander tediously repeating the information about which bus to take and where to catch it, and I am relieved that it is Ellen and not me on the receiving end of his pointed instructions. The next morning, Alexander once again repeats to Ellen, "You must take the 1A into Athens. I will write it down for you." Ellen shoots me a subtle eye- roll, though we both know that Alexander is just looking out for us.

We stroll through Platia Voula as shopkeepers are opening their doors and the sidewalks are filling with the smell of strong coffee and fresh-baked bread. The sunglass shop with its Dolce & Gabbana and Chanel sunglasses has not yet opened, but a young man is raising the awnings of the kiosk which sells gum, magazines, candy, and phone cards. A few men sit at outdoor tables sipping Greek coffee and watching with mild interest as the five of us chatter on our way to the bus stop. We sit on a long bench to wait for the 1A, which is scheduled to arrive every fifteen minutes. Several taxis slow to a stop, buses stop to pick up passengers, and young men on loud mopeds sputter by. Still, after twenty five minutes there is no 1A. We are feeling apprehensive when Ellen jumps up and points, "there it is!" The bus rolls to a stop and we board, happy to be on our way.

The driver turns down the hill from Voula, and makes a right on the main highway towards Athens. Behind billboards touting cars, vodka, and nightclubs, the sea glistens to our left. Traffic is heavy as small Citroens and motorcycles weave in and out of the lanes, between cars. Ellen and I are sitting in the front, perpendicular to a short, stout old woman in a babushka and black dress, and a wizened old man who sits behind the driver, facing the door. Ellen's daughters are in the elevated row behind us and Alexandra is across from them next to an attractive middle-aged blond woman. The bus stops, and a young, dark-haired man sprints on and sits next to the old man. I realize that we have been driving for some time, with the sea still on our left.

"*Signomi*, excuse me," I say to the old man in front of me. "Is this bus going to Athens?"

He lifts his chin upward, uttering "tsss," the familiar Greek gesture for "no."

I grab the silver pole in front of me, and lean in towards the bus driver. "Signomi," I say, "is this bus going to Athens?"

"Piraeus," he replies.

"Piraeus?" I turn and look at Ellen. "Apparently this bus is going to Piraeus."

Her eyes widen.

"Signomi," I ask the bus driver. "Isn't this the 1A?"

"2A." I give Ellen a fixed stare.

The old man and woman pick up on our dilemma, and become embroiled in a vigorous discussion. "No, no, no!" the old woman spits at the man, and vehemently chatters in Greek.

The old man turns to me. "Where you want to go?" he asks in English.

"We want to go to the Parthenon."

"Oh no. You are very far from the Parthenon. You must get off at the next stop and take the Metro for two or three stops. You will then take a train to Athens. After this you will find a bus to the Parthenon."

"Can't we just get off at the next stop and take a taxi?"

"A taxi from here would be fifty euros."

The old woman pulls at his sleeve. "*Ti tin eipes* - what did you tell her?" The argument ensues, and now the young man joins in.

The rumble continues, and I notice that the blonde woman is watching. She catches my eye and subtly shakes her head, as if to say, "don't listen to them." The bus pulls to the next stop, and she gets up to disembark. She nods her head towards the door.

"Come on," I say to my entourage. "Let's go."

"What?" they exclaim, startled at this call to action.

"Let's GO," I say, and we hurriedly disembark, leaving a stream of uninterrupted argument behind us.

We form a nervous circle around the blonde woman, who tells us to follow her, and we do. She tells me that she moved to Greece from Bulgaria four years ago, taught herself the language, and had to learn her way around. She points us in the direction of the train station, instructs us how to buy our tickets, and tells us to get off in Monasteraki, at the bottom of the Acropolis. We thank her for her kindness, and ten minutes later we are on a train bound for Athens.

The side-to-side motion and gentle rumble of the train eases our tension.

"How did you know to follow her?" Ellen asks after a few minutes.

"I don't know. Something about her."

"She could have been setting us up."

"For what?" I ask.

"I don't know."

We sit in silence for a few minutes.

"I'm sorry," she says.

"Me too."

"For what?"

"I guess I could have looked at the bus number as easily as you did."

"It's ok," she says. "Just don't tell Alexander!"

We spend the next few days visiting with our relatives. My Greek lessons have paid off, and this time I am able to converse with Aunt Loula as we sit outside on the balcony after breakfast. She talks of growing up in both Greece and America, and I realize how little I know about my aunt's life. I had heard stories of how my relatives knew King Constantine and Queen Annamarie, and how Loula's youngest daughter, Aliki, was a companion to the King's sister, Princess Irene, and accompanied her on a trip to the states, touring with the pianist, Gina Bachauer. I had been to my aunt's lovely apartment in Colonaki, with its marble floors and modern furnishings. But now, as Aunt Loula leans back in her chair and pauses to speak, she reveals an unexpected world to me. I had always known World War II to be something that affected my family in America. I knew that my father and uncles had all served in the armed forces, but I did not understand the extent of the German Occupation of Greece. Aunt Loula tells me that under German occupation, food and clothing was scarce, as the Germans confiscated these, and even buildings. If they found a building that they wanted, they threw furniture into the streets and occupied it, leaving its former residents homeless. Loula was inventive with the clothing, which she would darn over and over, until the garment was no longer wearable. She learned how to make a coat out of a blanket, and to undo sweaters, wash the wool, wrap it, and knit new sweaters, socks, and gloves. Food was a different story. There was little food within the city of Athens – what vegetables that were grown in the small city gardens and what meat was available had been commandeered by the soldiers.

The lack of electricity resulted in the closing of schools and public transportation. Pregnant, Loula was forced to walk several miles to the hospital in order to deliver her first child, my cousin Helen. Loula's husband Kosta would go by foot to the countryside in Kifissia, fifteen kilometers from the center of Athens, in order to get fresh milk for their baby. I think of Kifissia with its high-end apartment buildings and designer boutiques, and I have trouble reconciling the Athens that I know with the Athens of Aunt Loula's story, but she tells me that the gardens in Kifissia were rich with potatoes, asparagus, and strawberry fields, and that, most importantly, fresh milk was available. But, in the summer, by the time Kosta would walk the fifteen kilometers back to Athens, the milk would have soured.

I think of the photos that I have seen of Loula as a young lady in her early twenties living in Pittsburgh – she and Aunt Sassa in fashionable satin dresses, their hair in soft curls, and their perfect lipstick smiles. I look at her now, still a presence with her stylish closely-cropped silver hair and bright, dark eyes, and I am aware that there is much that I don't know about my aunt. I have many questions, but Aunt Loula is getting tired. I have been greatly moved by what she has told me, and I realize that there is much that I want to learn about my family.

We all travel to Marathon to spend a few days with our cousins Roi and Rena. Ellen and the girls stay with Rena and John, and Alexandra and I stay in the guest house next to Roi and Niko's house. Alexandra, like I did at her age, falls in love with Roi and Niko. We meet second cousins and their children, we swim in the sea or the pool and dine in the platia at night. Each afternoon, Roi and Rena cook dinner and we eat outside on the large covered patio: *souzoukakia* – Greek hamburgers in tomato sauce, *spanakopita* – spinach pie, fried eggplant, tomato and feta salads, *moussaka* – potato and ground meat casserole, fresh peaches and cherries. We linger over coffee and sweets long after the main course is finished.

We return to Athens a few days later. Ellen and the girls return to the states, and Alexandra and I enjoy a quiet day in Voula. We eat succulent souvlaki at the "Tasty Corner," one of my father's favorite restaurants, and stop at Starbucks for her tall carmel frappucino and a chance to flirt with the handsome barista, before heading back to the apartment to pack. Thanos is planning to pick us up at 7:30 a.m. to travel to Sparta, where my friends Panos and Helen have offered us their apartment.

On our way to Sparta the next morning, we stop at Epithauros, the ancient Greek amphitheater known for its amazing acoustics. We climb up the fifty-five rows of seats to the top, and listen as a man drops a coin, and we hear it land. After stopping in Napflion for lunch, we begin the final leg of the journey, a harrowing trip through the mountains. This takes twice as long as necessary as unfortunately, Thanos drives us over the wrong mountain. We discover this at a gas station at the bottom of a very steep and windy road, where the attendant tells us that the sign for the Sparta interchange had fallen, and no one had bothered to pick it up. Alexandra and I are close to tears when we realize we have to turn around and head back up the mountain and down another. It doesn't help that on the way Alexandra has counted twenty-two *eikonostasis* - small icons that are erected as memorials to people who have died, presumably in accidents on the road. It doesn't help that I am prone to motion sickness. And it doesn't help that Thanos is a chain-smoker, fumbling in his car for cigarettes and lighter, swerving while a cloud of smoke hangs in the car.

When we arrive in Sparta around 6 p.m., we go to pick up the apartment key from Panos' cousin Terry. His wife, Haroula, has prepared coffee and sweets. She looks much younger than Terry, who is fifty, and I learn that she is only thirty-eight. She is quiet and speaks no English. I try to make conversation with her in Greek, but she smiles politely and does not answer. Terry takes us to the apartment, and insists that we must come back later to see his son perform in an outdoor rock concert next to his house.

The apartment is a ten-minute walk from the downtown area. It is cool and spacious, and it is tempting to forego the concert and dinner, and flop on the beds for the night. But we wash our faces, revive ourselves, and walk into town to catch the end of Terry's 14-year old son on drums. Terry urges us to stay to hear the next band, and the next. It is clear that he is popular with the kids, and he seems to thrive on their energy and attention. The bands are not bad for teenage "garage" bands, and Alexandra is enjoying the lively vibe and the attention of the boys who are checking out the gorgeous American girl. But the music is loud rock and heavy metal, and I see Thanos's jaw clenching. So, as "Wasteless" takes the stage, and the moshing begins in the dust in front of the makeshift stage, we leave to eat dinner.

    I awake the next morning to the crowing of roosters. The apartment is in downtown Sparta, and I'm having a little trouble making sense of the cacophony of church bells, construction workers, and chickens. I learn that it is customary for one to sell his land to a builder, with the caveat that he keep an apartment in the building for himself. In this case, the landowner keeps chickens, and from the window of the apartment, I see a dozen brown hens and a large rooster strutting around the small fenced-in area next to the building. It is very hot. Alexandra is still sleeping, and Thanos and I walk into town for breakfast. By the time we walk back up the hill, we are drenched in sweat, and we scrap our sightseeing plans, opting instead for the beach. We stop in the port town of Gytheio and have lunch at one of the many tavernas along the water. The moussaka is delicious, and Alexandra's *bistekia* - Greek hamburger - is mouthwatering. I could linger in the shade of the canvas roof stretched out over the tables all day, but Alexandra is anxious to head to the beach. I tell Thanos about a beach that my friend Helen has told us about, a few minutes from Gytheio, and he nods.

We have come off of the main road from Gytheio, and have been driving for about ten minutes on a narrow two-lane road with no shoulder to speak of. "Thanos," I say from the back seat, "Helen told us the beach was two miles the other direction."

    "Ah, yes," Thanos replies, "but I think there is a beach along here somewhere. My parents used to take me camping there. I think I will find it."

    Alexandra turns to me from the front seat and mouths, "Make Him Stop!"

I shrug my shoulders. "Thanos," I call over the hot wind coming through all four open windows. "I think the beach was much closer to Gythio."

"It is just a little while," he says, and Alexandra turns to glare at me.

Thanos slows down the car and peers through the open window. "I think this must be it," he says, and slowly turns left onto a one-lane dirt road. We drive past dried fields of grass until we see a small dirt parking area, and he pulls the car into the lot. It is desolate, with the exception of a large, rusted white van about twenty feet away from us. A family of gypsies is getting out of the van. They glance at us, then walk to the beach.

Our clothes stick to us as we stretch our legs and get out of the car. "Is it safe here?" I ask.

"Of course," Thanos says. He pulls a small canvas beach chair out of the trunk.

We walk onto the deserted beach, and find a spot in the shade of a small tree. Thanos opens up the chair, sits down, takes off his shirt, leans back, and covers his eyes with the shirt. This is not the beach Helen told me about. Where are the lounge chairs and large umbrellas? The concession stands? The waitresses with drinks? The toilet facilities? People? Alexandra and I lay our towels on the sand, pull off our bathing-suit cover-ups, and sit down.

In five minutes Thanos is softly snoring, so we go for a walk. The air is hot and dry, and the sand burns the soles of our feet. There is plenty of shoreline, and we run for it. We look down the beach and see in the distance what appears to be a small stand renting paddle boats. I run back to the towel and grab some money from my bag.

We push the pedals of the paddleboat with our bare feet in a futile attempt to generate some sort of breeze. We are baking in the afternoon sun, and drag our fingertips in the water. The world around us is a deep wavy midnight blue. Now people fleck the shoreline, and as we paddle in to shore, one of them approaches the paddleboat. He is a tall young man, about Alexandra's age. He says something to her, but she replies, "*Den milo Ellinika poli kala* – I don't speak Greek very well," and he smiles.

"Oh, you are American!" he says, and introduces himself as Stratos. He asks in broken English if she would like to ride on a raft with him and his friends. I'm skeptical about letting her go out on a raft, pulled by a boat, with four strangers, as cute as they may be. As we wait for the boat to come in, we chat with the boys with our limited vocabularies. We learn that they all go to English school in Sparta, and that their teacher is actually Panos's cousin, Terry. The driver of the boat tells me that I can ride in the boat with him if it would make me feel better. It does. The kids all put on bright red life vests. Alexandra lays down on one of the rafts with Stratos, and the others get on rafts. I climb into the boat and the driver starts the motor. We accelerate quickly and soon we're dragging the kids behind us on long yellow ropes, cruising through the waves, and I'm getting splashed almost as much as they are. Suddenly, Thanos' beach isn't so bad. Three of the boys, Stratos, Stelios, and Antonis, flirt with Alexandra. John, the fourth boy, does not. When we finish the ride, Alex is chilly, and Stratos and Stelios offer her their towels. She ignores them. "Could I use your towel?" she asks John. Whether or not it is intentional, John has captured Alexandra's attention by not vying for it.

    The boys figure out that where they live in Sparta is close to Helen's apartment. They ask if Alexandra can go out with them that night. I don't give a definite answer – they seem to be nice boys, but I don't really know them. That evening Alexandra and I go out to dinner in Mystra with Thanos, Terry, and his family, where waiters fill pitchers with cold water which flows directly through the rock walls of an underground spring. I ask Terry about the boys from the beach, and he assures me that they are good boys. For the next three days, Alexandra splits her time between me and the boys. They are enamored with her, and she is torn between Stratos's crazy personality, Stelios and his endearing smile, and John, with his quiet intensity. "I can see you falling in love with John," I say, not realizing the veracity of that statement. Terry has taken me and Thanos to dinner, and Alexandra is out with the boys. Terry's wife does not come with us. After dinner, Terry asks if we would like to go to a club to hear Greek music. Thanos declines, but I am eager for a little nightlife. We drop Thanos off and drive onto a side road, not far from the center of Sparta. The building sits alone in the parking lot, a large backlit sign indicating "Alexander's." We walk in, and my eyes take a moment to adjust to the darkness. Terry leads me to a booth, and a waitress comes over to take our drink orders. Greek music plays over the speakers mounted in the corner. I am disappointed, as I was expecting a live band. The décor is red – red walls, red tufted leather seats, and red barstools. In the dim lighting I notice several men at the bar. A young blond woman in a low cut dress approaches the man at the end of the bar. He raises his chin, and she moves on to the next one. Terry leans across the small table. "You see this woman? She wants him to buy her a drink." He winks at me.

"What is this place?" I ask.

Terry explains that the male patrons of the bar buy drinks for the ladies – at an elevated price. The ladies will keep them company as long as the drinks keep coming. "Most of them are from Romania," he says. "They come here to find work."

"They come here to become whores?" I ask.

He shrugs.

The waitress delivers our drinks, and I glance back at the bar. The woman is now sitting down. Her legs are crossed as she sits on the barstool, her skirt hiked high on her thigh. She leans in toward the man, her eyes staring into his, her hand on his thigh, close to his crotch. Another woman approaches a man at the end of the bar.

"I don't like this place," I say.

"Finish your drink, and we will leave."

Terry talks about his job at the English school, his children, and his wife. He tells me that she was only fifteen when they married and that she wasn't always fat. She is not fat, and I find myself getting angry at this man who has been so gracious to us. I am sad for Haroula whom I imagine at fifteen being told to marry a twenty-seven year old man, clean his house, cook for him, and bear his children.

I sip my bourbon and water and try to relax, but I have an uncomfortable feeling. "Why did you bring me here?"

"I thought you would like to see this place," Terry replies. Under the table, I feel his hand on my leg.

"What are you doing?" I sit up and stare at him.

"Rita, I thought you might like to have a little fun."

I'm not interested in a boyfriend, and I'm certainly not interested in Terry. "I don't want a boyfriend," I say.

"Why not?"

"I'm married."

He shrugs again. "So am I."
I tell him that I want to leave. He wants to finish our drinks first, because they were expensive.

We leave the club shortly. Terry calls his son who tells him that Alexandra is in the platia in Sparta with her new friends. We drive back to Sparta and park the car, and Terry walks me to an outside bar, where I find Alexandra and the boys sitting at a high top table. It is close to midnight, and the square is alive with the electricity of the rock music which pours out from inside the bars and mingles with the laughter and conversation outside.

Terry glances at his watch, and makes a show of stifling a yawn. "I am very tired," he says. "I'm going to go home." I would bet money that he is heading back to Alexander's.

Alexandra raises an eyebrow at me, and I tell her only that the situation with Terry was awkward. She gives me a hug and pushes a stool back from the table for me. I enjoy the fresh air and young laughter in contrast to the oppressive darkness of Alexander's. There doesn't appear to be a drinking age here, yet no one appears to be drunk. I look around and realize that, while the majority of the patrons are in their twenties, there are enough older adults at the bar to keep me from feeling out of place.

The scene is a little different when, at someone's suggestion, we leave to go to a club. The atmosphere is a blaze of music and strobe lights. People are crowded around the bar, but no one is dancing. Alexandra and I remedy that, and soon the boys join us. The loud music and late hour is catching up with me, and I step outside. The cool night air feels good after the heat of the dance floor, and I sit on the concrete steps and appreciate the relative quiet. The music spills from the doorway as one by one, the kids come outside, and soon they're all there. I check my watch and realize that it's almost four a.m., and I tell Alexandra that we need to go. "Please can she stay out just a little more?" John asks.

"Please, Mom," Alexandra echoes.

My ears are buzzing from the music and the alcohol. I look at her – she is happy and we are in Greece. As my father did with me so many years before in Greece, I consent. "Ok," I say, "but somebody has to take me home."

"I will!" Stratos says, and he disappears to get his car. A few minutes later he pulls up in a '75 grey Alpha Romeo and skids to a stop. He jumps out, comes around, and opens the door, and I turn to hug Alexandra. "I'll be fine, Mom," she says. I get in the car, and I am still looking for the seat belt as he shifts it into gear and we speed up the road. There is no traffic on the streets and the air feels fresh coming in the windows. When I get back to the apartment, the stale smoke from Thanos's cigarettes lingers in the living room, despite the fact that I have asked him not to smoke inside, and I hope that we will be able to air out the apartment before we leave. I go to bed, wondering what my husband would think if he knew I let Alexandra stay out until 5 a.m. with a group of boys she had only met two days ago. I can't see this happening back in Pittsburgh, yet here I have no concern for her safety. I am comfortable in this place, with these people. Somehow, I know she is in good hands.

On Saturday, our last day in Sparta, Terry comes to the apartment to take me and Thanos to *Paleochori,* Panos' village, and to *Xirokambi,* the birthplace of my grandmother Olga. Alexandra has chosen to sleep in. Terry makes no mention of the previous night, nor do I. Helen has shown me photographs of vivid yellow and purple flowers she had taken outside of Paleochori, but it is summertime, and as we drive up the hill on the dusty one-lane road, I see only dried grass and weeds, with a few lone purple blooms. When I listened to Panos talk of his village, I pictured a village square, houses, storefronts, and people, but as we near the end of the road, I see only a cliff in the distance. Panos's house is an ancient two-story stone house with a red tile roof, which is being renovated. Several of the village houses are either under renovation, or abandoned. Underneath the house is a cool dark cellar with a wood door leading inside, and metal bars on the pane-less window. The yard is dust, rocks, and weeds. The houses are spread out above and below the road, and there are no signs of life on this sunny summer morning. The next house on the road is similar in structure, and also under renovation. This house boasts a patio and an outdoor fourno. It also has a dish antenna and a tall metal pole with electric wires, along with a large solar pane sitting on the roof in opposition to the natural setting of the home. Having seen Helen and Panos' house, we drive back down the hill to Xirokambi, park the car, and walk into the platia.

We walk up one of the side streets to the house where my mother's cousin George lives. It was his brother Gus and his sister Kiki who stayed with my mother's family so many years ago in Pittsburgh. We are told by a woman who is watering plants in his garden that he is out of the country. We return to the platia where we sit on cushioned chairs outside of one of the many restaurants, under the shade of an enormous plane tree whose ancient branches span the width of the platia. I cannot help the feeling that I belong here. It is overwhelming and comforting at once. Terry speaks with the waiter and, despite the fact that it is not yet noon, the waiter returns with a tray of water, small glasses of ouzo, and *mezzethes* – cheese, olives, almonds, and pita. The platia is bordered on all four sides by small grocery stores, fruit stands, bakeries, and butcher shops. I feel a connection to the village, and I want to explore it further. I know that I will return to Xirokambi.

    We return to Sparta and, after the sun, the walking, and the ouzo, we nap heavily and easily. When I wake up, the apartment is dark and cool, and I go outside to sit on the balcony. The symphony of crowing roosters, braying donkeys, and honking horns is my background music as I write in my journal while I wait for Alexandra, who has gone out for coffee with John. When Alexandra returns, we walk down to the platia in Sparta for some dinner. We are both moody, but we don't let it keep us from enjoying the freshly baked feta and Gouda pizza, and Greek salad with olive oil and oregano. She has one more night with John, and dreads saying goodbye. I have one more night with Thanos, and I am torn between annoyance, appreciation, and frustration.

    Alexandra goes to a party with the boys that night. Thanos and I stroll down to the platia which is alive with chatter as several restaurants have set up large screens on the sidewalks, and televisions echo each other as the announcers call the World Cup Soccer game. We sit down and order a chicken souvlaki and wine, and join the crowd watching Argentina play Mexico. When Argentina wins in overtime, the restaurant patrons cheer as if they are all Argentinians, but I realize that they are simply soccer fans. It is a soft, beautiful night, and I ask Thanos if he would like to walk for a while, but after about five minutes he says he is tired and we walk back to the apartment.

    Alexandra and John arrive around two a.m. It is clear that they have been crying. I let John stay with Alexandra, and give up the bed so that they can spend the night together in each other's arms. In the morning, Alexandra is crying again, or still, and John is on the verge of tears. What I think was a sweet summer romance has taken on a life of its own. In the car on the way back to Voula, through tears and sobs, Alexandra tells me that John has the kindest heart of any nineteen-year-old boy that she has ever met. "He has so much respect for people and he has a brilliant mind. I can't get over how smart he is, or the way that I feel when he smiles at me." She starts to talk about all the boys and what a good time she has had in Sparta, and I am both happy that she has had this experience, and sad to know that her heart is breaking. I tell her that in time she will get over this, but there is something about this boy that makes me think this is more than just an ordinary summer romance.

On the way back to Voula we stop at my paternal grandfather's village, *Vlachokerasia* - "Village of Cherries." It is aptly named. We pull into the main square of the village, which is much smaller than the platia at Xirokambi. It consists of a church, a cafeteria, and a monument to those inhabitants who have emigrated from the village. Across from the church is a large directional sign, with black arrows pointing in several different directions. Painted in white on the arrows are the names of cities: Toronto, Montreal, Reading, Atlanta, Pittsburgh. Thanos tells me that these are destinations to which Vlachokerasioti emigrated.
   Church has just let out, and the cafeteria is busy. Alexandra and I find a table while Thanos goes up to the bar to order us coffee, and inquire as to whether there are any remaining Langas's who might still live in the village. Next to us sit two men and two young boys with black hair and large eyes almost as black. The small boy sips a milkshake through a straw as he eyes us suspiciously. The men nod at us, and one asks where we are from. I tell them, and ask if they know of any Langas's remaining in the village. They do! The man explains how to get to the house – Mr. Langas is old, and no longer attends church, he explains. And, though it is a small village, the directions are confusing. "Gianni," he says to the older boy, "*pare sto Langka* – take them to Langas." Gianni's eyes widen as he looks from his father to us. "*Aide, re* – go on!" and he shoos him toward us with his hand.

We get in the car, and Gianni directs us down a winding dirt road. We drive to the bottom of a long hill before stopping in front of a two story white stone and stucco house which sits elevated upon a large cellar, and park next to a fence to which a white goat is tied. Large red bougainvillea and yellow rosebushes surround the base of the house and line the steps, which are covered by a canopy of grapevines. We walk up the steps onto a covered porch, and Gianni knocks on the door. It is answered by a handsome white-haired man with deep-set startling blue eyes. His name is Costas Langas – his father is the "old man," asleep upstairs. He, Costas says, would know more, but he is old and does not remember much. We sit outside on the porch, and a woman brings us lemonade. Costas tells us that there was another Langas in the neighboring village, but he is long gone. He thinks that his father and my grandfather were cousins, which makes us some sort of distant cousin. I look at his facial structure – the deep set eyes and wide mouth of my father – and I am sure of it.

Gianni has relaxed, and he and Alexandra talk in their broken English and Greek. She learns that Gianni is from Sparta, and visits his family in Vlachokerasia on the weekends. Thanos and Costas become embroiled in some sort of political conversation – the rapid Greek is too much for me to comprehend, and I sit back and relax, feeling again the comfort of a familiar place, although it is the first time I have been here.

When we leave Vlachokerasia, Alexandra's mind returns to Sparta, and John.

Back in Voula, Helen has moved our things to the upstairs apartment, where Ellen and the girls had been staying. The air-conditioning is a cool respite from the hot air that blows through the open balcony doors of Loula's apartment. We sit at the small table in Helen's kitchen and tell her about our trip, and Alexandra goes upstairs to call John. He is in no better shape than she is, and they spend the evening talking to each other, while I plan our next move. We want to spend a few days on an island. Helen and Aliki confer by phone, and help us to decide on Spetses – not too far by ferry, easily walkable, with clear beaches and small hotels. And, in June, we will have no trouble finding a place to stay.

I go upstairs to tell Alexandra about our destination. She is on the phone with John. "For God's sake," I say, "Just tell him to come to Spetses if you are going to spend all of your time talking to him.

"Mom says you can come to Spetses," she tells John. They chat for another minute, and then hang up. Alexandra tells me that John's mother, after listening to him pour his heart out about Alexandra all day, has told John, "Okay, what's the problem? Go find her wherever she goes, have fun while it lasts. You are very young, and these are experiences that you are going to remember for the rest of your life."

Two days later Alexandra and I board the Flying Dolphin, a "super-fast" hydrofoil, smaller than the ferryboat. At first we are delighted – it looks more like an airplane than a boat, with sleek interior and comfortable leather seats. As the boat picks up speed, our pleasure wears off. The trip on the hydrofoil to Spetses is two-and-a-half hours of turbulent Hell, and I fight the urge to throw up for the majority of the time.

John has told Alexandra that he and Stelios will come to Spetses. To do this, they must take two buses and the hydrofoil – a much longer trip than ours from Piraeus. We aren't sure when, or if, to expect them. She wants to meet them at the dock whenever they arrive, but our fatigue from the trip makes us drop like potato sacks, and we take long, hard naps. We awake to a phone call. Perhaps it is fate, perhaps coincidence – John and Stelios have arrived, and, not knowing where we were staying, have found a room in our hotel. It is the room next to ours.

The next few days are spent on the beach with its clear, cool water, in the tavernas eating delicious pastitso, souvlaki, and mezzethes, and exploring the town. We enjoy the continental breakfast at our hotel – breads, cheeses, meats, fresh fruit, juice and coffee, and the small town with its outdoor rooftop movie theater, bakeries, and artisan shops. At breakfast one morning I see a flyer for the "Athens Centre" which is featuring readings by American poets, and I take the opportunity to give myself some alone time, and the kids some time to themselves. But, we all are hoping for a little nightlife. We ask the locals who tell us that things don't get hopping in Spetses until August, and that the only real nightlife in June is at the Old Port, about a ten-minute walk from our hotel. There we will find live music and dance clubs. Alexandra and I put on dresses and heels, and we all walk in the direction of the Old Port as the sun is setting over the sea. After traveling on a quiet two-lane road for about ten minutes, we stop an old woman wearing a babushka and ask her if we are near the old port. *"Ekei,"* she waves her hand in the direction we are headed. *"Deka lepta me pothi,* ten-minutes by foot." We sigh, and continue walking. After another ten minutes on the same road, darkness falls, and we see no other people on the street. We became concerned that perhaps we are on the wrong road. An old man sits outside, leaning back on a wooden chair, barely visible in the dim light coming from his house.

*"Signom*i - excuse me," John says. *"Pou enai to Palio Limani -* where is the Old Port?" The man nods his head in the direction we are headed. *"Posa makria –* how far?" John asks.

The man shrugs. *"Deka lepta."*

Another ten minutes and Alexandra and I regret wearing heels. We arrive at a small port, empty except for a few fishing boats. Across the street from the docks, up on a slight hill, two large buildings overlook the street. The bass beat of dance music comes from one of them. A man passes by on the street. We ask him where the Old Port is. He spreads his hands out, palms up. *"Etho,"* he says. "Here." We climb the steps to the bar. Inside is a dance floor with loud music and no dancers. Three people sit at the bar. The air is soft, and we choose to sit outside at a high-top table. The boys decide to make the best of it by ordering rounds of a variety of drinks. I, who never, ever, mix alcoholic beverages, join them in each round of shots: Urses red vodka, Smirnoff Apple, Jack Daniels and Amaretto, and to top it off, an *elephantaki* - "little elephant" - made up of beer and tequila. And it doesn't matter that the club is dead, that we have walked for miles, or that the music is bad. There are no clocks to watch, no chores to do, no bosses to answer to, no restrictions. We are in Greece.

I don't expect to survive the night without the room spinning...or worse. But when the taxi takes us back, I fall straight to sleep and find myself wide awake at eight o'clock the next morning. I rent a bicycle and bike to the beach where I stay for several hours until the kids, looking much the worse for wear, eventually join me.

I leave them there, passed out on their beach chairs, and bike to a taverna across the street from the sea. The waiter seats me at a table on a small deck overlooking the water, and my mouth waters when they serve me a Greek salad with tomatoes, feta and oregano, fried eggplant, *keftethes* – Greek meatballs, and fresh bread. I am entertained by the Big Daddy of all seagulls whom Alexandra and I had watched the day before. We had thrown out crumbs of bread, thinking he wanted some, but he ignored the bread, and several small fish came up to nip at it. *Stupid seagull*, I had thought. I think perhaps the crumbs were too small, and throw out a large piece, but just as he did before, he bobs right past the bread without giving it a second look. I shake my head at the bird's stupidity, and once more I throw some bread which he ignores, although it floats only inches away from him. Suddenly he swoops in for the kill, grabbing a small fish who is going after the breadcrumb, and after carrying his prey to the shore, finishes him off in a few bites.

    I am pensive today – it is our last full day on Spetses, and in a few days we will be leaving for the United States. I could not have asked for a better vacation. We have connected with our relatives, we have swum in the sea, drunk the wine, inhaled the air, and embraced the culture. Alexandra has had one hell of a summer romance – how many girls can claim that a boy followed them to an island? But, knowing my daughter, I also know that her feelings transcend the definition of a "summer romance." I watch her and John together and think, *this is serious*.

    We have to check out of the hotel in the morning, but our ferry isn't coming until noon. We leave our suitcases at the ferry station by the pier, and go for a walk in town, peering into shop windows selling jewelry, *koboloi* – Greek worry beads, and pottery. John asks me to distract Alexandra, so I take her into a shop to show her a bracelet that I like. (It is delicate, both silver and gold with small dark beads, and I end up buying it!) When we come back out, John hands Alexandra a small package. It is a necklace with blue stones, the colors of the Aegean.

    The romance of the moment is broken when Stelios announces, "I have to find a place to *shit*."

    Alexandra and I look at each other and start to laugh, surprised at his language. "I haven't seen any public bathrooms," I say. Stelios looks at me quizzically.

    "No, I want to *sheet*!" he says, and now I'm the one who is confused.

    "*Vre Malaka*," John says. "It's *sit*, not *shit*! You want to find a place to *sit*."

When we find a place to sit, our mood darkens as reality sets in. If I had thought the first goodbye was heart-wrenching, it was nothing compared to the second. On the Hydrofoil ride back, Stelios and I sit with each other so that Alexandra and John can sit together. Stelios turns his head and peers several rows back. "How are they doing?" I ask.
"I think they are crying," he says.
At the pier, we hail taxis. I hug John and Stelios, and then Alexandra and John embrace. If time could stand still for only one moment, I'm guessing this is the one that Alexandra might have chosen. "*Ela* – come on!" the boys' taxi driver yells, and they depart. There is nothing that I can say on the ride home that will quell the tears of my heart-broken daughter.

We return to the United States, and in less than ten hours, Alexandra is on her way to Virginia for her senior trip with her two closest friends. That commitment (and my reluctance to say to her father, "Where is Alexandra, you ask? Oh, I left her in Greece with a boy she met in Sparta") may be the only thing keeping her from staying in Greece for the summer. But Alexandra believes that she will see John again. John apparently does not. For a while they send each other messages and talk on the phone. But suddenly, John stops communicating. It is as if they have separated all over again. I had wanted the trip to Greece to be a summer that Alexandra would always remember. I would never have wanted it to be one that she would remember with such heartache. I was so excited to be able to take her to Greece for her graduation because of the memories of my own trip. I had my summer romance with a handsome Greek boy from Baltimore. I fell in love with my relatives, and I fell in love with the country. I wanted her to have the same experience.

YOUNG LOVE - *Nei Agape*: ΝΕΟΙ ΑΓΆΠΗ

Despite believing that she could make a long-distance romance work – even if the distance is the Atlantic Ocean - the lack of communication from John forces her to admit that it is time to move on. She eventually dates and has her share of boyfriends and breakups, none as intense as her experience with John. In November of her junior year, after a tearful breakup with a boyfriend, she comes home for a weekend for some much-needed catharsis. After a venting session with me, she goes across the street to find her best friend, Athena, lying stomach down on her bed, watching classic music videos on TV. Alexandra sits down cross-legged on the Athena's bed, leans against the wall, and shares the details of the past week. She absent-mindedly roams MySpace on her laptop, when she sees a message: *Coming back from Korea in two months. We should hang out.* Alexandra replies: *Here's my phone number, call me when you get back.*

"Hey, remember that kid from St. Mary's we met at the Pirate game – Matt?" she asks Athena. "He just My-Spaced me. I guess he's in the army."

"Oh yeah," Athena says. "The one who gave you his shirt after that other guy spilled mustard on it?"

Alexandra has not spoken to him for over two years, but as she and Athena recall the incident at the baseball game, her phone rings. It is Matt, calling her from Korea.

A few days before Christmas, Alexandra is in the master bathroom that we share through Jack-and-Jill doors between our bedrooms. Through the halfway open door, I see her applying mascara while I fold clothes on the bed. "Where are you going?" I call to her.

"Nowhere," she replies, curling a few loose tendrils in the front of her hair. She eases a navy blue hoodie over her head, careful not to disturb her hair, and disappears into her room. I can't figure out why she is putting makeup on if she isn't going out. She emerges from her room an hour later.

"Hey sweetie, what have you been up to?" I ask.

"Talking to Matt on Skype," she replies. The next night, the hour stretches to two.

"Alexandra," I warn, "do not get serious with this kid. He's overseas. You hardly know him. Take it slowly." I should know better. On New Year's Eve, she tells me that she spent most of the night outside of the bar as the snowflakes softly fell, talking to Matt on the phone, and I know that my words might as well have been burned with the trash. Matt comes home from Korea in early January. His first stop is Clarion University to see Alexandra. They visit us one weekend and I meet Matt – he is handsome and muscular with an easy smile and short cropped army hair. He is reserved, perhaps because it's the first time he's met our family, but I don't get a sense of his personality from this brief meeting.

They spend the month commuting the hour and a half between Clarion and St. Mary's, Matt hitching a ride mid-week, Alexandra driving him home each weekend. By the time he leaves for his next duty in Savannah, they are officially a couple.

Matt drives north during a four-day leave to see Alexandra and spend Easter with his family. It is one of those soft, balmy days when the air smells like spring, and we have decided to grill steaks for dinner. Alexandra is in the living room watching TV. Matt comes out to the backyard where I am lighting the grill, and without preamble tells me that he wants to marry Alexandra. He asks me where John is because he wants to properly ask for his daughter's hand in marriage. The late afternoon sun is warm on our faces; I pause to collect my thoughts. My first is that it is way too soon, but my mother's reaction to my engagement to John echoes in my mind. She had said that I was too young. (I was 22 – the same age as Alexandra).

I also remember what my father said about matters of the heart. His opinion that one should not interfere was a surprising contradiction to the vast majority of Greek parents who insist on their children marrying only Greeks. "Matt," I say, tempering my concern, "don't you think you guys are a little young for this? Aren't you rushing it?"

"No, ma'am," he says, looking me straight in the eye. "I love your daughter."

I find John and send him back to talk with Matt. As I go into the kitchen, I intercept Alexandra who is on her way to see what everyone is up to. She notices my discomfort.

"What is wrong with you?" she asks.

"I don't know," I say. "It's just that you and Matt have gotten so serious so quickly. It feels like you're moving so fast."

"Mom, I've already heard it from Athena and April. I don't need to hear it from you. I already know that I'm going to marry him someday," she says.

Matt proposes on Easter Sunday in St. Mary's in front of both families. It is sweet and romantic – he has hidden the engagement ring in a blue plastic Easter egg, and his family has staged an Easter egg hunt in the backyard. Despite this, I have an anxious feeling gnawing at me. "What if she wants to say no?" I think to myself. The setting makes it impossible. But when she finds the egg, and Matt gets down on one knee to recite the poem that he has written for her, she smiles and says yes, and I am, for the moment, comforted by her reaction.

The wedding is planned to be in two years, when Matt gets out of the service. Alexandra moves to Georgia with Matt for the summer. We make plans to meet in Florida, so that my mother and father who are living in Clearwater can meet Matt. My father is in the progressive stages of Alzheimer's disease, and while he is often aware of whom my mother and I are, the arrival of Matt and Alexandra confuses him. I feel a sense of loss that this vital, outspoken, wise man can no longer provide me with advice and counsel as I navigate life's decisions. As is our tradition when visiting my parents, we walk across the street for the early bird special at the Island Way Grill. As we all chatter away over cocktails at a large round table, my father leans in to my mother and says, "I feel dumb. Who are these people?"

My mother patiently reminds him who I, my husband, my son, and my daughter are. She then nods toward Matt and says, "This is Matthew. He and Alexandra are going to be married."

My father draws his eyebrows together, looks at Matt and says, "Why?"

"Sir?" Matt asks.

"Daddy," I say, thinking he hasn't understood. "Matt and Alexandra are engaged. They're going to get married."

With a devilish glint in his eyes, my father says to Matt, "I feel sorry for you!"

The next day we drive to Tarpon Springs to see our close friends Deeda and Jim, Alexandra's godparents.

As we sip iced tea on the porch, Deeda asks Alexandra when they are planning to get married.

"When Matt gets out of the service," Alexandra says. "Not next year, but the year after."

"You know," Deeda says, casting a loving eye towards her husband of thirty nine years, "Jim and I got married when he was home on leave from the Air Force."

Alexandra and Matt turn to each other, beaming as if they have discovered buried treasure. John and I turn our heads slowly towards each other, and then towards Deeda, I am ready to kill her. We are still making tuition payments, and now we will not have an extra year to save for the wedding. With one innocent comment from Deeda, my daughter is now getting married in less than a year. Gone are our plans for finding a new house. Gone is the Caribbean cruise. But, most crucial, gone is the time they need to get to know each other, and more importantly, their own hearts.

Nick and I remain in Florida for a few more days to stay with my mother and father. Daddy isn't talking much. He joins us at the table for meals, but says little. He seems to know who we are, and for that I am thankful.

One evening, I sit down next to him on the couch, and he asks me about my teaching job: how I teach my students, what my classroom is like, how I like teaching. He tells me that he is proud of me for teaching. I had always thought that he was disappointed when I left a lucrative banking job and pursued my education degree. Until that moment, I had not known how proud he was of me.

He reminisces about his days at Robert Morris, the Greek picnics at our home in Moon Township, the long-lasting friendships from his early years in Oakland.

"I love your mother," he says. "And you, and Ellen." His eyes well up with tears. "And my grandparents. You never knew such wonderful people." He looks away and pauses.

"I've had a good life," he says.

August brings with it Alexandra's return to school. September brings a tearful farewell, as she flies to Georgia to say goodbye to Matt, who is departing for Iraq. Alexandra comes home most weekends for wedding tasks – finding a hall, working on the guest list, looking for a dress, supervising fittings for bridesmaids. I cherish the time with my daughter, but I have a nagging lump in my throat as we move forward with the preparations. I have spent little time with Matt, and do not know him well. I am daunted by the speed with which the wedding is approaching, and still feel that Alexandra and Matt are rushing into marriage. I think back to my mother's concerns about me, and wonder if this is how she felt. If she was wrong about John, could I be wrong about *this* marriage? Still, I am concerned that Matt may not be the right person for her. I don't see in their relationship the intensity of feelings that I witnessed between Alexandra and John in Greece. I tell myself that this was due to the circumstances: a vacation romance by its very nature creates a heightened sense of romance and desperation – the kind of operatic drama where a couple meets in the first act and falls in love by Act II. But, I had imagined that when Alexandra did get married, it might be to someone who was older, educated, and establishing a career - not someone who joined the army because he felt he had no other options, and was unprepared for life after the service. No matter how successful his time in the army has been, and no matter how crazy Alexandra seems to be about him, I am worried. Alexandra and I are sitting outside at Starbucks on an unseasonably warm Saturday afternoon in November, sipping our coffee, when I broach the subject.
"Honey," I say, "are you sure that you're ready for this?"

"What are you talking about?" she asks.

"You just seem to be in such a hurry. You guys are so young."

"*You* were twenty three when you got married."

I begin to say that it was "different" back then, but decide that reasoning will fall on defensive ears. "You hardly know Matt. Is he the right person for you?"

"Why wouldn't he be?"

"I just never saw you with someone like Matt. He's so different from anyone you've ever dated."

"What do you mean?"

I know the destructive power of words. When I became engaged to my husband, a friend of mine said, "Are you sure about this? I don't think he's smart enough for you. I think you'll grow tired of him." That tiny seed of doubt that she cast caused me unnecessary uncertainty for years. I don't want to do the same thing to Alexandra.

"Honey," I say, "I always saw you living in a city, maybe working for an ad agency, or a newspaper or magazine. You're such a city girl. I never pictured you living in a small town, or listening to country music. I guess I always pictured you with someone else."

"Mom," she laughs. "I never pictured myself with anyone like Matt. You can't help who you love."

DADDY - BABA: ΜΠΑΜΠΑ

I am talking with my mother on the phone in mid-November and ask how my father is doing.

"Oh, he's fine, Rita," she says, but something in her voice tells me that he is not.

"Do you need me to come down there, Mom? Is he worse?"

"Well," Mom says, "He's more forgetful. I don't think the medicine is working anymore."

I go to Florida the following weekend and get out of the Super Shuttle at the condo with a mixture of anticipation and anxiety. I ring the bell and Mom buzzes me in, and I pull my suitcase down the first-floor hallway to their condo. Mom has propped open the door, and I go in. The water is running in the sink, and she calls "hello" from the kitchen. My father is sitting at the white dinette table.

"Hi Daddy," I greet him, smiling.

He stares at me. Not at me, but through me, as if he doesn't see me. His deep set eyes look like two black coal pieces, impassive of emotion, boring into my heart. He says nothing. I burst into sobs and go into the bathroom. My mother comes in a few minutes later.

"Oh, Rita," she says. "I'm sorry. I thought I prepared you for this."

"Prepared me for this?" I shout through my tears. "You never told me how bad he was!" I am despondent and furious at the same time. But then I look at my mother. She is drawn and thin, and I can see that taking care of Daddy has taken its toll on her. I hug her tightly, splash my face, and pull myself together. I end up staying for a week. Mom tells me that she has been picking Daddy up when he falls. She has had someone come twice a week to bathe him. He has been docile and cooperative. I remember Daddy telling me that he once thought that if he could live until 40 and still have his hair, he would be fine with that. He would never have wanted to be in this position. It is clear that Mom cannot keep caring for my father at home. She has acquired information on nursing homes, and at the end of the week we move my father into a home ten minutes from her condo. It is the most heartbreaking thing that I have ever done.

No sooner do I leave, but Ellen comes down to spend time with Mom and visit Daddy. I am sick that he is in a nursing home, imagining him not knowing where he is or why he is there. A week later, I receive a call from my mother.

"Your father fell. They've taken him to Hospice."

I'm sleeping the deep exhausted sleep that comes as the aftermath of tears. I wake up suddenly, foggy, and squint at the clock. It's a few minutes past two, and I wonder what woke me up. It wasn't a dream. I don't have to go to the bathroom. I close my eyes and lay my head back down and the telephone rings.

"Mrs. Wilson. This is the nurse at Sunshine Hospice. Your father passed away at 2:05 this morning."

I return to Florida two days later and spend a week with my mother. If I am there to comfort her, I am not doing a good job. When I break down at the crematorium, she is the one who comforts me, and I make an effort to hold it together. I am amazed at her strength and resilience, but I shouldn't be. She has always displayed these traits.

A few weeks later, I am at home upstairs in my bedroom folding clothes on the bed, when I hear Nick come in the front door. His footsteps are slow on the steps and I hear him approach the bedroom.

"Mom," he says, and something in his voice makes my breath catch. I turn to look at him.

"Nick, what is it?"

He stands still and his eyes fill with tears.

"Nick! What is it? What's wrong?"

He chokes out between sobs, "I miss Georgie."

I start to cry. "Oh, honey," I say, "I am so sorry."

He sits on the bed, and I sit next to him. "I am so sorry," I repeat. "I was so caught up in my own grief that I didn't realize how much you and Alexandra are hurting, too."

We sit together for a while, reminiscing about my father. As the only grandson, Nick had a different relationship with Daddy than the girls did. He was "Niko" and the recipient of Daddy's sage wisdom, war stories, and Greek aphorisms. In trying to put on a strong front and keep my grief inside, I had not allowed my children to express theirs.

 My mother flies to Pittsburgh for the Christmas Holidays and we hold a memorial service for my father. It has been almost forty days, in keeping with the Greek tradition. We rent a room in the back of Clark's restaurant, but underestimate the amount of people who wish to pay their respects, and soon co-workers from Robert Morris, fellow tennis players, old friends, and Greek friends pour out of the room and into the restaurant. I am wearing a red wrap dress and pearls, and Mom is dressed in a bright teal dress and a gold Greek pendant. The gathering is not somber as we celebrate my father's life with fondness and nostalgia. Each person who has come to pay respects for George Langas has a story about him ranging from his outspokenness, finesse on the tennis court, and ability to solve problems, to his luck with the ponies, strictness with his daughters and fierce devotion to his family. They tell these stories with affection and admiration, and I know that it is the kind of celebration Daddy would have wanted.

Greece II – View From the Deck, oil painting,
Joyce Werwie Perry

LEARNING - *Mathisi*: ΜΑΘΗΣΗ

Alexandra and Matt get married in May of 2010, one week after her graduation from Clarion University, during Matt's mid-tour leave. My mother flies up for the wedding. She is still very thin, and I am concerned about her, but she is happy to be with family, and assures me that she is doing well.

After a four-day honeymoon cruise, Matt returns to Iraq, and Alexandra moves temporarily into her childhood bedroom. I have been asked by my friend Karen, a German teacher at school, to help her chaperone a high-school trip to Germany and Switzerland. My first inclination after a long school year is to say no, but then it dawns on me that my flight across the Atlantic will be paid for. I have been hoping to return to Greece, and now I can afford it, if I simply spend ten days in Germany with a group of high school students, so I agree to chaperone. I tell Alexandra about my opportunity. "*I* want to go to Germany!" she says. I have forgotten that she studied German throughout high school, and has always been interested in the country. I have forgotten that she is part-German on her father's side. I have mixed emotions. She cannot afford the ticket to Germany. However, she is a great traveling companion and has the time available, and ultimately the decision is a no-brainer. She is not yet working, and in the midst of all of the wedding planning, her college graduation has gotten lost. I offer to take her to celebrate her graduation. I am happy to give her something to look forward to in June.

It is late May and the school year is wrapping up. Emmy, one of my artistic students, is showing me some of the work she has done recently. Her paintings are vibrant and textured.
"Is this oil?" I ask.
"Yes, but I didn't paint it with a brush, I painted it with a palette knife," she replies.
I notice the energy in her seascape and the vibrancy of her sky. "Where did you learn to paint like this, Emmy?"
Emmy tells me about her teacher, Joyce Werwie Perry, who has a gallery in nearby Crafton and is known for her knife painting technique. During my lunch period, I look up Joyce's website. Her paintings are realistic and abstract at the same time. Some of the paintings don't even have detailed faces, and yet with a few strokes of the knife are full of expression. I call my daughter and tell her about Joyce.
"I think I'm going to take lessons from her this summer," I say.
"You won't," she says.
"What do you mean, I won't?"
"Because you always say that you're going to take painting classes, and you never do."
My mind starts arguing with itself. I *am* going to Germany and after that to Greece. I'll miss two of the classes, maybe it's not worth it....but, I dial the number on the website and enroll in the summer class that Joyce is holding at Sweetwater Art Center, happy to know that I have something to look forward to after returning from Europe.

The trip to Germany far exceeds my expectations. Alexandra misses her husband, but is relieved to actually be in the same time zone as he is, and they spend time on the phone every night. The high school students love Alexandra, who is close enough to their age to be a friend and confidant, and old enough to earn their respect. The kids are fun, the tours of castles and churches are interesting, and the scenery is spectacular – especially in Switzerland, where we stay for two nights across from Lake Luzerne. We enjoy the city vibe in Munich and watching the U.S.

national soccer team on the large screen in the English Gardens. Alexandra decides that she wants to live in Lichtenstein, and I am impressed by Heidelberg's charm, but after the whirlwind of bus tours and group meals, we are excited and anxious to get to Greece.

Niko and Roi pick us up from the airport, and we head straight to Marathon. After the constant movement in Germany, we are still. We are surrounded by pots of red and pink geraniums, fragrant fruit trees, grape vines with hard green grapes, and cats. Twelve feral cats live on the grounds. Niko feeds them table scraps. He has a basket for them in the yard and a box on the patio where some of them sleep. Apparently they come and go. Some of them lurk outside of Roi's kitchen door, hoping for a scrap, or a dash inside the house, but Roi will have none of this. *"Fige apo etho* – get out of here!" She waves her hand, and they scatter. Our days pass quietly talking with Roi, watching World Cup matches with Niko, sunning by the pool, reading, playing with the kittens, or walking into town. Roi makes us frappes and cooks for every meal. We try for four days to take her and Niko out for dinner, but they refuse.

I spend hours talking with Roi on the covered patio. Alexandra spends hours in the room – sometimes talking with Matt on the phone, often sleeping. The last several months have been spent finishing her last semester in college with straight A's (a goal that she had set for herself and was determined to reach before graduating), planning the wedding, going on her honeymoon, saying goodbye to her husband, moving back to Pittsburgh, and then traveling in Germany. Between the stress of saying goodbye to Matt, and the constant motion of the past few months, it is no wonder that she is exhausted. The migraines, which had surfaced in high school, are once again plaguing her. We try to shake her headache and her mood by going into town. We walk down the narrow road to the main street of the small town of Marathon, past butcher shops, *tavernas, kafenieos*, and fruit markets. Alexandra stops at the kiosk to buy a pack of cigarettes, and we notice that the old lady across the street is staring at her. We pass a few men who are drinking coffee outside of a bar, and notice that they, too, are staring. Further down the street, the scenario is repeated, this time with a middle-aged woman. Alexandra feels unwelcome and awkward, and we return to the compound.

"Oh," Roi says, "it is probably your shorts. They are quite short."

We look down at Alexandra's white shorts, which she had worn comfortably all over Germany. We say this to Roi.

"Yes," she replies, "but this is a village."

It is no solace to Alexandra, and she decides to stay back to shower and relax while Niko and Roi take me for a *volta* - a ride - to Rafina, the nearby port city. We visit a small, quiet whitewashed chapel on the top of the mountain which overlooks the busy port, and Niko lights a candle and places it in a sandy tray. "For Johnny," he whispers to me, and I close my eyes and remember Rena's husband who passed away the previous year. When we return, Alexandra is refreshed and hungry. Roi serves a delicious spaghetti dinner and we watch the World Cup match between Chile and Brazil. It doesn't seem to matter who is playing - every four years, televisions all over Europe turn to the World Cup.

We have had enough relaxation, and decide that it is time to visit an island. "If you haven't been to Mykonos, you must go there!" Roi says. It is an easy trip from Rafina, and is one of the most well-known islands of Greece. "My mother first met my father there. They were young. Fourteen, I think. My father told her he wanted to marry her. Of course, she laughed. They didn't see each other again for years. She was out one night with some friends in Athens, near the Parthenon, I think, and they saw each other."

"And?"

"And, you see what happened. They got married!"

Our mouths drop open as we arrive at the Palladium Hotel which sits on the high side of a winding road on Mykonos. Everything about it is white, and elegant. The lobby beckons us with white marble floors and rounded stone walls. Our room has a white tile floor - white linen sheets are pulled tightly around the bed, which is covered by a puffy white comforter and pillows. We step out onto the large, private whitewashed balcony. Everything is white, except for the crystal aqua of the pool below our balcony, and the deep navy hue of the sea in the distance.

We cross the street and walk down the several rocky steps to Psarous Beach at the foot of the mountain. Beach umbrellas and chairs line the sand, and we order frappes from the snack bar behind the beach. Far out in the bay, where the water changes from midnight blue to teal, several yachts are moored. The sky is clear blue and cloudless. We drift into a peaceful sleep, but I am slowly awakened by the sounds of children shouting. They are close by in the water, and are yelling at each other in rapid Greek. Every fifth word or so is *malaka*, which translated literally means masturbator, but serves as the Greek counterpart to "asshole." I realize quickly that these boys are playing, and that they are only about seven or eight years old.

Mykonos town is something else: crowded narrow winding stone streets with store after store selling "authentic" Greek souvenirs, and bar after bar painted in black or hot pink with techno music blaring onto the streets. We explore two different areas, but both nights end up at "Mex," partly because we like the bartender, Matina, partly because we prefer the rock music on the speakers to the techno blasts of the other bars, and partly because it is close to the bus stop so that we can catch the last bus for the hotel at 2:00 a.m. Matina is tiny and energetic, with frizzy brown hair which she wears in pigtails, and she makes us feel welcome. She tells us that she is 31 and was educated in Athens, but came to Mykonos on holiday, and has been there bartending ever since. It is a story we have already heard. Spiros, our lobby bartender was studying hotel management when he came to Mykonos on holiday last year, and stayed to work. What he really wants to do is own or run a club and spin records on the side, maybe come to America. Stavros, our morning waiter, told us that he has private teaching experience in math and physics, but did not have his "papers" for public teaching, so he took a job as a waiter in Mykonos to feed his family, although he would prefer to live in the mountains. And our pool bartender wants to move to New York to be a bartender "like Tom Cruise in *Cocktail*." Talking to these people makes me realize that underneath the whitewashed glamour of Mykonos lays a level of discontent masked by the veneer that is required by an island which thrives on tourism.

We spend our last night in Mykonos close to home at the Blue Myth Taverna, where three athletic men dance in traditional Greek style. Two of the men are well built younger, tanner versions of Tom Cruise and John Stamos. While we are enjoying the show I wonder if the men enjoy performing, or if they, too, are simply biding their time in Mykonos until something better comes along.

Niko picks us up in Rafina, and we spend the night in Marathon before getting ready to go to Voula. On our last day in Marathon, Alexandra and I lie down for naps while we wait for the taxi. I wake up, and strip the sheets off the bed. The blood drains from my face.

"Alexandra!"

"What," she says, hearing the tone of my voice.

"Look!" I point at the dead, flattened creature, about two inches long, which lay in the middle of the bed where I had just been napping. "Is that....."

She answers. "It's a scorpion!"

I go into the house to find Roi and Niko.

"We don't have scorpions here," Niko says.

I insist that there is a scorpion in my bed. He laughs, and repeats that there are no scorpions in Marathon. He follows me to the guest house. I point at the bed and he stares.

"What is this?" I ask.

He pauses and rubs his chin with his forefinger. "Hmmm. This, I believe, is a scorpion."

We leave for Voula, where we will be spending five days before returning home. In the back of Alexandra's mind is her trip four years ago. It has been on my mind also. A part of her wants to see John. A part of her does not. I can understand her conflict. She sends John a message to let him know she is in Voula. He is studying in Patras, about two and a half hours away, and it will be difficult to see her. He wishes her well. A part of her is relieved. A part of her is not.

We spend most of our time in Voula visiting relatives. Thanos comes from Psihiko to take us out to dinner, and tells us stories about his stepfather, our great uncle Mike. We learn of his daring escapades as a pilot, but even more interesting is that we hear about our great-grandfather, Elias, who Thanos tells us lived to over 100 years of age, and died during an argument in a taverna, defending the Venizelos political party, when he fell after being pushed. My interest is peaked.

I have learned much about my ancestors on this trip. And though I am able to carry on a decent conversation in Greek, I yearn to improve. I vow to find another source for Greek lessons. On a visit to see Aunt Helen in Kifisia, Rena shows us a video on which were several excursions that she and John took with my mother and father. It is melancholy to see all those who have recently passed away: my father, Uncle Dino, Uncle Bill, and Rena's husband, John. I don't want to let too much time pass before I return to see my beloved aunts and cousins. I cry when I say goodbye to Aunt Loula. She is frail and very emotional, and often complains that her bones are hurting. They have not told her that her brother George has died – they are afraid of her reaction. I pledge to return as soon as I can afford the trip.

It is a morning in July, shortly after our return from Greece. I pour myself a cup of coffee and call my mother to tell her about my trip. She is delighted to hear all of the news about the relatives, and interested in the stories that I tell her that Loula and Thanos have told me. She sighs.

"I wish that I had talked to my mother more," she says. I don't know anything about her life when she was in Greece."

"You must have talked to her about it," I reply.

"No," she says, "we never really talked about things. We just went about our lives."

"Mom," I say. "I bet you know more than you think you do."

For the first time in 16 years of teaching, I do not enjoy my school year. I can't quite put my finger on it, but it seems to be a combination of a small unruly group of disrespectful basketball players coupled with continued sadness over my father's death, and the frantic feeling that my years with my mother are lessening. I look into taking a sabbatical and discover that there are no longer travel sabbaticals – only educational sabbaticals. And I realize that this is the answer: pursue a Master's degree in writing, which will allow me to study and improve upon my writing skills, and still give me the flexibility to spend time with my mother and hear her stories. I research a low-residency program at Carlow University which will allow me the freedom to travel and write while earning my MFA, and in February I move ahead with the application.

Bouzouki Player, oil painting, Wilson

GREEK NIGHT - Ellinika Vrathia: ΕΛΛΗΝΙΚΗ ΒΡΑΔΙΑ

The winter in Pittsburgh is long, cold, and gray. I rely on reading, writing, art classes, and an occasional long weekend to Florida to get me through. Sometimes the temptation to hibernate is strong, and it is easy to become apathetic about going out into twenty degree weather with the wind blowing the snow sideways. One thing that can knock me out of my inertia is "Greek Night." "Bouzouki, bouzouki, dancing, more dancing," the invitation on Facebook reads. "Plenty of parking, food, drink, and no cover!" The venue, a hot-dog joint/bar, is sketchy, but I know the entertainment is first rate. I ask John and my friends to go with me, but they say that nine o'clock is too late to get started. Although most Greeks in America have adopted American cultural behaviors, Greek nights tend to bring out the Greek spirit in them, and I am ready to relinquish my normal bedtime to recapture mine. I contemplate going by myself to listen to the music, dine on mezzethes, and hopefully not feel too conspicuous as a middle-aged woman alone in a bar. I am still sitting on the fence when Alexandra calls to say that she will go with me, but won't be off work until ten.

"Hmm, that's a little late to get started," I say, mentally calculating the hours of sleep I will miss.

"Well, if we're tired, we'll just stay in and watch a movie. I'll call when I get done with work."

After a glass of wine, and a long day, I am now thinking "movie" when the phone rings, and the chipper voice on the other end announces that she is on her way.

"I'll be ready in 10 minutes," she says, as she bursts through the front door at 10:15 and runs upstairs. "I'll just wear what I have on." I should know better by now. I follow her upstairs.

"Mom!" she calls through the bathroom door. "Do you have any black leggings?" I hand her my leggings which I retrieve from a shelf in the bedroom closet, only to hear the muffled voice yell, "Mom! I don't like this top with these. Do you have a top that I can wear with them?" I am already back in the closet dusting off a box of black pumps when I hear, "Mom.... do you have any heels that would match this?"

If only her outfit were the sole thing keeping us from departing. Deciding that she no longer likes her hairstyle with that outfit, she rattles through my brushes, combs, and hairspray. I take a moment to check my reflection in the bedroom mirror. In celebration of the fact that I am actually going to be out past midnight, I have decided on black jeans, a black lace top, a denim jacket and black boots. *Not too bad for a middle-aged woman*, I think, and spray on a little Rock Princess perfume. Fifteen minutes later Alexandra emerges, looking every bit as lovely as she had fifteen minutes before. We leave the house, now well after eleven, and she adds, "Oh, by the way, I borrowed your bracelet." We circle the block twice looking for the "ample parking" that was alluded to in the Facebook invitation. We find it several blocks away. The streets are dark and quiet, the single light glowing from the neon pink "Hot Franks" sign above the hot dog shop. Strains of bouzouki music greet us as we approach the door, which an elderly, smiling gentleman holds open for us. "Come in, come in, *ela!*" He shouts over the din of the band. The hot dog shop is deep and narrow, with a long counter along the right hand side. Sotiri's four-piece ensemble is set up in the front window, facing the patrons who stand in front of the band on the makeshift dance floor, a small tiled area about 15' x 15'. He looks up from his bouzouki, smiles and nods as we walk by, and I wave. Alexandra and I weave our way past the counter to the back, where a bar replaces the food counter, and we attempt to order drinks. Two deep at the small bar, we wedge our way in between the men who are sitting on the round stools at the counter. After a 10-minute wait, we persuade the guys on the barstools to order for us.

The long, narrow room affords no way to see the band above the heads of the patrons, and the wooden tables against the wall opposite the bar are all inhabited. We lean against the counter, and I take a sip of my Jack Daniels and water. I nearly spit it out.

"This is *not* Jack!"

"Let me taste," Alexandra says, and confirms my observation with a grimace. "Take it back," she says, but one look at the now three deep at the bar convinces me to sip slowly and suck it up. At this point I am beginning to think that I have made a mistake coming downtown. It is well past my bedtime, I am tired, and my drink tastes like hair spray. To top it off, we can't see the band, and there is nowhere to sit.

I consider calling it a night, when Alexandra spots the couple at the table across from us leaving. We quickly grab the chairs against the wall, which gives us prime seats to watch the diverse parade of patrons walking past us to the rest rooms or to the bar: white haired men who do amazingly limber things on the dance floor; dark-browed, furtive-looking young men who wish they could do those things; middle-aged women with dyed orange hair and leopard print blouses; women in tight skirts, false eyelashes, and four-inch heels; pretty young women with thick dark curls and bright red lipstick. It's an interesting cross-section of Greek American society, whose common bond for this night is Greek food, music, and company.

We have a partially obscured view of the band, which is loud enough to hear and low enough to allow conversation. I lean back in my chair, and listen to the familiar Grecian melodies. The ice has started to melt in my drink, taking the edge off of the medicinal quality. A tall, not unattractive grey haired gentleman in a grey sport coat and black shirt approaches from the bar, and signals to the chair across the table from me. "May I?" he smiles. I assume he plans to take it to another table and I nod, removing my boots from the chair where my legs have been comfortably elevated. I am surprised when he sits down and introduces himself as Dennis. "What are *you* doing here?" he asks. "You're obviously not Greek."

Despite my hair, which has been dyed to a dark blonde over the past few years, and my green eyes, I feel that somehow my spirit and character alone would convey the fact that I am most definitely and completely one hundred percent Greek. "*You* look

Greek," he says to my daughter, whose blue eyes surely should imply an impure mixture of some sort. She laughs, and I cross my arms, lean back, and turn my attention to the band. Dennis calls his friend Alec over to say hello. We engage in the customary Greek introductory ritual that goes something like this:

"What's your last name?"
"What's your maiden name?"
"Do you speak Greek?"
"Which church do you go to?"
"Have you been to Greece?"
"Where are you from?" This final question refers not to one's current domicile, but from which island, city in Greece, or village one's ancestors have descended.

Through this ritual we determine that in 1972, our families were on the same flight returning from the Icarian convention in Greece. I laugh as Alec insists that he sat next to me, fell in love with me, and has carried a torch for forty years.

Sotiri plays on without a break, and we order drinks and Greek appetizers – feta, olives, pita, and gyro. The small hot dog shop which had been close to capacity when we arrived before midnight, is packed even tighter now. Alexandra and I work our way past the counter to the dance floor, and stand on the perimeter. As the circle of dancers glides past us, I tap a woman on the shoulder, and she breaks hands with the woman next to her to take mine. Alexandra and I join the circle, and quickly pick up the rhythm. Sotiri moves seamlessly from one song to another, keeping the same 7/8ths beat. Some dancers drop out of the circle, others come in, but my daughter and I continue to dance. My Greek spirit soars. I am with my daughter, dancing to Greek music, feeling young, untroubled, and alive. The night is just about perfect. We return to our table, flushed from the heat, the music, the dancing, and probably the drinks. We sit down, and sip our drinks, which have been watered down by the melting ice cubes. I relax in the chair, and Dennis leans over the table, towards Alexandra, who looks radiant. He stares into her stunning blue eyes and says, "You know, your *mother* is a beautiful woman."

The compliment is unexpected, but Alexandra smiles and says, "I know."

View from Xirokambi
oil painting, Wilson

THE VILLAGE - *To Horio*: ΤΟ ΧΩΡΙΟ

It is June of 2013, and I am in Ireland for the residency portion of my MFA program. I have saved my tennis coaching money and decided to travel on to Greece after completing the 11-day residency in Dublin. This will be my first trip alone. I am surprised at how difficult it is to find an inexpensive direct flight to Athens, and end up with a short connection via London. The Aer Lingus flight attendants look stern. Their hair is pulled back tightly in buns, and they are dressed in dark green long sleeved jackets with scarves tied closely around their necks. I pay 2.50E for a cup of tea. I am not prepared for Heathrow Airport, and after a long security line for connections and an "enhanced" security search of my bag, I am more than a little stressed when I realize that I am required to take a bus to change terminals. My anxiety increases during my long, long walk through a maze of construction and underground tunnels, and lengthy lines of irritated international travelers, and I run to the Aegean Airlines gate, my carryon bag bouncing at my side, with only minutes to spare.

    I approach the gate and immediately see an old Greek woman with silver grey hair, a tan, weathered face, and that familiar side-to-side gait that so many short, heavy old Greek women have. Greek music plays over the speakers as I walk into the plane, and the smiling Aegean hostesses in their sleeveless navy blue dresses, with their hair in stylish, slicked back ponytails, greet us with the customary *"kalimera* and *yeia sas."* While we wait for takeoff they serve us a watermelon candy. Once we are airborne, they serve us pasta with feta and olives, along with an eggplant salad, and Greek wine. I am no longer anxious.

    I spend the next few days in Voula with Helen and Alexander recuperating from the non-stop action of the residency in Dublin. Helen asks me if I want to go see friends and is concerned that I might be bored, but all I want to do is relax in the upstairs apartment or sit on the balcony reading or writing, taking an occasional break to go to the balcony's edge and gaze at the sea in the distance. Greece is sweltering after the cool misty days of Ireland, and it takes a few days to acclimate. I spend hours sitting with Helen in her small kitchen, in the warm breeze coming in from the North through the open unscreened kitchen door. There are no screens on any of the doors or windows. After a few days I am rejuvenated, and ready for a road trip to the Peloponnese. I have rented a little red Hyundai five-speed, despite Alexander's concern. He worries about me driving on the windy roads that spiral up and down the mountains and tries to convince me to take the bus from Athens. After about two hours, and only one wrong turn, I pass through the city of Sparta. Having been to Xirokambi briefly three years before, I recall that it is only about fifteen minutes from Sparta. As I leave the city behind me, the stores and gas stations get fewer and farther between, and soon I am on a long stretch of a paved two-lane road. After a half hour I pull off the side of the road, and call the Hotel Taleton on my cell phone.

    "I think I am lost," I say in Greek to the woman who answers, and I tell her I am a half hour from Sparta. I don't know if I have taken the wrong road, but I have not seen a sign for Xirokambi.

    "Tell me what you see," she says, and I tell her I don't see anything but trees and sky.

    "Turn around and call me when you see something."

    I drive for about ten minutes until I spot a single airstrip, and a sign that says *Aerodromio* - Airport.

    "Ah, you have gone too far," she says when I call her. "You must come back. I think five minutes, and you will see the sign. Turn left. You will find us."

    I laugh when I see the sign. I have been looking for a small sign, but on my left is a large blue sign with five villages listed. Xirokambi is the first. I had also been looking for a town beginning with an "X". But Xirokambi in Greek begins with the letter Ξ. I didn't recognize the name.

I turn left and immediately the road narrows. It is flanked by olive groves and dried grass, and dust kicks up from my wheels. It is late June, and the village has not seen rain for weeks. I come to a fork in the road with no sign, and stay to my right, crossing my fingers on the steering wheel. A few minutes up the road I see a woman standing in front of a small brick building with no sign on the front. She is wearing a green tank top, and gauzy striped harem pants, and her dark hair is pulled into a bun on the top of her head. She waves and smiles.

Katerina shows me to my room. We pass through a fenced-in stone courtyard with wooden tables and chairs and a small fountain gurgling softly in the corner. It is late afternoon, and the red and yellow roses are in full bloom. "At night you come in through here," she points to a locked wrought iron gate that leads to an alley. "No one works here at night. But you will be ok."

I ask her how many people are staying at the hotel. "Tomorrow will be some people, but tonight, just you."

I have never met my mother's cousin George, who still lives in the village. I call him and arrange to meet him and his wife Pitsa that evening. After a short nap and shower, I walk through the main square, which is set up with plastic tables and chairs. I have arrived on *Ayios Pnevmatos*, the church's biggest holy day of the year, and consequently, the town's biggest party of the year. I meet George and Pitsa at their home, and we walk back to the square, which is now filling with people, and find a large table. We are soon joined by their friends, none of whom speak English, but my Greek is now more than passable. It doesn't matter, as the noise around us limits our talking when the band starts to play traditional Greek music. George walks over to a food stand, and comes back with two large aluminum trays filled with roast *hirina* – pork, and roast chicken. We drink wine out of plastic cups and eat tomato salad and thick homemade bread. The music has been playing for almost an hour, and I look towards the center of the square, which has been cleared to make room for dancers. "Why is no one dancing?" I ask.

"You want to dance?" George says. "Let's go."

We make our way past the dozens of tables towards the dance floor, and are joined by a half dozen others who join hands and begin to dance. I am surprised at how limber George is at eighty-six years old. *I am at a Greek dance in Greece* I think to myself. George goes back to the table after about five minutes, but I keep dancing. When the music finally stops, I return to the table, and realize what a long day it has been. The music starts up again, louder than before, and I feel my temples throbbing. There is now a chill in the clear night air and I put my sweater on. I thank my host and hostess, and excuse myself. In the black night I walk carefully back towards the hotel, through the narrow alley, and unlock the door to the courtyard.

Katerina is sitting at one of the tables, talking rapidly on her cell phone. She hangs up and smiles. "Did you enjoy the celebration?" she asks, and I tell her that I did. In the quiet of the courtyard, the music from the platia drifts in softly. She nods in the direction of the music. "That will go on all night," she says, "but you will not hear it in your room." She pauses, then asks, "Would you like some wine?" She brings out a bottle of dry white wine. As we sip the wine I tell her about my family and my friend from the states, Helen, who is married to Panos, who immigrated from Paliohori, the next village up the mountain. They visit Greece often, and Helen has armed me with photographs of a dozen people that they know from Paliohori and Xirokambi, so that I might recognize people when I see them. I show these to Katerina, and she laughs and points to one of the photos. "That is my godfather! I will call him tomorrow and you will meet him!" We chat for a while, and I realize that my headache has disappeared.

I visit with George and Pitsa every day. They speak no English, so we speak in Greek. They are warm and hospitable. They feed me: *spanakopita, hirina,* tomato salad with olive oil and feta, fresh baked bread, ripe cherries and sweet honeydew melons from the village. Their home is one of the larger homes in Xirokambi. George retired from a successful business career and now spends his time in the garden, and Pitsa prepares traditional meals for his lunch and dinner. George grew up in Kamenia, near his Aunt Stavroula, the woman who raised my Uncle Nick when he was stuck for so many years in Greece. Although he was a few years younger than Nick, George was close to his cousin and played with him every day as a child. When Uncle Nick died, my Aunt Anneliese brought his ashes back to Greece, as he wished. George has offered to take me to the cemetery and to the house where Nick grew up.

    I shift the little red Hyundai into low gear as we turn off the main road and down a narrow one-lane road. George tells me to stop. "Over there," he points out of the passenger window. I look past him through the thick brush to a few piles of rocks. "That was the house," he says. I pull the car half into the grass, put it in neutral and pull the emergency brake, thinking that I will get out and take a photo. The house is separated from the road by a gully which is actually a dry streambed. In the winter, George explains, water runs down from the surrounding mountains, but in the summer it is dirt, pebbles, and boulders. I look doubtfully at the hill leading down to it, and with even more apprehension at the hill going up the other side to the old homestead. The brush has grown heavy, but I can see a faint path up to the yard. "When we were little," George says, "we would cross the river to get to the house. It wasn't too deep." He points to a large boulder. "We walked here."

    He takes my hand as we plant our feet solidly, one at a time, to avoid sliding down the dusty hill. *This is the epitome of chivalry,* I think, an eighty-six year old man making sure that *I* don't lose *my* footing. We reach the bottom of the hill, and walk about twenty feet up the dried riverbed until we find a clearing, and carefully navigate the rocky hillside. We push aside prickly brown weeds whose thorns catch on my clothing, and I realize that my sandals and sundress were not the best choice for this outing.

    The yard is flat with dried grass. To the left of us is a grove of olive trees growing out of the dusty soil, their trunks gnarled and silver in the late afternoon sun. To the right is a tall rusty fence. Large cactus plants with wide flat prickly leaves grow outside of the fence. Inside the fence are the rocky remnants of Great Aunt Stavroula's house. The footprint of the house is small. George explains that there had been a kitchen, two bedrooms, and a cool cement cellar to store cheeses and meats. The kitchen housed a large wood burning *fourno,* or oven. In the summer, the baking was done in the large clay oven in the back yard. All that remains of the house now are four short pillars of stone.

I peer through the fence and imagine Uncle Nick as a boy, playing in the front yard. He was tall for his age, with dark brown hair and hazel eyes. He must have been brown from the sun, like the village children I had seen playing soccer in the schoolyard. And clever. George had told me that Nick would construct cars out of a light wood, and they would play with them in the yard for hours while Aunt Stavroula tended to the cooking, bread-baking, and the laundry. I picture the two boys gathering dried brushwood from the olive grove to build the fire in the *fourno*, and then playing in the front yard with their homemade cars while the smell of baking bread hung in the air.

My reverie is broken when I hear a sound beyond the riverbed. I peer through the bushes and see the sun's glare reflecting off the red car. There doesn't appear to be anyone there, yet I continue to hear thrashing in the bushes. "What's that?" I call to George, my imagination getting the best of me. I envision the Albanian gypsies I had seen in town taking my purse out of the car, or worse, taking the car. But George has walked towards the back of the house, so I tentatively approach the streambed myself. From the top of the hill, I look down the river bottom toward the source of the noise. Looking up at me is a surprised dark-haired man holding a walking stick in his left hand. Behind him, a flock of bearded goats, white, tan, brown, and black, munch eagerly at the foliage on the hillside. A sheen of sweat exaggerates every muscle under the man's sun-browned skin. He has thick black hair, dark eyes, and a handsome, rugged face. He wears a dark grey tank top and green khaki pants. They fit him well.

I break into a smile, and he smiles back. Time is suspended. A scene from *The Quiet Man* flashes before me: Sean Thornton (John Wayne) has just seen Mary Kate Daneher (Maureen O'Hara), as she tends sheep in the emerald Irish fields. Their eyes lock, and Thornton is mesmerized by her long red hair and flashing eyes.

I hear a rustle in the field behind me. "Oh, it's just Michael, the goatherd," George says. "*Yiassou Mihali,* hello Michael!" he calls.

I look at the rocky hill which appears to be steeper going down than it had been coming up. George looks down at Michael and points to me. "*Pare to heri tis* - take her hand," he says.

Michael climbs halfway up the hill and reaches up to me. I take his rough, strong brown hand, and he guides me down the hill. *Forget the movie*, I think. This is the classic romance novel. *Michael the goatherd takes me in his arms, and in the dappled shadows of the trees along the riverbed we find a clearing. He leans over me on his powerful arms, and then.....*I catch the pungent whiff of goat. It smells like a blend of wet dog and moldy cheese. I scrunch up my nose at the smell, and Uncle George laughs. "We are in Greece," he says, and shrugs. The animals have made their way up the streambed, chomping on leaves and branches, and are closing in on us. "Give me your hand, quickly," says Uncle George, who has caught up with me. He reaches down from the hill where he has begun to climb back up towards the car. But in half a dozen quick, decisive steps, I bound up the hill, past George, and now look back down at Michael the goatherd and his herd of goats. *"Yeia sas,"* I say, and wave goodbye. As I walk to the car, I turn around to glance back at Michael, who is still watching me, and I wonder if behind his shy smile there might be a hint of fire.

"He lives next door to me," George says, as we get into the car. "He is a very good man."

"Is he married?" I ask.

"No, he lives with his mother, father, and sister. I asked him why he had not married, and he said, 'where would I find a wife who wants to stay in the village?'"

I drift back into my reverie. *Michael comes home from a long day of herding goats, sweat glistening on his arms, smelling of the man-scent of hard work. I am in the garden, tending to the baby vines we have planted that will yield sweet grapes. I stand up and wipe the dirt from my hands on my sheer cotton dress. Michael turns me around and I taste his passionate kiss as he clutches my skirt and pulls me toward him.* Wait. I have seen this scene before. Kevin Kline and Meg Ryan in *French Kiss*. Okay, then. *I am inside taking a shower when Michael comes in. I hear the creak of the bathroom door and he pulls the shower curtain aside. I can see that work has not tired him. I reach for him and sponge the sweat from his muscular chest, the soap forming ringlets of his dark chest hair. The water from the shower head sprays us both....*

"Margarita!" Uncle George says. He taps my hand which is clutching the gear shift. "Let's go!"

We drive over to a large brick schoolhouse that my uncle and George attended when they were children, and then to a small chapel and cemetery in Kamenia. Behind the chapel is a small stone building. George explains to me that the Greek custom, because of the shortage of graves, is to lease a grave at the local cemetery. After three years, the grave is opened, the remains are exhumed, and the bones are removed, washed in red wine, and kept in an *osteofilakio* - a bone chamber, or ossuary.

"But, Uncle Nick was cremated," I say.

"Shh!" Uncle George cautions me. "I made this special box for him," he says as we enter the ossuary. "He is here, among the bones. The church does not allow cremation, but your uncle wished to be cremated, and so I have arranged to keep him here."

Uncle George takes a wooden box from a shelf, and opens the lid. Inside is another box wrapped in thick plastic. He unwraps the plastic to find a black box, and we open this one. Inside is a plastic bag which holds Nick's ashes. George begins to unwrap the ashes, but I touch his hand. I take the bag with my Uncle Nick's ashes. I close my eyes and remember him, not only in his final days as a sick cancer patient, but as a young boy in Kamenia playing in the fields, and as my handsome uncle with his dark mustache and distinct brows. I kiss my index finger and place it on the bag. "*S'agapo*, I love you," I whisper, and place the bag back in the box. George smiles, pats me on the shoulder, and wraps the box. We drive back to Xirokambi where Pitsa has dinner waiting for us.

My friend Helen has emailed ahead of my arrival to introduce me to her Paleohori neighbor, Markos, a large bearded man who wears his hair in a ponytail and speaks excellent English. Markos, in turn, has introduced me to Niko, a short, stocky, silver-haired man with an ever-present smile. Niko is the former mayor of Kamenia. By day they help me to track down information on my ancestors – at night I meet them in the platia for dinner. They refuse my attempts to buy my own dinner. "In Greece a woman does not pay," Niko says. Something tells me that this is not true in Athens, but in the village I accept it as fact, and thank them. We sit nibbling *paidakai* - baby lamb chops - from the bone, and Markos sees a woman walking slowly through the alley. He elbows Niko and nods toward the alley, *"Yineka sou* – your wife," he says, and Niko grins sheepishly.

"*Se vrika*, I found you!" she says, smiling. Markos grabs a chair from another table and brings it up to ours. He introduces me to Lora, who is from Russia, born to Greek parents. She came to Greece when she was sixteen, and met Niko when she was cutting his hair at her shop. She has curled her dark hair, and put on lipstick and eye shadow. She is one of the few village women in the platia this evening and takes over the conversation. She is pleasant to me, yet I get the feeling that her presence there is not unlike a dog marking her territory.

Back at the hotel, Katerina tells me that many of her friends who moved to Athens in the 1990's have come back to the village, unable to find work as the unemployment rate hit record highs. Those that did find work made enough money to live on, but not enough money to buy a house, and have returned to their parents' homes. The jobs that they have found in the village are not the jobs they studied for: they are working in restaurants and stores, cleaning homes, or working in the family business, be it farming or olive oil. Katerina did not leave the area. She studied and worked in Sparta for three years before taking the job at the hotel in Xirokambi.

Katerina tells me she does not regret staying in Xirokambi. She likes that everyone knows her. When she walks into the platia, everyone says hello, and she can always find a friend to drink a coffee with.

"I don't like," she says, "that if you do something, they all know, and "blah, blah, blah..."

"What do you mean?"

"If you were divorced, you would not be able to find another husband, because everyone would know everything about you."

I try to tell her that I understand the way she feels about feeling at home in the platia, because I feel the same way, but something is lost in translation and she says, "Yes, that is because you are a beautiful woman that they talk about you. If you were ugly or fat, they would ignore you." As pleased as I am at her compliment, I am now wondering who is talking about me, and what they are saying.

The hotel business is slow, and Katerina does not know how long she can continue to work there. She hopes to stay in Xirokambi though, because, in the village, "you put a tomato and you eat tomato. You know?"

I have let the boys from Sparta know that I would be in Greece, and John has sent me his phone number. He is in Sparta on leave from the army for a few days, and suggests that we meet for coffee. We have arranged to meet at Taleton. I am writing in the courtyard as I wait for him.

"Here she is," I hear Katerina say as she enters the courtyard. Behind her walks John – a little taller, a little fuller, than he was when we met at the beach. I get up and reach up to give him a hug. "You've grown!" I say, and he smiles.

"Yes," he replies. "I think it has been eight years."

"Seven," I correct him. "Alexandra graduated in 2006."

Katerina offers to bring us frappe, and we sit down at the table. The sun has lessened in its intensity and the air is warm and pleasant. I ask about the boys, and John asks about my family. He wastes no time. "Why did you let her get married?" he asks.

"Me?" I said. "Why did *you* let her get married?"

"It wasn't up to me!" he said. "You are her mother. You should have stopped her."

"What could I have done to stop her? She's very stubborn. When she makes up her mind, there isn't much I can do to change it." These are the words I say to John, but in truth I have been asking myself for the last three years if there was something else I could have said to make her think twice.

"Why did you stop writing to her?" I ask. There is silence, and for a moment I think that John is not going to answer me.

"She was so far away." He looks down at the table, then back up at me. "She gave me something," he says, and points to his wrist, "to wear."

"I remember. It was a leather bracelet."

"Yes," he says. "I wore it for about a year. It finally came off in the bath." He pauses before speaking. "My friends told me that I had to get over her. I was hurting too much. They said that I would never see her again. That I had to move on."

"Ah, but your friends were wrong," I say. "She was already planning to come the next summer. She was even talking about coming back at Christmas. She was hurting too. When you stopped writing, she was devastated." I pause. "She was in love with you."

"I have only ever loved two girls," John tells me. "Your daughter was one of them."

Katerina comes out carrying a tray with two coffee frappes in tall slim glasses and two glasses of water and places it on the table.

I pick up my frappe and stir it around with the straw. *"Yeia mas,"* I say, holding the glass out to John, "to our health."

"Noooo, it is bad luck to toast with coffee," he says.

"Oh, really?" I smile. "Okay," I pick up my water glass, and lift it towards him.

"No, it is also bad luck to toast with water," he says. "You only toast with ouzo or beer."

"Well then, I guess we'll have to have some ouzo."

We finish our frappes and walk to the platia for a glass of ouzo. We move away from the past, and talk about the present. He is finishing his mandatory time in the army – a lot of paperwork and a lot of downtime. He catches me up on the boys, and I realize the economic downturn in Greece has affected all of them. John is concerned about finding an engineering job, Stelios has quit school and is working full-time as a waiter, Antonis is not working, and Stratos is working long hours as an accountant. John tells me that even if he does find a job, he will be lucky to make $1000 euros a month. There are too many people and not enough jobs, and he worries that he might have to leave Greece. "All my life, I couldn't wait to go to college, to get my masters, so that I could get a job and get married and have a family. And now, I'm scared."

He asks about Alexandra – her marriage, her job, her life. "I am never going to get married," he says. He doesn't elaborate. I tell him that he hasn't met the right girl, and that someday he will. But I tell him that somehow, I wish it could have been Alexandra.

It is my last morning in Xirokambi, and I don't want to leave. I am savoring my freshly-squeezed orange juice and homemade Greek yogurt before putting the rest of my things into the Hyundai. I walk into the platia to meet Markos who takes me to the Records Hall. I find information on the Savellos family, but I draw a blank with Nefopoulas. I guess that I will never know how Achilles arranged the marriage with Olga. We meet Niko for a cup of coffee in the platia. I am planning to stop in Vlachokerasia on the way to Marathon. Niko tells me to find Christos – a man with a large mustache who owns a restaurant. He might be able to give me some information about the Langas side of the family. The waiter brings the check, and I take it and pull out a few euros. "No," Markos and Niko say simultaneously, and they both reach for the check. I pull it away.
"I want to thank you for everything. You can at least let me pay for coffee!"
They look at each other.
"Okay, fine," Markos says. "You may pay for the coffee."
It is a small victory for women's liberation. But I have to admit, I have enjoyed their gallantry.

It is late morning when I pull into Vlachokerasia, and the village is quiet. I find the cafeteria that we had stopped at seven years before, and ask after a Christos. I am directed towards a narrow road, and I drive a minute or so past a small kafeneio and park the car. There are no signs of life at the coffee shop, but next door an older lady picks cherries from a tree. "*Signome*," I say, and I ask if she knows Christos. She smiles, but does not reply. She offers me a cherry.
I walk over to the coffee shop and am about to go in the open door, when a man with a thick grey mustache steps outside. "Are you Christos?" I ask in Greek. I tell him that Nikos has sent me to see him, thinking that he may be able to help me information about Langas.
"You are from Pittsburgh?" He asks. "My cousin George lives in Pittsburgh. I just talked to him last week. His name is

Mandros." The name is familiar, and I have a feeling that this George was a friend of my mother's.

Christos disappears, and returns in a few minutes with a cup of Greek coffee and a glass of water. He is not able to help me with the Langas search, and believes that Costas Langas, the man I met on my last trip, moved back to Athens after his father passed away. The woman from next door, Georgiana, comes over with a bowl of washed cherries, smiles, and sets them down in front of me. Another man approaches the shop, and Christos speaks with him quickly in Greek and nods toward me. "He will take you to the Records Hall. Perhaps they can help."

I am impressed by the warmth of these people in the villages, and thankful for the kindness of strangers. At the Records Hall, I learn that my great grandfather, Konstantino Langas, had three sons in addition to my grandfather, Basili: Panayiotis, Anastasios, and Emmanouli. This is the only record of any Langas in the village, but I realize that unless none of them had children, it is quite likely that I have Langas cousins.

Akrotiri Pots, oil painting, Wilson

CONNECTIONS - *Syndeseis*: ΣΥΝΔΕΣΕΙΣ

In Marathon I tell Niko and Roi about my adventures and my disappointment in trying to learn more about the Langas side of the family. "Ah," Roi says. "That is because Langas is not a Greek name."
"What?"
"The name Langas is Romanian. Our ancestors came from Vlachia to Vlachokerasia. The village is named after the Vlachies who settled there."
"But, where is Vlachia?" I ask.
"Romania."
"So we're part Romanian?"
"Not necessarily," Roi says. Many of the Vlachies moved here and married Greeks. So, maybe you are a little Romanian. Maybe not. It depends how far back you go."
She tells me about our grandmother Coula's mother, Eleni Daglari, who was from Aigio, in the Peloponnese. "Oh, she had beautiful eyes. Just like Elizabeth Taylor. I met her once."
"Eleni, or Elizabeth Taylor?" the grammarian in me clarifies.
"Tsss. Eleni. When I was six years old. But," she adds, "I saw Elizabeth Taylor when I was in Mykonos!"
She tells me that Eleni, with the beautiful eyes, eloped with Anastasis Constantinedes, a handsome man from Megara, near Corinth, who was taken with her beauty. "He was an *Alvanitis*," she says.
"An Alvanitis?"
"He was from Albania."

"So we are part Albanian?"

Roi tells me that in 1821, when the Greek revolution against the Turks began, after 400 years of slavery and oppression, many Albanians fought on the side of the Greeks. Several of them remained in Greece – many in Megara. In 1928 the Turkish troops left the Peloponnese for good, and Greece became a republic. Those who lived in Greece became citizens of Greece.

"So you see," Roi says, "we are all Greek."

Aunt Helen comes to visit for dinner, and I am incredulous that she will be 100 years old in December. Her skin is fair and smooth, and only a little plump. She walks occasionally, but deftly, with a cane, and she is bright and endearing. She speaks no English, aside from a few words, but we converse in Greek. We sit down at the table, and Niko pours wine into our glasses. Helen picks up her glass to toast, smiles at me, and says in perfect English, "Here's mud in your eye!"

I leave Sunday afternoon for Voula, where I will spend my last few days in Greece. I am still hoping to see the other boys from Sparta, and I know that I must also make a point to see Aunt Rita.

"She was very upset that you did not see her the last time," Cousin Helen tells me.

"I know," I say, but I hate doing things out of obligation.

"Beatrice will go with you," Helen says. She will meet you in Athens and you will go together.

I make plans to meet Stratos after work that evening, and to see Aunt Rita the next day. Stratos sends me a message that the auditing job he is doing is not going well, and that he will be very late.

I return from dinner at the platia with Helen and Alexander, and wait for Stratos. It is past eleven, and I sit out on the top floor balcony. The air is warm and the night is soft, and the sounds from the traffic on the boulevard are only a quiet hum. I hear the loud sputtering of a motorcycle and look over the balcony. I wave at Stratos, and motion him to wait, and I run down the stairs and out into the courtyard.

I give Stratos a hug, and step back to look at him. He is no longer the skinny kid that I met in Sparta seven years ago. Like John, he has filled out and he is taller, but he has the same enthusiastic smile.

"You've gotten so handsome!" I say.

"Yes, I am not a kid," he says, suddenly serious, but he pronounces it *keed*.

He asks if I want to go get a drink, but I point to the motorcycle.

"No, I want to go for a ride!"

He points to the denim shirt that I have tied around my waist. "Put *eet* on."

I mount the bike, and we are off, and I feel free and exhilarated as the air, now cooler, rouses me. For a moment I am sixteen again, experiencing the pleasure of my first nighttime motorcycle ride in Greece. We stop at a kiosk for a couple bottles of water, and ride down the boulevard to a small beach. I sit on one side of a white bench, leaning back on the arm of the seat, with my knees up, clasped between my folded arms. He sits across from me, and we catch up on seven years of life to the background music of ocean waves and not-so-distant traffic.

The next morning I tell Helen about my midnight motorcycle ride.

"Yes, we saw you from the balcony," she smiles. "But, now, you must go to meet Beatrice."

It is not that I dread the visit to Aunt Rita, although in a way I resent the command performance. Maybe it is her stately presence or her social standing, but Aunt Rita dictates what day and time people may see her or even call her on the telephone, and everyone seems to bow down to her wishes. I take the bus into Athens, and find Beatrice on the appointed street corner. We decide to buy some sweets to take to Aunt Rita, and find a specialty bakery. We buy a dozen small, elaborate iced petit fours, and the woman behind the counter wraps them in a fancy box with a large yellow bow. We are sure to please Aunt Rita.

The maid answers the door, and takes the box from Beatrice. We are instructed to sit and wait in the living room, and we sit quietly, except for an occasional childlike giggle. I feel like a child in the principal's office, and I'm not sure why.

Aunt Rita comes in from the bedroom. She is regal, as always, but her auburn hair is now short and white, and she has put on much weight. Still, she is dressed in a fashionable mauve caftan with gold trim, her hair is styled, and she wears bracelets, rings, and lipstick. Beatrice and I get up to kiss her. She looks at

Beatrice, and admonishes, "It takes a visit from Rita to get you to come see me?" and then turns to me, and accuses, "You didn't come to see me the last time you were in Greece."
I decide not to be defensive. "No, I'm sorry, I didn't. But I am here now."
She ponders for a moment and motions towards the couch. "Sit wherever you like," she says.
The maid brings out a tray of brownies, but there is no sign of the beautiful pastries that Beatrice and I brought. Once we have been chastised, the visit is pleasant, and we chat until Rita is tired and we are dismissed.

Beatrice and I go to lunch at a corner café in Kolonaki and she tells me that she is no longer working at the gallery on Paros. The economy has forced the closing of the art gallery where she has worked the last several summers. She now manages the apartment building where she and her boyfriend live in Athens. The economy, it seems, has affected everyone. Even those who have jobs and money have seen an increase in their costs of living. I learn that the cost of a car license is about $1500 per year. I already know that gas is expensive, because it took the equivalent of $80 to fill the tank of the small Hyundai. In Marathon, Roi told me that the cost to heat their small house is about $600 per month for the six months that require heat. Again, I wonder how people can survive in Greece on little or no income.

On my last morning in Greece I awaken to a mad chorus of birds. The fan I've set up in front of the window hums softly as it rotates the fresh outside air in and I wrap the sheet around me. I'm tired, but I want to see the sunrise. Although it's only 5:45, I get out of bed and go outside. From my vantage point on the roof I can see an almost white sky to my left, suffused by a pale pink pre-dawn light. The sun has yet to rise over the mountains. On the other side of the balcony, over the sea, the sky is the same light grey-blue as the water, and only the ripples in the waves differentiate sea from sky.

The birds' song is now accompanied by the whizzing of cars and the honking of horns on *Leoforos* Poseidon below. The hue of the sky in the east has changed. If I were to name a paint color, I would call it rose parchment. As the sun ascends it is diffused by a yellow gold. In its light, the ferry boats returning to

Piraeus from the islands are illuminated, and in the pink-gold glow, I spot a distant island that I have never seen in the haze of day. The sun emerges in its full brilliance and the soft pale sky is immediately sharpened by the sunlight which gives clarity to the buildings and the mountains. On the highest distant peak, a Greek flag waves.

    I suppose it is not a spectacular sunrise. Except for the fact that it is Greece, and perfect, and I have watched the sky and the world around me change colors, and I've listened to the sound of the birds go from full orchestra to a few random solos, and heard the coo-coo-coo of pigeons dim and the noise of traffic quicken. And now I can hear the sound of trucks up in the platia, and I have spent an hour waking up to sunrise on my last day in Greece, and know that I will miss it in my heart.

    Since I am up so early, I take a walk down to the beach. At 8:00 a.m. there are already several women bathing, and a few men lay on towels. I have not worn my swimsuit – I had not planned to swim. The sun is warm, and the water lures me. I find a discreet place behind a wall, take off my sundress, hang it on the stone wall, and plunge in wearing only my panties. I revel in the pleasure of cool water on my nearly naked skin.

    As I later eat toast and cheese with Helen in the kitchen, and sip my coffee, I am happy to have savored every minute of the morning.

When I return from Greece, I upload my photographs to my computer. Just before my trip, I had bought a new camera with a 50X Zoom capability in order to take candid shots of my potential painting subjects. During the trip, I took some photographs in "stealth mode," zooming in on people on street corners, in the *platias,* at restaurants, to capture unsuspecting subjects in interesting places. Ironically, when I look at these pictures, often the subjects of my "candid" shots are looking right at me!

    I am looking through these photographs of the village. A dark haired woman in a flowered blouse intently waters the plants in front of Dimitri's Restaurant with a green garden hose; another woman in a long grey cotton halter dress glances over the ripe melons and apples displayed in cardboard boxes in front of the grocery store. Two grey-haired men sit outside of a coffee shop and sip thick Greek coffee from small demitasse cups as they watch her go into the store. An old woman sits on the whitewashed steps in front of her house, hunched forward, the weight of her elbows on her knees. She looks past her grandson who rides his bicycle, a little wobbly on his training wheels. His curly-haired little sister wrinkles up her nose and makes a face. I laugh at this picture, which reminds me of Nick and Alexandra at that age. The Orthodox priest, tall in his long black robes and long grey beard squints to look across the street as he approaches the church; he holds sunglasses in his hand. There is an apparent absence of young adults in the platia, and I wonder where they are.

    I scroll to the next photograph. Four men sit at a table in front of a taverna. The chairs in the center of the platia obstruct my view of the table. I assume they are drinking coffee - they might be drinking ouzo. One man talks animatedly while one listens closely. A younger man with a short beard and a necklace is headed into the kafeneio. Another man is watching him. He has thick dark hair and sideburns and a day's growth of beard. He is wearing a grey tank top. It is Michael the Goatherd!

    Before my imagination begins to run amuck and I once again come dangerously close to cheap romance novel territory, I think about what he had said to Uncle George: "Where would I find a wife who would want to stay in the village?" The daydream of the shower was, after all, only a daydream. If my husband were to attempt to come into the shower with the grease from his dirt bike on his hands, and the sweat of the afternoon on him, chances are greater that I would say, "Wait until I'm finished," than, "Baby, come in and let me soap you off." The village is charming, and the country is simple, quaint, and serene. Yet, there is the reality of actually living in a small village versus vacationing in a boutique hotel. Walking up to the platia to have dinner with my friends each night would be far less likely than my cooking not only lunch, but dinner while my husband sips Greek coffee with his friends. My friend, Daniela, has returned to her parents' village in Italy and has had the same daydream. "But the reality," she says, "is also that there's no good shopping and internet is slow and expensive. There's weird anti-woman gossip in villages that keeps women in their houses, except at festival time. There's a lot of fun to be had as an American woman on vacation."

I wonder whether the romantic notion of life in the village is unrealistic. Perhaps the part of me that longs for a simple life in the village with a passionate Greek man would become bored with the sunshine, the sea, the passion...and the fresh lemons, cherries, and *horta*. When fall arrived would I content myself with the sweaters at night and the departure of the tourists, or would I miss hockey, opera, the changing of the leaves, and – dare I admit – Starbucks? What about the women who would become my friends? Would they be educated – able to discuss literature, art, and sports? Who would I talk to when my husband was not around? What would I talk about with him? Would I even have time to talk, or would I be busy watering the garden, pulling weeds, doing laundry, cooking, and keeping house? Would the oil paint under my nails be replaced by garden dirt? Would I be able to walk into the platia for coffee – would I be the only woman there – would *I* be the victim of anti-woman gossip?

I suppose that gossip has always existed in small towns. I know this because of the stories I have heard of my great aunt Loukia who, almost 100 years before, fell in love with Panos and was chastised for it. And because of the whispering of Yiayia Olga's friends, all immigrants from Greek villages, whose gossip turned Olga against my father.

I think about the women from the village with whom I've spoken. Pitsa has lived close to Xirokambi all of her life. Her father emigrated to America, where he had hoped to bring his family. But he lost what money he had, and returned to the village of Katsouleika. Pitsa was six years old in 1941 when her village was occupied by the Germans. Greece was suffering as the Germans appropriated livestock and farm production, and in the winter of '41 and '42, wide-scale famine resulted. Pitsa's mother planted beans so that they had something to eat other than the bread which they made from corn they ground into flour. Breakfast, lunch, and dinner were often identical. Resistance movements sprang up in the mountains and villages, and the Germans were on alert. Pitsa watched a villager from the small window in her kitchen as he walked down the dirt road past her house. A German soldier called out, and raised his rifle. The man put his hands up over his head. The German soldier shot him point blank. Pitsa slept with her mother after that. These are her childhood memories.

She is now close to eighty. She has never worked outside the home – her job has always been raising children and taking care of the home. She and George travel, but they have never considered leaving the village. Their daughter, Maria, grew up in Kamenia and Xirokambi, and like most of her friends, she left the village at age 18 after she finished high school. Some of her friends moved to Athens to find work, some like Maria studied there. Most of them did not return to the village. This was in the late seventies, after a decade of high economic growth and low unemployment.

Helen, my friend from the states, and her husband Panos visit Greece often and stay for several weeks. Helen is a champion of the environment. The stories in the American newspapers upset her, and she finds comfort in the village life. Panos's village, Paliochori, just up the mountain, is even smaller than Xirokambi. It has no platia, and only twenty-two houses, nine of which are occupied by year-round residents. In the 1950's when Panos was a child in Paliochori, over 200 people resided there. By 1960, the census placed the population of Paliochori at 155. Now there are less than twenty permanent residents. Some emigrated to Australia, some to America, some moved to Athens, some simply to larger villages. Children of the villagers left and did not return. The population is old, and with every citizen who passes away, gets smaller. The only hope is in people like Panos, who is remodeling his family home and hopes to spend much of his time in retirement in Paliochori.

I admit that when it comes to Greece, I am guilty of wearing rose-colored glasses. I see a small stucco cottage and smell the sweet lavender next to the path, and I think, "I could live here." The village air is fresh, and pollution-free, and smells of olive groves, citrus trees, and sweet dried grasses. The cicadas sing in the early morning and late evening. There is a charm to the whitewashed buildings against the bright blue sky, and the white shirts and colorful skirts which hang from the clotheslines in the yards. Clearly, life in Xirokambi is much different than it was a hundred years ago. Some of the buildings are still standing – the school that my uncle attended, the church where he worshipped – but many have been replaced with modern brick buildings with electricity. Most of the homes have indoor plumbing and internet access, and the romantic notion of village life is less a harkening back to life in the early 1900's than it is a contrast to city life.

At home I complain because the walk-in closet isn't large enough for all of my shoes, and I don't have a finished basement. And while I doubt that the village women still use *ventouzes* to lower a fever, I'm guessing that the medical facilities in Pittsburgh far exceed those of Greek villages. Yet, there is something pure, simple, and organic about village life, and when I think of Xirokambi, I long to be back in the village, waking early to the sound of the roosters announcing daybreak, and taking a morning walk past the ancient olive groves with their gnarled grey trunks, Mount Tayetos rising tall above the pines which grow thick at its base.

Soon after arriving back in the states, I prepare to leave for California. I have been trying to convince my husband to visit his cousins in San Diego. It has been several years since he has seen them, and after hearing me talk about my visits with my Greek cousins, he finally agrees that we should go. We fly to California in late July, and spend several days reacquainting ourselves with his cousins, aunt, and uncle. Towards the end of the week, we drive to Anaheim to visit my mother's brother Angelo and his wife Joyce. My cousin Lisa greets us at the door. "Dad has gotten forgetful," she says, "but he's glad that you're here." Uncle Angelo seems to know me, and he reminisces about his brothers and sister, and growing up in Oakland.

"Oh, guess who came to see me," he says. "Patrick."

"Patrick?" I ask. Angelo's son to Jane, who he had been forbidden to see? I am dumbfounded. The last I knew, Patrick did not know who his father was, let alone make contact with him.

"Yes," Angelo continues, cheerfully. "He looked me up, can you believe it? Here, I'll give you his number, if you want to call him." He writes down Patrick's address and phone number on a card.

When I return home, I send Patrick a letter, explaining who I am, and that I will be calling. I don't want to blindside him, and I don't know how receptive he will be. I go through my old files, and find the article and photograph that I had cut out of the Moon

Record over forty years ago. A few weeks later, I phone him at his home in Colorado. A woman answers.

"Hello," I say. "Is Patrick Nefos there?"

"Who's calling?"

"This is his.... cousin Rita in Pittsburgh."

We start the conversation tentatively. He was surprised to get my letter, as he had no idea that anyone knew of his existence. He, himself, had no idea who his father was until his mother died. Patrick's wife, Donna, was going through a box of old papers, and found a document from the railroad with the name "Angelo Nefos" on it. Donna did some research, and found Angelo in California. Patrick stopped to see him while on a business trip.

"I was surprised," he tells me. "I looked more like Angelo than his other children. It was a little awkward." Patrick confirms the story that I have heard – that Jane's uncle threw Angelo out of the hospital room. "I didn't know where he was," he says. "I thought he was in Greece. I never knew that I had family here."

We send each other photographs, and plan to stay in touch.

ROOTS - *Rizes*: ΡΙΖΕΣ

I make plans to return to Greece the following year. The pull of my roots is stronger than ever, and I have unfinished business. I want to return to Xirokambi, but this time, I want my mother to come.

We have talked about her traveling to Greece. She has traveled to California to visit her brother, and she has flown to Pittsburgh and Philadelphia several times. At the age of 87 she still plays tennis, and I am confident that she can weather the long flight to Greece. She has not been there since before my father passed away, and although she talks wistfully about the hours spent on Loula's balcony, and how much she misses everyone, when I ask her to go, she usually says, "We'll see. Maybe next year." I try a different tactic.

"Mom! Aunt Helen is *a hundred*!" I say. "How much longer are you going to wait?"

"Okay," she says.

"Okay? You'll go?"

"Yes, why not?"

We make plans to travel in June of 2014, and Ellen agrees to join us, although it will be a busy summer for her. She is getting remarried in September.

Alexandra and Matt separate in April, after four years of marriage. Their initial love for each other could not withstand their philosophical differences. Matt was from a small town where hunting was King, fishing was Queen, and Bud Light completed the triumvirate. Country music ruled the airwaves and higher education was an afterthought. Alexandra was a motivated, educated, responsible woman. She was lured by the romance of the situation, only to be disappointed by the reality of it. After a difficult year, and a very difficult decision, she is saddened and disillusioned. I ask Alexandra if she'd like to come with me to Greece. I imagine that it will do her a world of good. My friend, Joyce, the artist, has already expressed her desire to visit Greece, so we make our plans. They will join me for the last two weeks. Mom, Ellen, and I will travel over together first. Ellen can only stay for one week, and mom, despite my attempts to persuade her to stay longer, decides that she will return with Ellen.

We have one week to make sure that Mom sees everyone that she wants to see, and we are off on a whirlwind visit that takes us to Voula, Athens, Marathon, and Xirokambi. And somehow, with my little blue five-speed Jetta and a GPS system, we get Mom everywhere she needs to go.

Aunt Loula can no longer walk and relies on a wheelchair. She is overjoyed to see us, but her smile turns quickly to tears. Cousin Helen explains that her mother is very emotional and cries often. They have finally told her that her brother George passed away, but they will not tell her that her sister Sassa died the previous year. Loula is hard of hearing and cannot speak on the phone. There is no reason to upset her, they say, because there is no way for her to know.

My mother sits with Aunt Loula. Her calm manner has a soothing effect, and soon Loula is smiling. She says little, but holds my mother's hand in her palm, patting it with the other hand, and for the time being, is comforted.

We leave the next morning for Xirokambi, and Mom meets her cousin George for the first time. George takes us to the cemetery in Kamenia. Pitsa has cut light pink roses from her yard for us to place on the box that holds Uncle Nick's ashes. On the way, George tells us that his father and Mom's father, Ahileas, were first cousins. He then tells us that Ahileas was not from Xirokambi or Kamenia, but from the state of Mani, more specifically the village of Milea. I try to subdue my frustration at the spoon-feeding of ancestral information. Where was this information last year?

At least now I can speculate that it was on a visit to Kamenia to see relatives that Ahileas first saw Olga.

George, Mom, Ellen, and I crowd into the dark chamber that houses the boxes of bones, and the box with Nick's ashes. He pulls the box from the shelf, and this time, as he takes it out I notice some writing on the lid: ΝΙΦΑΚΟΣ.

"What does that say?" I ask George.
"It says Nifakos."
"What is that?
"What do you mean, what is that?" George asks.
"What does it mean?"

"It means Nifakos. It is your uncle. Nikos Nifakos."
"But, his name wasn't Nifakos," I say. It was Nefopoulas."
"No," George insists, "it was Nifakos. Nikolas Nifakos." Mom has never heard this name before. The immigration documentation from Ellis Island lists my grandfather as Ahileas Nifopoulos. We have no idea what to make of this.

The day has been a long one, and after a late dinner, we take Mom back to the hotel. Ellen and I have a full night ahead of us. With the wonders of modern technology, I have discovered George, the boy from Baltimore from so many years ago. We have corresponded, and discovered that his hometown is also in the Peloponnese, only 20 minutes from Xirokambi. He is in Greece, remodeling the village house, and will be in Sparta that night with his cousins at a new jazz club, Leski.

Ellen and I drive into Sparta around ten o'clock, but the directions we got were faulty. We have only a vague idea where we are, and we can't find a parking space. After about fifteen minutes, Ellen spots one, and we squeeze in. Music blares from nightclubs – the treble of bouzouki mixed with the bass of American dance music – and patrons sit outside of cafes drinking coffee or ouzo. We stop at the first café.

"*Signomi* - excuse me, can you tell me where Leski is?" I ask the group of twenty-somethings who are sitting at an outside table. The man closest to us rolls his eyes and nods toward the street, unsmiling. We have apparently parked right across the street from Leski. Outside in the square in front of the club a tall man with silver hair stands, scanning the area. He is handsome, dressed in off-white pants, a light pink shirt, and a cream-colored sweater tied over his shoulders. On his feet are loafers without socks.

"I bet that's him," Ellen giggles.
"Do you really think so?" I ask.
The man turns towards us and smiles, his teeth bright white against his tan face.

After forty years, I think that I expected perhaps a heart palpitation, but I don't recognize the boy from my memory with his dark wavy hair under his fisherman's cap. We pass a pleasant hour with George and his cousins, and he invites us to visit the village home when we have time. They are off to Krokees. Ellen and I have more socializing to do. We are meeting Stratos and John.

Stratos finds us in the square full of people heading to or from the myriad of bars and clubs that surround the platia. We follow him to a bar on a side street, where John sits outside. He is sporting a full beard and stands up and hugs me. Stratos, also with a full beard, a little more unruly than John's, leads us all inside, but it is dark and loud, and we have to shout over the music to be heard. Ellen, John, and I go back outside where it is easier to talk without the din of cranked up dance music. John tells us that he has still not found work and now stays with his mother and stepfather in Sparta. He is more somber than last year.

Stratos comes out to get us. He is full of energy and hopping around, but we are relaxed and enjoying the cool evening. He finally sits down.

"She wants to be your mother-in-law," he says to John, nodding towards me, and I laugh.

"Okay," John says, and smiles at me. "But you can't live with us."

The late hour has caught up with us, and Ellen and I get up to leave. John says that he looks forward to seeing Alexandra when we return to Sparta the next week.

We leave Xirokambi after lunch the next day and set out for Vlahokerasia. Mom and Ellen have not been to the village. I drive to the *kafeneio* that I had been to the previous year, in the hope of finding Christos Mandros again. Christos is not there, but his wife, Antonia, is working. It is mid-afternoon, and there are no other patrons at the café. Antonia remembers me from my brief visit the past summer. We sit on the covered porch, out of the midday sun. She prepares Greek coffee for me and hot mountain tea for Ellen and Mom. She asks if I have found any more information on the Langas family, and I tell her that I have not.

"Langas is not from Vlahokerasia," she says, and I sit back, my eyes large. (Now what am I going to find out? That we're from Turkey?) But, she continues, "They are actually from *Ker*asia. The next village over." She points down the road, and I let out the breath I have been holding. "That is my house," she says, pointing across the road. "I was born in the yard."

"The yard?" I say, thinking that I have mistranslated.
"Yes. When the Germans came they burned the village down. I was born in the yard. My father was a prisoner of war. They fed him potato skins."
"But, why did they burn the village down? Weren't they occupying the village?"
She shrugs – a gesture that is becoming familiar to me.

At the end of the week we take a day trip to Marathon to visit Cousin Rena, Roi and Niko. Rena's daughter and grandchildren are there, as is Aunt Helen, who is now 100 years old. Roi fixes us cold coffee frappes, and we set out sweets that we purchased early that morning in the platia at Voula. We sip our frappes on the covered patio as we tell them about our trip so far, and our stop in Vlahokerasia.

"Your Uncle Deno used to go to Vlahokerasia during the war," Roi says.

"Why would he go there? Wasn't it occupied by the Germans?" I asked.

"Before the Germans came, Deno would go back to the village to eat. Food was scarce in Athens, but in the villages they still had chickens, tomatoes...."

"So, there were still relatives there?"

"Yes," Roi says. "Some uncles, some relatives. I'm not sure. But Uncle Deno ate well, while the Italians ate cats and bitter oranges."

"I thought we were talking about the Germans?" I realize that it is time for a history lesson. On October 28, 1940 Italian Ambassador Emmanuel Grazzi presented Greek Premier Ioannis Metaxas with an ultimatum from the Italian dictator Benito Mussolini: Allow Axis forces to enter Greek territory and occupy certain strategic locations, or face war. Metaxas refused. This standing up to the Axis powers is celebrated in Greece every year on October 28. The holiday is called *OXI*, meaning NO. The Italian troops stationed in Albania attacked the Greek border that day, thrusting Greece into World War II. In March of 1941, with the bulk of the Greek army fighting the Italians in the mountains on the Albanian border, German troops invaded through Bulgaria. The German troops reached Athens in late April.

Our Uncle Deno was a student at the University of Athens when the hostilities broke out. Horrified by the actions of the Germans – public executions, the burning of homes and property, the withholding of food and water – he joined the resistance movement with the Greek People's Liberation Army, known as ELAS. He fled Athens with several other men in a rowboat, taking two weeks to get to Turkey, where he was given the responsibly of transporting British servicemen to Egypt. From there, Deno boarded a Liberty Ship to the United States to join the Allied Forces, and was assigned to a submarine which took him to Spain, France, and Belgium. Rena laughs as she tells me a story about Uncle Deno falling asleep in a field in Belgium, and waking up with a cow licking his face. Hearing this reminds me of my father's stories – we are shielded from battle stories, and tales of sorrow, but entertained by the humorous aspects of their service. Perhaps the reality of war is too painful. By the end of the occupation, Greece suffered over 400,000 casualties. Deno was awarded the U.S. Medal of Freedom.

Aunt Helen, who in the past has sat quietly listening to conversation and occasionally chiming in, jumps in to the topic of the war. Her memories of Athens during *H Katochi*, the occupation, are vivid.

"There was a boy from a poor family, I remember," she says in Greek. We had little food. But one young boy came to the door. '*Pinao, pinao* – I'm hungry,' he would say. And we would give him bread when we could. But sometimes we had nothing to give him. People would eat garbage. They died from the worms." Aunt Helen pauses, then continues. "When we could, we visited my mother-in-law in Glyfada. It took two days to get there from Athens." Glyfada was next to Voula. It was less than twenty miles from Athens. I am grateful for my Greek lessons, which have allowed me to understand most of the conversation, with very little clarification. I ask my aunt why it took so long to get to Glyfada.

"We would walk from Athens to Kolonaki. From there we would take a truck to Glyfada. Sometimes it took more than two days. But there was food in Glyfada. My in-laws had two goats, a hen, tomatoes, potatoes…" her voice trails off. "The Germans would carry fresh baked loaves of bread. Children would beg for just a piece of bread. They were so hungry. And the Germans kicked them away. I saw this." She again pauses, then continues, "There was a woman who lost her husband. My mother-in-law would make beans with onions. We would share with this woman. It was a small portion. Maybe one onion and some beans. And she would kiss my mother-in-law's hand for just this small amount of food."

Roi speaks. "I remember when they bombed Piraeus in 1944." She was only six years old then. "We could hear it all the way in Glyfada."

"Yes, I remember," says Aunt Helen. She pauses, recalling something else, and smiles. "I always liked fresh flowers," she says. "One day I went across the street to the park to cut flowers from the mulberry bushes. But there was a firefight. I had to run across the street. Your uncle yelled at me and told me never to do this again. But, I got the flowers," she says.

"Yes, I know this story," Rena frowns. "You were pregnant with me."

"When were you born?" I ask Rena.

"Ah, you don't know this?" she asks. "I was born on May 9, 1945. The Day of Peace. That is my name, *Irini*. It means peace."

Thanos meets us in Voula the next night, and the four of us walk to Platia Voula for dinner. I look at my mother across the table from me. It is twilight, early for dinner in Greece, and the tables in front of Antonis' Restaurant are empty, except for ours. Although the night is warm, my mother wears a lightweight white jacket. Her hair is drawn back into a low ponytail, but the breeze has captured some of the stray ends which now frame her face. She looks much younger than her eighty-seven years, despite the fact that she has been on the go for almost a week, has stayed up past midnight almost every night, and has seen more relatives in the last six days than she has in years. Soon the conversation turns to broader matters, and Thanos speaks pessimistically about Greece, the economy, and the laziness of the younger generation (his 38-year old son among them), while smoking one unfiltered cigarette after another.

I tell Thanos about our conversations in Marathon about the German occupation, and he in turn tells us a story about my great-aunt Chrysoula. All that I recall from previous conversations was that she and her husband had a kafeneio in the village.

"Chrysoula – she was your grandmother's oldest sister – you remember?" Thanos asks. I nod.

"She died during the German occupation," Thanos says.

"How?"

Chrysoula, Thanos continues, had appendicitis. She and her husband traveled to Athens for the appendectomy. They had little money, and hoped to barter for the doctor's fee. The doctor asked for four cans of olive oil to perform the operation, but they only had two.

"So what happened?" I asked.

"The doctor refused the operation," Thanos says, and takes a deep puff of his cigarette. He exhales slowly and presses the cigarette butt into the metal ash tray. "So she died."

Ellen and I sit, silent in our thoughts, but Thanos is not finished with the story.

"I don't know what happened to all of her children," he says. "One of Chrysoula's sons traveled with the carnival. Her daughter was very attractive – she became a prostitute, and *her* daughter followed in her footsteps."

"What happened to them?" I ask.

Thanos raises his eyebrows and shrugs.

Mom and Ellen leave the next morning. I have two days to myself before Alexandra and Joyce come in. I spend the first day hanging out with Cousin Helen and catching up with laundry and a few errands in the platia. It's about seven in the evening – the breeze is a little cooler after a very hot day. I decide to treat myself to a lemonade at one of the restaurants in the square. Few people sit under the umbrellas at this odd hour. I order a *Lemonita*, which I discover is a carbonated lemon drink. It's not what I expected, but it's cold, delicious, and served with a glass of ice and a lemon slice. I reflect back on the week, still amazed that I really did manage to get mom to see everyone that she needed to see. I guess Ellen was right – a week was all they needed, but I can't imagine only going to Greece for a week. Each time that I visit Greece, I want to stay longer. I'm not even sure that three weeks will be enough this year.

I return to the apartment, and Helen and I go downstairs to spend some time with Aunt Loula. She is in a talkative mood, and tells me about her days in Oakland, when she lived in the states.

"We lived in Oakland," she says in Greek, "in a house next to a friend of my mother."

"Your mother was back in Greece?" I asked

"Yes, I lived with my father and Sassa. I was engaged to Costa. I didn't want to stay in America. But my father wanted me to come."

"Did my father live with you?"

"No, he lived in a rooming house. He worked at the restaurant."

"Did you work there, too?"

Loula laughs. "Me? No. Sassa and I didn't work."

"What did you do?"

"We shopped," she says. "And we cooked. Sassa asked your father to come to dinner many times. But, he refused to wear a tie, so she would not let him in!"

I laugh, because I know that he was the only Director at Robert Morris College who refused to wear a tie to work. Old habits die hard.

Aunt Loula reflects. "It was hard to live without my mother. Kiria Sikioti lived next door. She taught us things. She was the one who told us about shaving our legs and our underarms. We didn't know."

Cousin Helen interrupts. "Mama, isn't she the sister of Ritsou, the one who...."

Aunt Loula laughs, and replies rapidly in Greek, and I can't follow her conversation.

Helen explains. "Kiria Sikioti's sister, Kiria Ritsou was your grandmother Coula's best friend. She was getting divorced, and Coula told her to go to Saryas, her husband. Well...they fell in love. He divorced Coula and married Kiria Ritsou!"

"But isn't that what happened when Saryas met Yiayia Coula?"

"Yes," Helen says. "She should have known better. But, I think that she loved him. She was very sad." She and Aunt Loula exchange a few more words. "There is a lot of, how do you say - scandal, in the family," she laughs. Your Aunt Rita had several affairs. You didn't know this?"

I'm surprised that this is common knowledge, yet not surprised that I didn't know. My father never talked about his family. Everything is a discovery to me. I had always taken my relatives' prosperity for granted. I had no idea of their struggles during the war years and the things that my ancestors had to do just to survive. I have learned of relatives whom I had not known existed, and have realized that I am most likely not "one-hundred percent Greek." I wonder what else I have yet to discover.

By the Acropolis, oil painting, Wilson

ATHENS - *Athina*: ΑΘΗΝΑ

The next morning I grab an hour of beach time before I have to pack and return the rental car in Glyfada. It's the next suburb in the direction of Athens, and I figure that it would be easier to return the car here than in the busy city. I am sorely mistaken. I follow the GPS directions, but when I get to the street that Budget Rental Car is on, I see nothing but department stores, boutiques, restaurants, and offices. I don't remember Glyfada being so busy. I call Budget from my phone, and a woman tells me to turn around.
"The sign is out front," she says.
I make a U-turn and drive a few blocks, but I still don't see it. I call again. "It is next to the department store," she says. I slow down, look around, but I see no rental car sign and no parking lot with rental cars. I call again. This time, a man answers, and I explain my dilemma. He laughs. "Come back down the street. I will go outside and wait for you." I start to drive. "I see you," he says. "Make a U-turn, and I will wave to you!"
I see a young man in a light blue shirt and jeans waving, and I double park next to another car. There is nowhere to park on this busy street. "Where is the rental car office?" I ask. He points to an office building.
"It's on the second floor."

"Where is the sign?" I ask. He points back to the office building. On the second floor, in a window, is a small sign, about one foot by one foot, which reads "Budget."
"You have got to be kidding!" I say, and he laughs again.
"Where is the parking lot?" I ask.
"Parking lot?"
"I was looking for a parking lot. For the rental cars."
"Oh, we have no parking lot here. We just park on the street."
I am sweltering in the mid-afternoon sun. It is about ninety degrees. It took me only fifteen minutes to get to Glyfada, but a half hour to find Budget. My nerves are frayed. "Can you call me a taxi to take me to Athens?"
He points down the street. "Go down there a few blocks. You will be able to find a taxi."
I drag both of my suitcases behind me on the rough pavement as they wobble like sliding doors off their tracks. I stand on the corner, attempting to wave down a taxi, and after about five minutes, one pulls over. The driver gets out, puts my suitcases in the trunk, and I get in.
"*Pou pas* - where are you going?"
"*This*sio," I reply.
"*Pou?*" he asks, as he pulls away from the curb.
"*Thissio*," I say, thinking perhaps I have put the accent on the wrong syllable.
He reaches into the glove compartment, his left hand still on the wheel, and pulls out a city atlas. Driving with one eye on the road, he flips the pages and scans the maps with the other eye.
"Maybe I should get another taxi?" I say.
"No, no. I will find it."

He does find it, after about a half hour, and I realize that I am actually early for checking into the apartment. "I understand that there are some coffee shops around here. Do you mind dropping me off at one, and I'll just walk over to the apartment when it's ready."
"*Vevaios* - of course," he says, and drives around the block in search of a coffee shop. "Ah, I know where this is now!" he says. "I recognize this place." He pulls expertly into a small parking spot.

"Would you like to have coffee with me?" he asks. "Do you mind if I join you?"

I'm glad to have company while I wait in a strange neighborhood. "No, I don't mind. That would be nice."

We cross the road, and walk up a street that is lined on each side with kafenios and restaurants. It is one-thirty in the afternoon, and although it is quite hot again today, the umbrellas over the tables and chairs provide enough shade to make sitting outside pleasant. The taxi driver's name is Dimitri. He is from New Zealand, Greek by nationality. We order frappes, and pass the time talking about New Zealand, Pittsburgh, art, the Greek economy. And now, I am late for my appointment at the apartment. "Oh, I have to go!" I say. I reach for the bill.

"No, no. I have it," he says. I am about to argue, but think back to Niko and Markos in Xirokambi.

"*Efharisto*, Thank you."

We walk back to the taxi. He pulls up in front of the apartment, and I ask for the fare. I notice that the meter reads thirteen euros. "Ten euros," he says.

"I know it's more than that," I say. "What do I owe you?"

"Ten euros is fine," he says. I get out, and he writes his number down on a piece of paper and hands it to me. "If you need anything," he says, and smiles.

The ad for the apartment on tripadvisor.com read, "Live Like An Athenian In Athens!" Except for staying in Athens during my first trip to Greece as a child, I have only spent a day here and there visiting the Acropolis or a museum. I want to see what it is like to "live like an Athenian." I unpack and try to take a nap, but my head is full of chatter. I hear the voices of my relatives, some in Greek, and some in broken English, and I give up on the nap. I shower and go for a walk, trying to follow the small map that the landlord has given me. I pass the same coffee shop that I had gone to earlier, and I'm pleased with the sudden sense of familiarity. I walk up a slight grade, and when I get to the end of the cobblestone street, I am awestruck. Ahead of me, on top of the mountain, sits the Parthenon, shining white against a backdrop of crystal clear cerulean sky. The sun is still bright at 7:30 p.m., and I take a seat at Athvaion Politeia, where I can continue to view the Acropolis. A glass of white wine; a bacon, feta, and spinach crepe;

and the cool mist of a spray from the awnings makes me forget that it is close to ninety degrees. I'm looking forward to seeing Joyce and Alexandra, but after the whirlwind of activity the last week, I savor this brief bit of independence.

Joyce and Alexandra arrive the next morning, and we live like Athenians for four days. Three women and one bathroom is a challenge, especially when we blow the hairdryer up and lose our electricity, but we cohabitate well. We walk almost everywhere, including the nearby *kafenieos*, restaurants, *Monasteraki* (the Greek souvenir shopper's paradise), bars, museums, the Acropolis. We find that the best restaurants are those hidden up stairways and down alleys – not frequented by tourists. On our first night we eat early for Greece – around six o'clock, as Joyce and Alexandra have not yet acclimated to Greek time. We discover an open restaurant off the main street and up a flight of steps. World Cup soccer plays on the television over the bar, and we sit outside across from it. We are the only patrons in the restaurant. We order a mezze platter. Whether it is our hunger, our joy at simply being together in Greece, or the fact that this may actually be the best thing that we have ever eaten in our lives, we savor every bite of the creamy feta cheese drizzled with olive oil and sprinkled with fresh oregano; the tender *keftedes* – small Greek meatballs soft in the inside and fried crunchy on the outside; spicy Greek sausage; crisp cucumbers and ripe juicy tomatoes; tangy, smooth *melitzanasalada* – eggplant salad; garlicky *taramousalata* spread; and of course, lemony *dolmadakia* - stuffed grape leaves – ground meat and rice seasoned expertly and rolled into bitter, savory grape leaves, accompanied by a glass of dry white wine.

    We return to the apartment to freshen up before walking to Monasteraki. We are meeting the boys from Sparta – the ones who we had met during our trip eight years ago. John is not in Athens, but the others are, and Stratos has asked us to meet him at a club where he "does some work." Because of the maze of streets in the area, Stratos comes to meet us at the church – a landmark in the area - and hurries us to the club. He deposits us at an outside high-top table, where his friends get up to give us their seats, and disappears into the bar. We are happy to see Stelios who looks the same as he did eight years ago, although he now wears a beard and mustache. He introduces us to his girlfriend, Vasiliki, who is studying for her master's degree while working full time at a job in communications. We order drinks – Stelio and Vasia have come on motorcycle and are only drinking water. Stelios tells us that he is working as a waiter – many hours, but that Vasia has encouraged him to return to school to finish his math studies. He is still lighthearted and humorous, but I'm impressed with his sense of responsibility.

We meet several of their friends as we sit at the table. There are many bars in the area, each with an inside bar with loud music, and an outside area for talking. Stelios and Vasia leave at about midnight. He hugs us warmly, and invites us to go to dinner with him on Saturday – he wants to take us to a favorite restaurant in Plaka, another old area at the base of the Acropolis.

They walk away from the bar, and Stratos appears at the table. He watches them depart, turns to us, and sneers. "They are in love." He draws out the word *love* distastefully.

"What's wrong with that?" I ask.

"I don't have a good feeling."

I don't understand, so I press. "Why?"

"She is not for him." He tries to explain his thoughts in broken English. The closest that I can come is *manipulative*.

"Why?" I say. "Because she wants him to go back to school?"

He shrugs. "Look at her," he says. "Do you think they belong together?"

"What do you mean?"

"Are they equal?" he says.

"Are they equal?" I ask. I hope that I am misunderstanding what he is saying. "Do you mean that she is not equal to him in looks?"

"Yes," Stratos says. "Look at Stelios and look at her. You will see what I mean."

"You are shallow!" I say.

"What you mean?" he says, but he knows from the tone of my voice that it is not a compliment.

"Shallow." I place my hand out flat and push it down to the table. "Shallow. Not deep. You see only the surface."

"I am not shallow," he says, and disappears once again to work the crowd.

We linger for a while, enjoying the company and the energy of the city. It is late, and the day has been long, so we leave to walk back. Stratos points us in the direction of the church. "It is not difficult," he says. "You will find it. From there you will know the way."

Within five minutes we are lost. The streets are quiet, and while we are not afraid, we are mildly concerned about finding our apartment. We turn the corner at the end of a narrow street, and see in front of us a large sign: LOUKOUMATHES. "Loukoumathes!" I say. The sweet smell wafts from the shop, which has a counter open to the sidewalk. We realize that it has been hours since we have eaten, and the thought and smell of these honeyed fried dough balls lures us across the street. I approach the young man behind the counter. "Can we get six loukoumathes?"

"I can only give you twelve," he says.

"Hmm. I don't think we can eat twelve."

He glances up at the clock, which now reads 2 a.m. "I will *give* you twelve," he says. "But you must eat them over there." He points to a picnic bench on the sidewalk.

"You'll *give* us twelve? Oh!" I realize. "You are closing!"

He smiles and nods. He turns and drops a dozen spoonfuls of dough into a vat of hot oil. Soon the sweet doughballs are fried to perfection, and he spoons them out. He places them on a paper plate and drizzles Nutella on them. I have never seen loukoumathes with Nutella. I am not complaining. We thank him profusely, and take our loukoumathes to the picnic table. Two young men are already sitting there next to each other, and we sit across from them. We have barely taken our seats before the young man in the shop is pulling down the shade.

Each bite of the sweet, doughy loukoumathes is better that the previous. As we savor our late-night dessert, we listen to the men across from us. A serious looking man with dark hair and glasses, perhaps in his late twenties or early thirties, is patiently correcting the Greek of a soft-spoken blond man of similar age. They, in turn, have been listening to us and realize that we have only an inkling of how to get home. "We will walk you there," the dark-haired man says. The other agrees.

As we walk down the deserted streets, their story unfolds. Mantea, the blond, is originally from Spain, but lives and works in

Denmark. He is on holiday by himself in Greece. He speaks softly, and his accent reminds me of Rafa Nadal, the tennis player, with his high-pitched resonance and thick accent. He and Dimitri met online, and have spent the last week together. Mantea walks with me and Alexandra. Dimitri walks up ahead with Joyce. Each tells his story, and we learn that it is their last night together.

"You don't have to walk us all the way," I say. "We can probably find it from here."

"No, it's okay," says Dimitri. "We don't mind walking." The night is warm and still. We have passed through the platia and are walking past the subway tunnel. Graffiti covers the concrete walls behind the subway track: 'Earth Metal' sprayed in English in large round yellow letters on one wall, *Lefteria stous kratoumenous* - 'Freedom to prisoners' sprayed in Greek in black on another. Across from, and between the restaurants which line the street across from the subway, every wall is decorated with graffiti.

"I don't understand this," I say. "Why are they destroying these buildings?"

Dimitri hears me and turns around. "Some, I think, is just for attention, you know? But some, it is desperate." He cites a statistic that we have come to know – fifty percent of citizens between the ages of twenty one and thirty are unemployed. "Fifty percent!" he repeats. It is a sobering statistic.

We reach a spot that we recognize, thank them profusely, and hug them goodbye. "I hope that you are able to come back to Greece," I say to Manthea.

"Oh, yes," he says. "I plan to come back!"

I look at Dimitri, and see the doubt in his smile.

The next morning, I am awakened by a phone call from George, one of the Greek students whom I taught at Robert Morris almost twenty years ago.

"You are sleeping?" he asks, and I mumble yes. "You came to Greece to sleep?" He is in Athens running errands the day before his wedding, and has invited me to go for coffee. Joyce and Alexandra are sleeping off their jet lag, and perhaps the wine from the night before. The taxi driver was not the only person who could not find the address – I walk a few blocks to an address that George recognizes, and he picks me up in his sedan.

"Why don't we just have coffee here?" I ask. "There are some very nice coffee shops close to the apartment."

"No," he says. "It is not so nice here. I want to take you somewhere in Piraeus. You have been to Piraeus?"

My recollection of Piraeus is the plethora of cruise ships and their loud, low horns, the glut of taxis and motorcycles, and the tearful goodbye that Alexandra and John had. It is a warm, hazy Friday morning around ten o'clock, and the traffic is as I remembered – bumper to bumper. Horns honk periodically, George's air conditioner is struggling, and I am wondering why we are driving to Piraeus. After about 20 minutes we pass the port to our left, drive around the bay, and park on a narrow side street. We walk up a set of stairs which open out onto a large covered restaurant. In the middle is a long bar. On either side of the bar are aluminum tables and chairs next to large open windows. We sit on the bay side, overlooking the water, the long shoreline, and mountains in the distance. A lone fishing boat with a single fisherman is anchored in the bay, the Greek flag waving from its port side. A little further out is a single sailboat, its sails still furled. A cool cross breeze blows through the restaurant. It must be ten degrees cooler here than in the center of Athens, less that twenty minutes away.

"Yes," George says. "That is why I brought you here." He sits across from me, sunglasses pushed back on his head, over his black hair which is now graying at the temples. He is no longer the twenty-two year old student I taught at Robert Morris, and it strikes me that I am not the forty-year old teacher that he said goodbye to almost twenty years ago. I find it hard to reconcile the person I am on the outside – a woman approaching sixty - with the young spirit that I have inside me, especially when I am in Greece. But I am not about to let this age-old conundrum ruin the delicious breeze, good company, and tasty cold frappe.

On Saturday, we travel to Marathon to visit Niko and Roi. We are getting comfortable living like Athenians, and take the metro to Kifisia, the end of the line, where we pick up a taxi the rest of the way. It is sweltering in Athens, and only slightly less warm in Kifisia, where a hot breeze persists. We arrive midday at Marathon and are warmly greeted by Niko, Roi, and Rena. They are interested in Joyce's art, and we sit outside and drink cold frappes while Joyce shows them photos of her artwork on her cell phone. We move inside for lunch; the large living-dining room with its cool tile floors and whitewashed walls feels cooler than the porch. Roi is also an artist, but she has not painted for several years. The walls of her living room are hung with her oil paintings: a seascape, a still life with flowers, a portrait of Niko. I ask her when she is going to paint again, but she tells me that she is finished. I try to entice her into a deal – I will create a painting for her if she will create one for me. But she lifts her chin, and that is the end of that.

Niko tells us that the bus into Athens is a better alternative than the taxi. He walks us into Marathon to show us where to wait. The bus is late, and Niko checks at the Kiosk down the street. "We have a new schedule," he says. "It is now July. It will be here in fifteen minutes, I think. It will come from there," he points down the road.

"It's okay," I say. "You don't have to wait with us."

But I am pleased when Niko replies, "No, no, no. I will wait. It is not a problem."

It is hard to leave these relatives when I don't know when I will see them again, and I savor the few extra minutes on the sidewalk with Niko until the bus to Athens pulls up, and we hug him goodbye.

That night Stelios meets us back at the Platia, motorcycle helmet in hand. The Platia is a cacophony of laughter, chatter, and music. From a makeshift stage, African drumbeats sound as dancers furiously stomp to the beat. Vendors hawk souvenirs from wooden stands and card tables, and men walk through the crowd selling neon braided bracelets. This could be any tourist town anywhere, and I am relieved when Stelios comes to rescue us. We weave through the crowd and follow him through a maze of narrow streets to Plaka, the oldest area in Athens, at the base of the Acropolis. We turn onto another narrow street, and arrive at a long flight of wide stone steps. Restaurants line each side of the steps, constructed unevenly to adjust to the steep slope of the hill. In front of each restaurant are one or two small tables, and as many wooden or metal chairs as can fit around the tables. Barely a path exists between the tables, and we climb, single file, to the top of the steps. Stelios spies a lone table and chairs among the crowds and speaks to a waitress. She moves some of the patrons around in order to seat us. Four others join us, including Stratos and a friend of his, and they squeeze in more chairs. We are practically on top of each other. We have to speak loudly over the laughter and chatter which bounces off of the restaurant walls in the narrow space. We hear only Greek around us. Stelios orders for us. This is his favorite place, and I am touched by his eagerness to share it with us.

It is fun to be in Athens with the boys from Sparta, but Alexandra was hoping that John would have come to Athens. He has told her that he cannot afford the trip, and that he will see her in Sparta. Stratos tells her not to expect things to be the same. "What do you mean?" She asks.

"You guys were kids," he says. "It was long ago. It's very different now. I don't think he has those feelings anymore." His comments add to the anxiety that she is already feeling.

Stratos introduces us to his friend Margaritas, a professional drift car racer. He has a dark mustache and beard, a huge smile, and is wearing a tight fitting "Superman" tee shirt. He speaks the least English of the group, but it doesn't keep him from trying. He is apparently successful in Greece, having won the title of "King of Europe" the previous year in the European drift racing circuit. It's not Europe that Margaritas is focused on. "I like Miami," he says. He tells me he went to America to compete, but did not have enough funds to complete the tour. "The women are beautiful. I like America. I would like to live there," he says. I'm doubtful that anyone in America is going to sponsor a thirty-year old Greek drift car racer, however entertaining he might be.

When we finish dinner Stelios leaves with two of his friends, and we are left with Stratos, Margaritas, and a large plate of watermelon, which Stratos eats voraciously. Two men next to us laugh, and offer their plate of watermelon to Stratos, and he takes it. Stratos decides that Joyce and Margaritas would make a good couple, despite the considerable difference in their ages. "Why not?" he says, as he leans over his plate and cuts a large chunk of watermelon with his fork. "I know women. You like him," he says to Joyce, pointing the fork with a large chunk of watermelon on it at her. "I know this."

"You know women?" Joyce asks Stratos, not amused.
"Yes," Margaritas says, nodding towards Stratos. "He is a guru." He laughs at the word.
"Really, Stratos?" Joyce says. "Lay some of that wisdom on me. Go ahead, tell me how you know everything about women."
The young men next to us make no attempt to hide their laughter. Stratos pouts, and stabs another piece of watermelon. Margaritas does not comprehend the conversation. He turns to me and asks me if I think that he has a chance to make it in America. We pay our bill, get up from our tables, and wonder how we will be able to weave our way down the steps between the tables and the people who are now sitting on the steps between the tables and chairs. One of the young men who has been sitting next to us stops Alexandra as she squeezes by. "I wanted to tell you that I've been looking at you all night," he says. "You are so pretty."
She smiles.
"Can I have a kiss?" he asks, and points to his cheek. "Please?"
She laughs and says, "Why not?" and bends down to gives him a kiss on the cheek.
"Yes!" he says.

Sunday is our last day in Athens, and despite the temperature in the nineties, we scale the Acropolis. It is not overly crowded. I overhear a man saying, "The last time I was here, you couldn't even move on these steps!" The marble steps he refers to have been worn smooth over hundreds of years of foot traffic. They lead up through a marble archway which opens up to the Parthenon, built over 2,000 years ago to pay tribute to the goddess Athena. Alexandra and I have been here before – it still renders us speechless. Joyce is struck with the artistic magnificence of the Doric temple, and even though the Parthenon has suffered erosion and damage over the centuries, its basic structure remains intact. From the Acropolis we look down at Plaka, where we had dinner last night. Beyond this is Syntagma Square, and the Athens National Garden, where I went after I visited Aunt Rita last year. In the background is Mt. Lycavittos, where Uncle Nick and Aunt Annaliese fell in love. North of the Acropolis is the Platia where we have walked for the past few days. Joyce and Alexandra are ready to leave Athens and head to Santorini, but I feel the familiar pang of loss at leaving a place that I have come to love.

Stelios has invited us to a party at his apartment to watch Greece vs. Costa Rica in the World Cup soccer tournament. We are a little weary and need to pack because we are waking up at five the next morning to get the ferry to Santorini. We consider passing on the invitation, but Stratos insists that Stelios is excited to have us come to see his apartment and host us for the party, so we acquiesce. The taxi ride is only fifteen minutes to Nea Psihiko. We are buzzed into a large two-story apartment where Stelios lives with three other roommates. Vasia greets us and shows us around, but apologizes that she will not be able to watch the game with us – she has homework. Stratos is preparing a dish with ground meat, potatoes, and of course, watermelon. Stelios ushers us upstairs to the roof, where he has set up his computer, a projector, a large screen, and a large cooler of beer, which he offers us. Around the perimeter of the rooftop is a bamboo fence. I walk toward it.

"Don't lean on that!" Stelios says. "You will fall!" I realize that it is a makeshift fence, and I'm shocked to realize that if you were to lean on it, you would fall over the balcony and onto the street. We sit down in an assortment of chairs which have been placed around a table across from the large screen, and Stelios gets the projector working. The game is about to begin when Stratos comes up with the plate of food, sets it down in front of himself, and tackles it ravenously. It is quiet on the rooftop. Only the announcers on the television and our conversation interrupt the stillness of the night, until Greece moves aggressively toward the goal at the ninety minute mark in hope of tying the game. From across the rooftops, we hear cheers. A second later, Greece scores on a rebound by Sokratis Papastathopoulous, and we realize that our computer feed is on a delay.

The game progresses into extra time, something that we do not understand, and then finally, a shootout, something that we, as hockey fans, do understand. We also understand the total silence in which these diehard fans are watching the end of the game. When Costa Rica scores to win in overtime, we realize that there is nothing that we can say to our friends at this moment. It is late – after one a.m. – and we wait a respectable five minutes or so before getting up to say our goodbyes and thank yous. Stratos grabs his motorcycle helmet and walks us to the corner to hail a taxi. The streets are desolate in this section of Athens, and we wait about fifteen minutes before we finally spot a taxi. We are hungry and tired, and we know that we only have about three hours of sleep ahead of us before we head to the port of Piraeus.

Santorini Blue, oil painting, Wilson

SANTORINI - *Fira*: ΦHPΆ

The cool breeze in Santorini is a welcome change from the sweltering temperatures in Athens. The view from Hotel Theoxenia, our boutique hotel in Thira, is of clear blue sky, ocean, and mountains on the horizon. We have no need for air-conditioning. Our room is on the third floor of the hotel, across the street from the cliff. Our doors open onto a small balcony and a patio, providing us with a fresh cross-breeze. Breakfast is served to us daily on the patio, and Alexandra's dream of wearing one of those fluffy white hotel robes comes true as we sit, overlooking the caldera, drinking strong coffee and eating an assortment of eggs, pastries, fruits, fresh yogurt, meats, and cheese pies.

We are indulging in our breakfast on our second day on the island, when three other guests of the hotel join us on the patio. They overhear us contemplating plans for the day, and a young woman says, "Oh, you should rent quads. We rented them yesterday. Had a blast!" She gives us the information, and within an hour we have booked a reservation for two quads. The guys from the rental place meet us at the end of the narrow street, and take us, one by one on motorcycles to the rental place. Alexandra goes first. The man returns for Joyce, and she stands, looking at the bike. "Go ahead, get on," I say, and still she hesitates. The man on the bike turns around to look at Joyce and repeats, "Get on!" She straddles the bike awkwardly, and grabs onto the man's stomach as he takes off with a lurch. He comes back for me in a few minutes. When I arrive, Joyce is laughing nervously.

"What's wrong?" I say.

"I've never been on a motorcycle before!"

"Oh, my god. I'm so sorry. I didn't realize that!" I pause. "Are you sure you're okay with renting a quad?"

"Yes, but *I'm* not driving it."

We rent one quad for Alexandra, and one for me and Joyce. The man at the desk is a swarthy looking man in his mid-thirties. His neon green tee shirt reveals a geometric tattoo covering his arm. He sports a small chin beard and silver rings on his ears. He reminds me of Captain Jack Sparrow. He asks whether we want the bigger engine, and when we hesitate he suggests that we start off with the smaller one.

We've taken some fruit and bread from breakfast and put that in the storage area in back of the quads, along with sunscreen, beach towels, and our purses. We're a little giddy at the prospect of driving the quads, and a little nervous about driving them on the main roads, which we'll be sharing with trucks, motorcycles, cars, and buses. We're feeling bold, and we take off to explore the island. Our goal, after a stop in Oia, is to find the black sand beach on the other side of the island.

We spend the morning traveling to Oia. After coffee and a sweet at a restaurant overlooking the sea, we consult the tourist map provided by the rental place, and head for the black sand beaches. After about an hour along the coast, we realize that we are lost. We drive up the hill to see if we might find some sort of civilization there among the dusty fields and small farms. I pull ahead into a crossroad, and spot a quad rental place on the corner. "Look!" I say. "They'll be able to tell us where to go!" I'm thrilled that there is a rental place on this side of the island.

I hop off the bike, hang my helmet on the handlebars, and approach the man behind the desk. He is a swarthy looking man in his mid-thirties, and I recognize him from the morning. "Hi!" I say, "I remember you!" He doesn't seem impressed. I wonder if he works at both places, but then I look around. The desk and rental area seem familiar. "Wait," I say, "Is this the same place I rented the bike from?"

"No," he says, with the tedium of someone who would rather be elsewhere. "I have a twin and he rented you the bike somewhere else."

I'm incredulous that after all of that driving, we ended up at the place we started this morning. I attempt to stave off humiliation and pretend that I know where I am, and I ask how to get to the black sand beach. He takes me out into the street and points the way. We ride for about an hour, and perceive that we are no closer to a black sand beach than we had been earlier. And we are hungry. The snacks in the storage compartment are long gone. We are riding up a long, steep hill. At this point we realize that we should have gotten the more powerful bikes, as every truck, motorcycle, bus, and quad passes us on the grade. We pull into a large dirt parking lot to stop and check our maps. Next to us is a big wooden storefront with the word TAVERNA hand painted across the front in large letters. "Let's eat here," I say, my stomach growling in agreement.

"Here?" Joyce asks. There doesn't appear to be anything *here*, but we notice a few cars in the parking lot. There is no way in to the building, but outside to the left are a set of steps, and we have nothing to lose. We walk down the steps, which open out onto a covered patio where several patrons sit at wooden tables and chairs overlooking the valley. We are tired, sweaty, and dirty. The waitress seats us and brings us complimentary cheese and olives, and some sort of clear drink in a short glass while we wait, in awe of the expansive valley below. The meal is superb, and ends with a complimentary dessert and warm red wine in shot glasses, which we only sip, as we may or may not have miles to go.

Once again, we ask directions, and finally, after about an hour, we find the black sand beach – Perissa. It is half past five, but the air is still warm, and there are empty lounge chairs on the beach. Alexandra and Joyce collect pebbles. I swim for a few minutes, and then relax in the lounge chair to rest up for the trek back to Thira, hoping that the route back will be more direct than the one we took to get here!

Santorini is one of the more popular and scenic islands in Greece. It's the one that all the post cards show of the whitewashed churches and hotels built into the Cliffside overlooking the caldera.

Its capital, Thira, is known for excellent souvenir shopping, mouth-watering restaurants, and a vibrant nightlife. I wanted Joyce and Alexandra to experience it, because if you don't get to Greece often, this is one island that you should see. But I would have preferred a small, less touristy island, and after three days, I am ready to return to the mainland, and to Xirokambi. We all have our reasons to be excited. Joyce has heard me talk of Xirokambi, seen my photos and paintings, and is anxious to see and photograph it for herself, I am looking forward to spending more time in a place where I feel so at home. And Alexandra is excited to be back in Sparta – and nervous about seeing John.

Tayetos, oil painting, Wilson, after photo by Louis Vlahakis

REUNITED - *Epanenomeni*: ΕΠΑΝΕΝΩΜΈΝΗ

We pull into Xirokambi around three o'clock on Friday afternoon. We are quite hungry, but the platia is empty. We find one restaurant serving food, and order beer and mezzethes. As with every plate we have ordered since landing in Greece, this too is delicious: tomato salad, keftethes, potatoes. We go back to Hotel Taleton to rest, although Alexandra is too nervous to sleep. She has plans to meet John that evening.

At 7:30 Alexandra shoos us away from the courtyard as she waits for John. Joyce and I peek through the curtains in the window, but the tree branches are in our way, and our visibility is limited. We hear voices, but can't see anything, so we sit down on the bed. "Well, now what do we do?" I ask. We sit for a few minutes, and then Alexandra bursts through the door.

"What are you guys doing sitting here in the dark?" she laughs.

We go outside to greet John. I give him a Pittsburgh Pirates tee-shirt that I brought from the states. "I will put it on now," he says, and goes into the room to change.

"Are you okay?" I ask Alexandra. Her face is flushed and she appears nervous. John comes back out and we chat for a few minutes. Neither of the kids seem relaxed.

"Hey," I say to John. "What happened to speaking only Greek?" an agreement we had made the previous week.

He replies, *"Tha milame argotera na me katalavenies,"* and I am confused: *We will talk later so that you will understand me. What does he mean by this?* I wonder.

Joyce and I leave to meet Panos at the square for ouzo and *oktopodi* - grilled octopus. I tell him about the discovery that my ancestors were called Nifakos, not Nefopoulas, the name for which I had been searching.

"Ah, yes," he says. "This name is from Milea, in Mani. I think that I also have relatives who came from Mani. Would you like to go there?"

We make plans to visit Mani on Sunday. We then walk over to Dimitri's restaurant, where I have come to know I will find Marko and Niko in their usual spots, and we join them for dinner. I am surprised when Alexandra approaches us about an hour later.

I introduce her to the men, who greet her and pull up a chair for her. Again I ask, "Are you okay?" John has told Alexandra that he met a girl about two weeks ago, and that he is hoping that things will work out with her. But he has told Alexandra that he would like to see her again the following evening.

We drive to Krokees on Saturday morning to meet George from Baltimore. He has invited us to see his village home, which he is having remodeled, and to spend the day at the beach. He is waiting outside when we arrive, and asks if we would like a tour of the home. It is unlike any village home I have ever seen. Although not yet furnished, it is easy to see that the home could easily grace the pages of *House Beautiful* magazine with its updated appliances, ceramic tile floors, clean whitewashed walls, high ceilings, and expert woodwork. We walk back outside where a short, sunburned, dark-haired stone mason sits on the ground at the end of a large yard, surrounded by a pile of large dusty stones. We can see where he has fit some of the individual stones together to form a flooring. "Is this a patio?" I ask George.

"No, it's the driveway."

I've never seen such an artistic driveway. The stone mason smiles and waves to us from across the yard, and I wave back. George leans in and whispers to me, "He's Albanian. I only pay him five euros an hour. Can you believe it? What a steal!" I am stunned and bothered by this revelation. To be paid only five euros an hour for this expert craftsmanship is a crime, and I wonder if this mason who is chipping away at the stones is happy to earn this. Still, it troubles me.

We spend the morning at Mavrovouni Beach, and afterwards have lunch with George. Perhaps it is the sun, or the food, or the stress of waiting for John to contact her, but Alexandra is not feeling well, and we return to the hotel for a nap. That evening, we are sitting in the courtyard having a fredo cappuccino, when John finally contacts Alexandra, only to tell her that he cannot see her again. The girl he likes has told him that if he wants things to work with her, he should not see Alexandra. She is hurt and disappointed. There are still things she had wanted to say. But, just like that, after eight years of "what might have been" and "what could still be," he is gone.

Neither Joyce nor I know what to say, and perhaps there is nothing that we can say. Alexandra is quiet as we drive to Sparta for a late dinner. We have yet to eat gyros in Greece, and on the recommendation of a few men sitting at an outside bar, we walk down a side street to The Parthenon restaurant. "It's so anticlimactic," Alexandra says, as we sip our beers. "I thought maybe we could rekindle something. You think it will be like *The Notebook* – a recurrence of all of those feelings. But, I guess in a way it released me. Now I don't have to live life wondering *what if* anymore."

I know what she means. Many of my thoughts about Greece begin with "what if." I wonder how much of my hoping that she and John would work out have to do with my own yearnings.

After dinner we head to the Ministry Music Hall to meet up with Louis, a friend whom Alexandra had met on our first trip to Sparta, when we listened to the bands next to Terry's house. He has recently competed on the Greek version of "The Voice," and has been working on advancing his singing career. We find Louis near the front of the bar watching "The Burning Sticks," a rock band with an intense female lead singer. His once long, shaggy hair is now short and curly. His eyes are dark brown and deep set, covered with thick dark eyebrows. He wears a goatee, but his face is boyish. He tells us that he will come back and talk to us in a few minutes, as soon as the show is over. As the members of the

Burning Sticks take their bows, the owner of the club comes on the microphone and invites Louis and his band to play. We have watched videos of Louis singing and playing guitar on the internet – he has a smooth, mellow voice, well-suited to his acoustic covers of pop rock tunes. So we are surprised, amused, and delighted when we hear the first guitar notes of "Play That Funky Music, White Boy," and Louis rocks out. After a few other American rock covers, he joins us back by the bar, where the bartenders have been pouring us complimentary assorted fruity shots. We chat for a while, but the bar is loud, and the music over the speakers is now "techno" music, so I go outside. A few minutes later, Louis comes outside to join me. He tells me that he works at a pizza shop to make ends meet, he is remodeling his house, and he is trying to make it as a singer. Joyce and Alexandra soon join us, along with Louis's cousins and his bandmates. I have stopped drinking - Louis has warned me about DUI checkpoints on the road back to Xirokambi. Nevertheless, it is almost 4 a.m. when the group asks us if we want to leave and go get a drink at another bar. We are still wide awake, and there is something enticing about staying up all night, but we have plans the next morning and decline. We are walking towards the car, and Louis says to me, "I have friends, I have family. I have the beaches, my music. I have everything I need in Sparti. What more is there?"

"Nothing," I reply. "You're right. You have everything here."

Sunday's phone call from Panos comes at nine a.m. "Are you ready?" he asks. I look at Alexandra sound asleep next to me, and hear no stirring from Joyce downstairs, and I give him a more realistic departure time of 10:30. It is a late start for all that is planned for the day, but he is surprisingly accommodating. I have always had the impression that he is impatient, but something about the village life softens the harsh edges.

On the way to Mani we pass some of the most spectacular scenery that I have seen in Greece. Mountain roads with hairpin turns weave up and back down the hills, lavender grows freely on the mountainsides, and steep cliffs overlook the ocean with patterns of deep midnight blue and turquoise water swirling around the rocks. We stop for frappes at an isolated hotel which overlooks Iteli, a small seaside town, its stone houses with their yellow and orange tile roofs built up to the water's edge on large rock formations, and take several photographs there and along the way. We are thankful that Ana from the hotel has packed us sandwiches and fruit. It is 1:00 p.m. and we have yet to arrive at Milea. The roads are more narrow now, and shortly we pull into a small platia, but there is no life in the square. Panos and the others look around the square. I wander up an uneven narrow road between old stone houses, and up a short flight of steps, and come upon three middle aged men sitting on a patio in front of a sturdy stone building. Two of them wear jeans; one wears khaki shorts and a straw hat. They sit on plastic chairs at a table covered with a brightly flowered plastic tablecloth, next to a stack of empty red plastic Amstel crates, sipping water, or perhaps ouzo. They ask with some curiosity how I got there. I tell them that I am looking for Nifakos, and they direct me to the "lower town," and tell me to find Calliope. "She knows everything," The men tell me. Before they let me go, they want to chat about America, and the man in a straw hat tells me enthusiastically that he has been to Pittsburgh and that he loves baseball.

    We drive the short distance to Lower Milea, and pull into the platia. The only sign of life is a woman on a balcony, shaking her rug over the railing. "*Signomi* - excuse me," I call, and I explain that we are looking for Nifakos.

    "*Ena* lepta - one minute," she says. "I will call my neighbor. I expect her to go into the house to use the phone, but she goes over to the side of the balcony, cups her hands, and yells, "Calliope!" I hear voices in rapid-fire Greek. The woman returns to the middle of the balcony and says, "Wait here. She is coming."

    I look down the steep hill which leads to a few homes and say, "We can go down to see her – she doesn't have to come up."

    "No, no," the woman says. "She wants to come up here."

    It is several minutes before we see a short, slightly stout woman in sunglasses, a flowered blouse, and long blue skirt climbing up the hill. She uses a cane to walk slowly up the path. She is about ten yards away from us when she stops and asks us what we want. I tell her that I am the granddaughter of Ahileas Nifakos, and that I have come to find information about him.

    "Ahileas?" she asks. "*Apo* – from - Xirokambi?"

    "Yes," I reply.

She raises both arms, dangling the cane from her hand, smiles, and says, "*Eimaste emma* - We are blood!"

We finish introductions, and Calliope Nifakos goes to a large building on the other side of the square. She emerges a few minutes later with a tray of sweets and orangeade, and we sit in the shade of a large plane tree on white plastic chairs at a marble-topped table to talk. Calliope knows no English and speaks in Greek, mostly to Panos, about her brother, nieces, nephews. Our connection is that her grandfather and my grandfather were second cousins. We ask to take a photograph, and she takes off her large, dark sunglasses. I catch my breath. Her eyes are the same shape, depth, and hazel color of my mother's. "She has Angie's eyes!" Alexandra says.

"She has your coloring," Panos says to me. I have always wondered where my reddish complexion came from. My sister, her children, my daughter, all have a golden glow when they are tan. My son and my father turn brown in the sun, but Nick has always said that I look like an Indian when I've been in the sun. And in front of me is Calliope, with the same reddish glow to her complexion.

Calliope walks us over to a small monument with a metal bust on the top of it. "*Keeteh* -look," she says. The plaque below the bust reads:

ΝΙΚΙΤΑΣ ΝΗΦΑΚΟΣ	NIKITAS NIFAKOS
ΠΟΙΗΤΗΖ	Poet
1748 – 1818	1748 – 1818
Ακριβεστατη μου πατρισ	My dearest country
ψεννητρια, τροφοσ μου,	Birthplace of my light,
ωραια μου κθμοπολισ	My beautiful small city,
Μηλεα, γλυκυ φοσ μου	Milea, my sweet light.

"He was your ancestor," Calliope tells me. "We are all related to him."

"He was a writer!" I say.

Calliope asks me to walk with her down the hill to her home, and Alexandra and I follow her. We stop at a small chapel on the way. The door is locked, and Calliope unlocks it so that we can go in. Eight high-backed wooden chairs face a small altar.

Icons and pictures of the saints in gold frames cover the whitewashed walls. The faint scent of incense lingers in the small space. We walk out and approach a locked wrought iron fence. I am surprised that Calliope locks it in a village this small; only about 35 people reside permanently in each of the upper and lower villages. She unlocks the gate, and we walk into a yard that is something out of a fantasy book. Large trees and grapevines overhang the stone patio, letting the sunlight peek in between dappled shadows. The courtyard is surrounded by uneven stone walls held together with thick cement. Weeds push through the cracks in the cement, and large zucchinis suspend from the arbor above the patio. Clothes, rugs, and sheets hang from rope lines and iron railings. A large table with an oversized plastic flowered tablecloth sits in a corner, surrounded by mismatched plastic chairs. A set of small metal steps lined with tiny orange pumpkins leads to a plateau of weeds and tall brown grasses. Large pots of bright red geraniums, pink flowers, and herbs line the steps leading to Calliope's house. The courtyard is mystical. Calliope disappears inside the house, and reappears with two large metal cans of honey. "It is from Milea," she says. "It is the best." Calliope asks if we can return in August. She tells me there is a large celebration on August 15, and all the Nifakos' return to Milea. "You can meet everyone!" she says.

"I wish that I could," I say, smiling at the notion, yet knowing that time constraints, money, and the resumption of everyday life make this impossible.

On our way back to Voula the following day, we stop in Napflion, the port city at the base of Palamidi prison. From the foot of the mountain we can see the walls of the fortress, and the winding path made of up the 999 steps that lead up to the prison compound. We have driven over two hours to arrive here, and I picture my great-grandmother, Zoitsa, making this trip on a donkey to bring food to my great-grandfather. I can't imagine the courage and strength that it took to travel through the mountains in harsh conditions to keep her husband from starving. I think about the pride that I felt about navigating the mountain roads in a foreign country with a six-speed and a GPS, and I am humbled.

From Milea, oil painting, Wilson

DISCOVERY - *Anevresi*: ΑΝΕΥΡΕΣΗ

It is late summer, back in Pittsburgh, and Joyce and I have gone to Central Diner to have lunch after art class. The former Denny's restaurant has been bought and remodeled by Greeks, and now has a large patio out front with wrought iron tables and chairs under shady umbrellas. We are eating our Greek salads on the outside patio when Dimitri, the owner, stops by to say hello.

"How is everything?" Dimitri asks. He is a handsome middle-aged man with short-cropped greying hair who rarely smiles, I suspect because he is so busy running the restaurant.

"Great!" I reply.

"Good," he nods, half talking to me, and half glancing inside through the windows to make sure that everything is under control. "How are you?"

"Good," I reply. "I was in Greece this summer."

"Where did you go?"

"Athens, Santorini, Xirokambi. It's a small village...."

He cuts me off. "Yes, I know it," he says, still unsmiling.

"You know Xirokambi?"

"Yes. I am from there."

"You're from Xirokambi!"

"Yes," he replies. Dimitri's level of excitement clearly does not match mine.

"What is your last name?" I ask.

"Takos."

"Takos? It's like Nifakos. It has the same ending." I explain my search for Nefopoulas, and my discovery that the original name was Nifakos.

"Yes," he says. "You know why that is?"

"No...."

He explains. "The Maniotis were a vengeful people. Violent. They settled disputes with guns. There was no law. They even built bridges on the second floors of their houses to go across from one house to the other, so that they would not be killed in the streets. Finally, people had enough. They began to leave the village. They moved to small villages outside of Sparti."

"That would explain why they were in Xirokambi," I said. "But what about the name?"

"Ah," Dimitri said. "Some of them changed the name to get rid of the 'akos' so that people would not trace them back to Mani. So – your Nifakos, it becomes Nifopoulos."

I remember my cousin Thanos once referring to my great grandfather Elias Savellos as Savelakos. I turn to Joyce. "So, the families could have known each other in Milea," I say. "I may never know how my grandparents actually met, but now it makes more sense."

I call my cousin Patrick to chat, and to tell him about the Nifakos discovery. He tells me that he and Donna will be going to New Jersey the first week of September for vacation.

"My sister Ellen is getting married that Saturday," I say. "She lives outside of Philadelphia. That's only two hours away. Maybe there's a way that we can meet?" Ellen is hosting a post-wedding brunch on Sunday morning. I invite Patrick, and tell him that he will be able to meet the whole family if he is able to come. He says that he will try.

The morning of the brunch John and I are running a few minutes late. We arrive at Ellen and Brian's home in Haverford, a former carriage house whose stall doors have been replaced with floor to ceiling windows, which beam sunlight into the massive great room. Standing there, talking with my mother, is the younger version of my Uncle Angelo. I walk up to Patrick and hug him. I finally meet the cousin whom I so wanted to know over forty years ago.

On a Wednesday evening in October I am back in my office, reading my email and savoring a cup of green tea, when my cell phone rings.

"Mom," Alexandra says, and I can tell in that one syllable that something is wrong.

"What is it, Alexandra?"

"I have something to tell you. I don't think you know – if you did, you would have told me."

A sense of dread crawls through my body. I set my tea down and lean back in my chair. "What?"

"You know Kathleen from Marathon?" Kathleen is married to Niko and Roi's son, Vasili. I'm caught off guard and not sure where this is going. "She posted something on Facebook about her father-in-law. That's Niko, isn't it?"

"Yes."

"He had a stroke, Mom. He's in a coma. She says that it's just a matter of days."

My eyes well up with tears. I whisper, "No."

It is seven hours later in Greece – too late to contact anyone, and I send a message to Kathleen. When I wake up, she has messaged me back. Niko passed away that morning, with his family around him. My heart goes out to Roi.

It is a week before I can finally connect with her on the phone. "It was so sudden," Roi says. "He had had pneumonia, but the doctors said he was fine. He was in good health. It was so unexpected." Her voice is tired. I tell her how much I love them both, but she already knows this. "I tell you," she says, "the only good thing is that he would not have wanted to live like this, with someone having to feed him, to help him to do everything." She talks of what a good life they had together, how important their family has been to them, what a good man he was. "The only things you have are memories. And I have very good memories. But, in the end, I am alone."

I have never known Roi without Niko. They are always together in my thoughts. But she is a strong woman, as is Rena, who lost her husband recently, and Aunt Helen, who lost hers only a few years ago. Marathon is no longer home to John and Rena, Niko and Roi, but there is new life there. Rena's daughter Eleni and her husband Pandalis now live full-time at Marathon, as he attempts to forge a career as a doctor in Greece, rather than move for a more lucrative position to Saudi Arabia or London. Her other daughter, Christina, spends weekends in Marathon with her husband and twins. Roi's son Vasili has moved permanently into the guest house with his wife, Kathleen.

"How is your mother?" I ask Roi about my Aunt Helen who, at 100 years old has seen three of her four younger siblings and now both of her sons-in-law go before her.

"She is fine," Roi said. "She is a strong woman. Do you know how amazing she is? We have the fish dinner after the funeral. Everyone was too busy. And, do you know what she did? She came in a taxi, by herself." It does not surprise me. The last time that I spoke with Roi, she told me with a mixture of angst and admiration that Aunt Helen walked up the three flights of steps to her apartment when the elevator was broken. "What did you expect me to do?" her mother asked her. "Wait there?"

As generations move on, they leave a legacy. It is up to us to keep the ties. My Greek relations fill my head and heart with love, joy, and a sense of belonging. They nurture me and awaken my soul. My identity is intertwined with the people whom I have come to know. When I am in Athens or Voula, Vlahokerasia or Xirokambi, I have a sense of those who have come before me and paved the way: my great grandmother Zoitsa, who had the sagacity to send her daughter Olga away for a better life than the one in the village, and to give her son Mike the precious money needed to become a pilot. My great-grandmother Eleni who gave up the grandson she loved, George, knowing that he needed the discipline that only his father could provide, even if it meant his leaving for America. My great-aunt, Loukia, who had the courage to leave the village, build a career in days when most women did not have careers, and live life on her own terms. My grandmother, Olga, widowed with five children, who did what she must to keep her family afloat. My parents, whose love and devotion to each other created a family where, despite their over-protection, my sister and I were ultimately encouraged to become independent and assertive women. "We didn't know how to be parents," my mother has said. "You learn as you go – sometimes you make mistakes." As an adult, I recognize that any mistakes were made in the fierce love that only a parent has for a child. When she looks back on her own life, my mother observes, "We didn't know that we were poor. We just knew our lives." She has only two regrets, both about Olga. "I wish that mother had accepted George. She really missed out. He was such a good man, and she let the rumors get in the way. She never took the time to get to know him." She reflects upon her bond with her mother: "I love the relationship that I have with you and Ellen. And that you have with your girls. I wish that I had talked more to my mother when she was alive." That was a different time. Trying to survive the Depression in a foreign land, widowed, with five young children leaves little time for coffee at the dining room table. But through her, I have learned to cherish every drop of coffee that I drink with my mother, and every precious moment with my children.

    The reality is, I may never live in Greece. My roots run deep, and a Greek song can stir a longing in my core that can bring me to tears. But, my legacy is in America, where my father came to be a better man. It is where my grandmother raised five children, as a widow on welfare, so that their children would thrive. It is where so many of the Greeks that I have met still dream of coming. It is where I hope to watch my grandchildren grow and prosper someday. If I am so blessed, they will know about the toils and struggles of their Greek ancestors, the passions and pleasures of their forefathers, and the joy and pride that comes with being a Greek American.

Epilog

In September of 2009 my mom received a phone call from her brother, Stanley. "We lost Irene," he said, and they talked for the first time in more than thirty years. The following year Stanley and his daughter Rosemary took a trip to Florida and stopped to visit my mother. In October of 2012, Stanley and his youngest daughter, Susan, traveled again to Florida, and my daughter and I flew down to see them. I was happy to meet them, after so many decades, but part of me was bitter for all of the lost years and heartache my mother had experienced. I asked Mom if they had ever discussed Stanley's estrangement from his family. "No," she said, "that's over and done with. I'm just happy that Stanley is happy and living a good life." They continue to stay in touch. Mom has moved to an assisted living facility and is happily involved in all of the activities there – including Yoga and Corn Hole! My visits to Florida have become more frequent as I feel the passage of time more intensely. My father's sisters, my Aunt Loula and my Aunt Sassa have both passed away, leaving their older sister, Aunt Helen at 102 years old, the last remaining sibling.

Family research is never-ending. I discovered that Michel, the daughter of Mom and Dad's friend Jimmy Tsouris is a distant cousin of mine through her mother and my father's side. She is an artist now living in Florida, and we have reconnected after several decades. I have discovered another Nifakos relative living in Athens, whom I hope to meet this summer. As I bring this to a close, I am looking forward to a trip to Greece with my husband, John, who will finally be able to meet all of the relatives whom I have been talking and writing about as we travel throughout the Athens area and the Peloponnese. Of course, I can't help but wonder what new discoveries I will make as I chat with cousin Helen in her kitchen.

Acknowledgements

About five years ago my mother and I sat at the kitchen table in her apartment in Florida, catching up on news over a cup of coffee. As I brought her up to date on the latest happenings with my daughter, my mother said, "You have such a nice relationship with Alexandra. I wish that I had the kind of relationship with my mother that you and your daughter have, or that you and I have. I never really talked to my mother. I don't really know much about her life."

"I bet you know more than you think you do," I replied. A seed was planted.

What began as an exploration of my grandmother's life took on new energy once I enrolled in the Carlow University MFA program. I had the extreme pleasure of learning Creative Non Fiction with two talented MFA candidates, Lisa Costa and Elizabeth Tamburri – lovely women whose support and encouragement is unwavering, and whose new-found friendships I cherish. Learning from countless Irish and American authors in the residency workshops and lectures, and working with talented and knowledgeable mentors Carlo Gebler, Leslie Rubinkowski, Sean Hardie, and Brian Leyden allowed me to hone my writing skills and turn my ideas and essays into what would eventually become "Greek Lessons." Dr. Ellie Wymard's guidance and direction and Brian Leyden's keen eye for detail and patient mentoring inspired me to create a manuscript that went far beyond my initial expectations. What started out as a simple family history became the story of an ancestral line of strong Greek women. More importantly, researching and writing the book has allowed me to explore the powerful effect that the Greek culture has had on me and my family.

I owe a debt of gratitude to the West Allegheny School District for approving and encouraging my sabbatical so that I could undertake this ambitious project, and to my fellow teacher, Elizabeth Shannon, who read my work, voiced her opinion, and let me vent when I was stuck or exhausted. I could not have finished this book without the patience and encouragement of my relatives

– my dear aunts, uncles, and cousins in both Greece and the United States who tolerated my many questions with patience and humor. Cousin Thanos, whose shared stories of the Savellos family, and acted as driver and guide for my first trip to Xirokambi. Helen and Panos, who gave me their home, their support and their friendship. My dear friend, Daniela Buccilli, whose candid input helped me to polish the final draft. My traveling partners – Jean, Joyce, and of course Mom, Ellen, and Alexandra, who made every trip to Greece a joy and an adventure. My new friends in Xirokambi, Markos and Niko, who were kind enough to help me in my quest for roots, and Uncle George and Aunt Pitsa who made me feel at home in the village.

    I am overwhelmed by the help and the support that I received from my family: my daughter, Alexandra, who patiently recounted details, some difficult, and generously gave her input and advice. My son, Nick, whose honest criticism and sharp editing enabled me to refine the manuscript. My sister, Ellen, who acted as advisor, empathizer, and sounding board, whenever needed. My mother, Angie, who patiently responded to the hours of questions, and never wavered, even when my own patience was wearing thin. And especially, my husband, John, who recognized when I was engaged in the writing process, even when I was sitting at the dinner table. His patience as I spent hours and days at my computer never faltered.

    It is with a mixture of joy and sadness that I finish writing this book. The memoir may be finished, but the journey is not. I look forward to continuing to fill in pieces of the family puzzle, and to what the future holds for our next generation.

Made in the USA
Columbia, SC
09 September 2018